Burke Aaron Hinsdale

President Garfield and Education

Hiram college memorial

Burke Aaron Hinsdale

President Garfield and Education
Hiram college memorial

ISBN/EAN: 9783337093419

Printed in Europe, USA, Canada, Australia, Japan

Cover: Foto ©ninafisch / pixelio.de

More available books at **www.hansebooks.com**

PRESIDENT GARFIELD AND EDUCATION.

PRESIDENT GARFIELD

AND EDUCATION

Hiram College Memorial

BY

B. A. HINSDALE, A.M.

PRESIDENT OF HIRAM COLLEGE

BOSTON
JAMES R. OSGOOD AND COMPANY
1882

COPYRIGHT, 1881,
BY JAMES R. OSGOOD AND COMPANY.

All rights reserved.

Franklin Press:
RAND, AVERY, AND COMPANY,
BOSTON.

PREFACE.

THE propriety of a Hiram College Memorial to President Garfield will be admitted on all hands. It was in Hiram that he fitted for college, and that he made his reputation as a teacher and school-administrator. Hiram was his home for twenty-six years. Much of that time, probably one-half of it, he spent in other places and duties, — college, the army, and Congress; but Hiram was the place to which he looked for residence and rest. To those who have become acquainted with him, his name or fame, the last four years, Mentor means more than Hiram; but to all of his earlier friends Hiram means as much more than Mentor, as his residence in the one place was longer than his residence in the other.

Nor can there be two opinions as to the fitness of such a memorial as is here attempted. General Garfield was a scholar and an educator. His earliest fame was won in study and in teaching. He was always the friend and advocate of education. It was in Hiram school that his happiest days were spent, and that he performed the work which in late years he looked back upon with most satisfaction. Hence, such of his utterances concerning education and educators as have been preserved, attended by suitable memorials of his Hiram life, could not fail deeply to interest educators and cultivated men generally, especially such as belong to the Hiram fellowship. That this volume will measurably draw out this interest, is the hope of its compiler and of others whom he has consulted in its preparation.

Some remarks upon the number and quality of the speeches and addresses included, will be found in another place; but it is proper to say here, that the personal sketch is by no means exhaustive. An interesting and inspiring volume could be prepared on his Hiram life. Here the aim is to make a Garfield book in the sense of his being its author, and not simply its subject. At the same time, the personal sketch is a comprehensive survey, embracing all salient points of his Hiram life and character, filled in with sufficient *memorabilia* to answer the purpose of illustration. What is more, the memorial speeches made at Cleveland supplement the sketch, and show the impressions made by Teacher Garfield upon their authors, who are simply the representatives and mouth-pieces of thousands.

This book has been prepared, and is now published,

in the confident belief that no more appropriate memorial to the lamented dead could go forth from President Garfield's old home. It is also believed that none could go forth, which, were he living, would give him so much pleasure.

It is proper to add, that this memorial has Mrs. Garfield's cordial approval. The pictures of the President and herself she has chosen. Writing at Mentor, Oct. 28, 1881, she says, "*I quite approve of your plan in regard to the memorial volume. It would be most appropriate that the speeches to which you refer should appear in such a volume.*"

B. A. HINSDALL.

HIRAM COLLEGE, HIRAM, O.,
   Nov. 19, 1881.

CONTENTS.

PART I.

MEMORIALS OF PRESIDENT GARFIELD IN HIRAM.

		PAGE
I.	GENERAL SKETCH	15
	I. HIRAM AND HIRAM SCHOOL	15
	II. GARFIELD THE HIRAM STUDENT	24
	III. THE WILLIAMS COLLEGE INTERREGNUM	39
	IV. GARFIELD PRESIDENT OF HIRAM	46
	V. GARFIELD'S OUTSIDE WORK	73
	VI. GARFIELD'S LATER HIRAM LIFE	87
II.	ADDRESSES AT HIRAM COLLEGE MEMORIAL SERVICE	114
	I. B. A. HINSDALE	114
	II. J. H. RHODES	124
	III. C. B. LOCKWOOD	133
	IV. C. D. WILBUR	138
	V. J. W. ROBBINS	145
	VI. A. H. PETTIBONE	147
	VII. H. C. WHITE	150
	VIII. H. N. ELDRIDGE	157

PART II.

PRESIDENT GARFIELD'S SPEECHES AND ADDRESSES ON EDUCATION AND EDUCATORS.

INTRODUCTION TO SPEECHES	161
I. THE STATE AND EDUCATION	162
1. The National Bureau of Education	162
2. The Army Post Schools	169
3. The "Hoar Bill"	173
4. Education and the South	173
II. THE STATE AND SCIENCE	174
III. STUDIES AND METHODS	176
IV. TRIBUTES TO EDUCATORS	178

CONTENTS.

                                              PAGE

I. THE NATIONAL BUREAU OF EDUCATION: *Speech in the House of Representatives, June 8, 1866* . . 181

II. NATIONAL AID TO EDUCATION: *Speech in the House of Representatives, Feb. 6, 1872* 215

III. SUFFRAGE AND SCHOOLS: *Extract from " The Future of the Republic: its Dangers and Hopes." An Address delivered before the Literary Societies of Western Reserve College, Hudson, O., July 2, 1873* . . 231

IV. POPULAR EDUCATION: *Extracts from the Letter of Acceptance, and the Inaugural Address, July 12, 1880, and March 4, 1881* 245

V. THE GIST OF THE "SOUTHERN QUESTION:" *Reply made at Mentor, to a Delegation of Colored Citizens from South Carolina and other Southern States, Jan. 14, 1881* 251

VI. RELATION OF THE NATIONAL GOVERNMENT TO SCIENCE: *Speech in the House of Representatives, Feb. 11, 1879* 257

VII. COLLEGE EDUCATION: *An Address before the Literary Societies of the Eclectic Institute, Hiram, O., June 14, 1867* 275

VIII. ELEMENTS OF SUCCESS: *Address before the Students of the Spencerian Business College, Washington, D.C., June 29, 1869* 315

IX. SOME TENDENCIES OF AMERICAN EDUCATION: *Speech before the Department of Superintendence of the National Education Association, Washington, D.C., Feb. 5, 1879* 335

X. S. F. B. MORSE: *An Address at the Morse Memorial Meeting, held in the Hall of the House of Representatives, April 16, 1872* 343

XI. JOSEPH HENRY: *Address at the Memorial Meeting, held in the Hall of the House of Representatives, Tuesday evening, Jan. 16, 1879* 353

XII. LIFE AND CHARACTER OF ALMEDA A. BOOTH: *An Address delivered at Hiram College, O., June 22, 1876* 365

APPENDIX 427

LIST OF ILLUSTRATIONS.

	PAGE
PORTRAIT OF PRESIDENT GARFIELD	*Frontispiece*
FACSIMILE LETTER OF PRESIDENT GARFIELD	15
VIEW OF HIRAM COLLEGE	24
PORTRAIT OF MISS BOOTH	28
FACSIMILE LETTER OF MISS BOOTH	30
PORTRAIT OF MRS. GARFIELD	86
FACSIMILE LETTER OF MRS. GARFIELD	90

PART I.

Memorials of President Garfield in Hiram.

STUDENT, TEACHER, AND CITIZEN.

EXECUTIVE MANSION
WASHINGTON March 26. 1881.

Dear Burke—

I throw you a line across the storm to let you know that I think, when, I have a moment between breaths, of the dear old quiet & peace of Hiram & Mentor— Let me hear from you.

As Ever Yours
J A Garfield

PRESIDENT GARFIELD AND EDUCATION.

I.

GENERAL SKETCH.

JAMES ABRAM GARFIELD first came to Hiram in August, 1851. An account of what Hiram then was, and of what he was, will be a fitting introduction to his Hiram life.

I.—HIRAM AND HIRAM SCHOOL.

In 1850 Hiram was a township of Western Reserve farmers; surface twenty-five square miles, population eleven hundred and six. The "Centre" was a cross-roads, with a post-office, one or two shops, two white churches, and three or four dwelling-houses. It was remote from any main thoroughfare or centre of population. No stage-coach wheels rolled within five miles of the place. Probably twenty farmhouses lay within a radius of a mile. And this was all. Here, on the eastern slope of the great "divide," and a mile from its crest, the Disciples of Christ, in the summer of 1850, planted the Western Reserve Eclectic Institute, the child of much consultation, prayer, and hope. The reasons that led to this location may properly be set down in this place.

In that day the Disciples of the Western Reserve were mostly rural people, sharing the old-fashioned prejudices against towns and cities. Thought, in Northern Ohio, was narrowly provincial in 1850. There were only two or three railroads in the State. No one dreamed of our present railroad system, or foresaw the centralization of wealth and population that the steam-locomotive has wrought. Travelling was done in wheeled vehicles or on horseback. People owned their own conveyances and horses. So the fathers asked, "Why can they not turn their horses' heads towards Hiram as well as towards any other place?" Hiram, then, offered the desired seclusion. Hiram had a vigorous church, that would furnish the desired religious environment. Hiram, too, offered a contingent subscription of four thousand dollars,—no mean inducement to the trustees of a school that was not expected, at its founding, to cost more than twice or thrice that sum. The aims of the school were both general and special. More narrowly they were these : —

1. To provide a sound scientific and literary education.
2. To temper and sweeten such education with moral and scriptural knowledge.
3. To educate young men for the ministry.

One peculiar tenet of the religious movement in which it originated was impressed upon the Eclectic Institute at its organization. The Disciples believed that the Bible had been in a degree obscured by theological speculations and ecclesiastical systems. Hence their religious movement was a revolt from the theology of the schools, and an overture to men to come face to face with the Scriptures. They believed, also, that to the Holy Writings belonged a larger place in general education than had yet been accorded to them. Accordingly, in all their educational institutions they have emphasized the Bible and its related branches of knowledge. This may be called the distinctive feature of their schools. The charter of the Eclectic Institute, therefore, declared the purpose of the institution to be "the instruction of youth of both sexes in the various branches of literature and science, especially of moral science as based on the facts and precepts of the Holy Scriptures."

It took time for Hiram to become what it is to-day, — a bright Ohio village;. white houses, green blinds, maples and elms, a handsome college building, and a beautiful campus. Soon the new school drew to itself three hundred scholars; and, although that number was not long maintained, Hiram has furnished tuition for more than five thousand individual pupils. At the re-union of 1880 General Garfield said, " To my mind, the history of Hiram College, and the institution on which it was built, divides itself into two chapters. The first, both in time and perhaps in importance, should be headed, ' What other people did for it; ' and the second, ' What Hiram did for itself.' " On that occasion he condensed much Hiram history — as well as much of his own history — into this short speech: — .

"LADIES AND GENTLEMEN, — I said there were two chapters in the history of this Institution. You have heard one relative to the founders.[1] They were pioneers in this Western Reserve. They were all men of energy, great force

[1] Referring to an historical address just delivered.

of character, and nearly all of them men of small means; but they planted this institution. In 1850 the campus was a cornfield with a solid, plain brick building in the centre of it; and almost all the rest has been done by the institution itself. This is the second chapter. It was without a dollar of endowment, without a powerful friend anywhere, but with a corps of teachers who were told to go on the ground, and see what they could make out of it, and to take their pay out of the tuitions that should be received; who invited students of their own spirit to come here, and find out by trial what they could make out of it; and the response has been their chapter of work, and the chief part of the response I see in the faces gathered before me to-day. It was a simple question of sinking or swimming. I know that we are all inclined to be a little clannish; perhaps we have a right to be: but I do not know of any place, I do not know of any institution, that has accomplished more, with so little means, than this school on Hiram Hill.

"I know of no place where the doctrine of self-help has had a fuller development, by necessity as well as by favor, than here on this hill. The doctrine of the survival of the fittest found its place amongst these men and women gathered here. As I said about them a great many years ago, the theory of Hiram was to throw its young men and women overboard, and let them try it for themselves; and all that were fit to get ashore got there, and I think we had few cases of drowning. Now, when I look over these faces, and mark the several geological ages so well represented by Mr. Atwater in his address, I note one curious fact where the geological analogy does not hold: I find no fossils, — no fossils at all. Some are dead, and glorious in our memories; but those who are alive are ALIVE, I think all. The teachers and the students of this school built it up in every sense, — made the cornfield into that handsome campus. These evergreens you see across the road, they planted. I well remember the day that they turned out and went into the woods to find beautiful maples, and brought them in; when they purchased these evergreens; when each young man for himself, and perhaps a second for some young lady that he loved, planted one or two trees on the campus, and named them after himself. There are many here with moist eyes to-day who can point out the tree that Bowler planted. Bowler was shot through the heart at Cedar Mountain. Many of you who point out trees, big trees now, called after you many years ago. I believe, outside of the physical features of the place, that there was a stronger pressure of work to the square inch in the boilers that ran this establishment, than any other I know of. Young men and women, rough, crude, untutored farmer-boys and farmer-girls, came here to try themselves, and find what manner of people they were. They came here to go on a voyage of discovery to discover themselves. In many cases I hope the discovery was fortunate in all that was worthy of trying; and the friendships that were formed out of that struggle have followed this group of people longer and farther than almost any I have ever known in my life. They are scattered all over the United States, in every field of activity; and if I should try to name them the sun would go down before I had finished."

Truth, if not modesty, would have allowed him to add with Father Æneas, "All of which I saw, and a great part of which I was."

When Garfield came to Hiram, every thing was new and crude. As he says in his address on "The Life and Character of Almeda A. Booth," "The Eclectic was compelled to create its own scholarship and culture. Very few of its early students had gone beyond the ordinary studies of the district school; and a large majority of them needed thorough discipline in the common English branches." Hiram gave the Institute a seat; the trustees gave a building and the first teachers; the regions farther and nearer, scholars; and then the spiritual Hiram developed itself. Society, traditions, and the peculiar genius of the place were evolved from the teachers and pupils, limited by the local and general environment.

The opening of this new school was coincident with three things important in this history: —

1. Coincident with a general educational awakening in the State of Ohio. In an important sense, the present school-system of the State dates from the year 1853.[1] Population had increased

[1] The date of the "Rice School Law."

in the State marvellously; the homes of the people were full of youth; and wealth had so grown, that men, in great part freed from the burden of sweeping away the forests, were enabled to pay greatly increased attention to the education of their children.

2. Coincident with an important epoch in the history of the Disciples of the Reserve. They were numerous and active: they now had a school of their own, in which they took the pride and interest that parents take in a first child.

3. Coincident with the young manhood of James A. Garfield. His family belonged to the Disciples' Church: so did the families of many neighbors. He himself had become a member a year and a half before. No better school was within his reach in 1851; but it must be said, that, for the most part, religious influences brought him to this place. Here, too, may be dropped a thought that cannot be fully developed.

No other church in the land could have given him the opportunity that the Disciples offered. This is true in a double sense. While there was an absence of license on the one hand, there was large freedom on the other. This gave him an opportunity to exercise his gifts, intellectual and religious, such as an older and more conservative body could not have given, which he improved much to the profit of his brethren and to his own advantage. But more, the Disciple habit of mind, especially the denominational method of handling the Scriptures, — which may be briefly defined as a brushing-aside of the Church creeds, as well as much of the traditionary theology, and a direct face-to-face study of the Bible, — was an important element in his history. Stress may also be laid upon the accepted canons of interpretation, both few and simple, as well as "dividing the word of truth" by the application of the principle of relativity; as, for instance, taking into account the period of divine revelation immediately in hand, whether the Patriarchal, the Mosaic, or the Christian. No one who is thoroughly familiar with President Garfield's history can doubt that this Disciple habit and method had a most important influence upon his mind, his whole life and character. At the same time, he was the farthest removed from a sectarian or denominationalist. His religious thought was ever broad, his spirit ever catholic.

II.—GARFIELD THE HIRAM STUDENT.

To this young school, young Garfield came the third term of its existence. In three months more he would be twenty years of age. An obvious and interesting analogy between the school and the pupil could be readily traced out. Both were in the formative period; both were full of strength and enthusiasm; but both needed growth and ripeness. He was strong-framed, deep-chested, six feet high, with a blue eye, and a massive head surmounted by a shock of tow-colored hair. Physically he was the Garfield of twenty years later, only he had the pulpy adolescence of twenty. Time had not yet rounded out his figure, browned and thinned his hair, and put into his face the lines of thought. The school was growing, and he was growing. His intellectual and moral qualities had already declared themselves. Having lost his father in his infancy, and having been thrown upon his own resources at an early age, in the midst of the pioneers of Ohio, his sense of responsibility, his judgment, and his self-helpfulness were developed much beyond the average. He was full of animal spirits and young joviality; but he had had his ear upon the human heart, and had heard its re-

HIRAM COLLEGE.

verberatory murmur in the minor key. Two years or more before, he had finished the studies of the Orange district school. At Chester, O., where he had attended Geauga Seminary four terms in 1849 and 1850, he had studied natural philosophy, algebra, and botany, and begun Latin and Greek. He had taught district-school two terms, and received a full measure of the benefit which comes from that valuable discipline. He had already put his early longings for the lake and the sea behind him, and had determined to have the best education that he could obtain. His coming to Hiram was the next step towards carrying out this resolution. His address on Miss Booth contains some interesting description and autobiography. This extract lets in a strong side-light upon his mind in 1851: —

"A few days after the beginning of the term, I saw a class of three reciting in mathematics, — geometry, I think. They sat on one of the red benches, in the centre aisle of the lower chapel. I had never seen a geometry; and, regarding both teacher and class with a feeling of reverential awe for the intellectual heights to which they had climbed, I studied their faces so closely that I seem to see them now as distinctly as I saw them then."

All scholars who had few books and other educational advantages in youth can take in this picture at once, — teacher, class, and the honest, open-eyed youth of twenty years, full of wonder, appreciation, and reverence.

Having looked at Garfield's new surroundings, and equipped him, let us now see him at his work.

First, he came to Hiram poor in every thing but faculties and character. He was wholly dependent upon his own resources. He sought and obtained the position of janitor, — a position reserved in those days for poor students who wanted a chance to help themselves. Two terms he made fires, swept the floors, and rang the bell. Scores of men and women can now be found who well remember seeing the future President of the United States at the end of the Hiram bell-rope. One who has added her rill to this stream of reminiscence, and whose memory goes back to the bell-ringing days, says, "His large head and massive frame had a suggestion of the overgrown; but he escaped awkwardness by the thought and purpose that controlled his actions. His clothes had a poor-student look. At the close of the morning lecture, before the students left the room, he would leave the chapel, and ring the bell. His tread was firm and free, and the same unconscious dignity followed him then that attended him when he ascended the eastern portico of the Capitol to deliver his Inaugural Address. He was modest and self-possessed, without vanity or self-consciousness, and then and always absolutely free from any affectation whatever." A house is still pointed out in Hiram, the clapboards of which he planed in one of his vacations. But bell-ropes and jack-planes do not make men great: if they did, the road to greatness would be easy enough. So we pass on to things more important.

On his arrival at Hiram in August, 1851, Mr. Garfield took up his studies where he had dropped them at Chester. After one term's work as student and janitor, he retired for a term to teach his last district-school. In the spring of 1852 he returned, and continued in Hiram until he went to Williamstown in 1854. Principal Hayden and teachers Dunshee, Munnell, and Hull were his instructors. To Dunshee he probably recited more than to all the rest put together. Garfield always appreciated and respected his Hiram teachers; but it is perfectly just to them to say that Miss Booth, who never was a teacher of his, but rather a fellow-student, did much more than they did to mould his character and give direction to his life. That he so felt, any one can see by reading between the lines his noble tribute to her character and work. Not only so, but he says in words, —

"On my own behalf, I take this occasion to say, that for her generous and powerful aid, so often and so efficiently rendered, for her quick and never-failing sympathy, and for her intelligent, unselfish, and unswerving friendship, I owe her a debt of gratitude and affection, for the payment of which the longest term of life would have been too short."

But it may be said, "This was in the presence of the Hiram fellowship." Let it be said, then, that before the Williams College fellowship he bore a similar testimony. At the Williams banquet, held in Cleveland, Jan. 10, 1881, after recognizing his obligation to the common schools of Ohio and to Williams College, he said, —

"I am glad to say, reverently, in the presence of the many ladies here to-night, that I owe to a woman who has long since been asleep, perhaps a higher debt intellectually than I owe to any one else. After that comes my debt to Williams College."

He called no name, but it was Almeda Booth. Probably the best account of Garfield's Hiram

studies that can be given without access to his diary is his account of Miss Booth's studies. Let the reader substitute his name for hers, in the following paragraphs: —

"I remember that she and I were members of the class that began Xenophon's 'Anabasis,' in the fall term of 1852. Near the close of that term I also began to teach in the Eclectic, and thereafter, like her, could keep up my studies only outside of my own class hours. In mathematics and the physical sciences, I was far behind her; but we were nearly at the same place in Greek and Latin, each having studied them about three terms. She had made her home at President Hayden's, almost from the first; and I became a member of his family at the beginning of the winter term of 1852-53. Thereafter, for nearly two years, she and I studied together, and recited in the same classes (frequently without other associates), till we had nearly completed the classical course.

"From a diary which I then kept, and in which my own studies are recorded, I am able to state, quite accurately, what she accomplished in the classics, from term to term, in the two following years. During the winter and spring terms of 1853, she read Xenophon's 'Memorabilia' entire, reciting to Professor Dunshee. In the summer vacation of 1853, twelve of the more advanced students engaged Professor Dunshee as a tutor for one month. John Harnit, II. W. Everest, Philip Burns, C. C. Foote, Miss Booth, and I were of the number. A literary society was formed, in which all took part. During those four weeks, besides taking an active part in the literary exercises of the society, Miss Booth read thoroughly, and for the first time, the Pastorals of Virgil, — that is, the 'Georgics' and 'Bucolics' entire, and the first six books of Homer's 'Iliad,' accompanied by a thorough drill in the Latin or Greek grammar at each recitation. I am sure that none of those who recited with her would say she was behind the foremost in the thoroughness of her work or the elegance of her translations.

"During the fall term of 1853, she read one hundred pages of Herodotus, and about the same amount of Livy. During that term also, Professors Dunshee and Hull, Miss Booth and I, met at her room two evenings of each week, to make a joint translation of the book of Romans. Professor Dunshee contributed his studies of the German commentators, De Wette and Tholuck; and each of the translators made some special study for each meeting. How nearly we completed the translation, I do not remember; but I do remember that the contributions and criticisms of Miss Booth were remarkable for suggestiveness and sound judgment. Our work was more thorough than rapid; for I find this entry in my diary for Dec. 15, 1853: 'Translation Society sat three hours at Miss Booth's room, and agreed upon the translation of nine verses.'

"During the winter term of 1853–54, she continued to read Livy, and also read the whole of Demosthenes 'On the Crown.' The members of the class in Demosthenes were Miss Booth, A. Hull, C. C. Foote, and myself.

"During the spring term of 1854, she read the 'Germania' and 'Agricola' of Tacitus, and a portion of Hesiod."

Cuy. Falls May 8th.

Burke,

O yes my "recollections
in as mind". Those first-
Societies of the Eclectic!
- Pousfuis? And dont I
be they were always sissing
lways sure under a full
of steam, with many a
us explosion? And I
now as I think how ear—
tic, how crude, how cra—
and withal how capable
ally and collectively were.

Truly Yours, A. A. Booth.

Garfield was in Hiram only eight terms, averaging thirteen weeks in length, before he went to college. Six of these terms, as will soon be more fully stated, he taught in the Institute several hours each day. In those eight terms he carried his studies to the junior year of the Williams College course. This included nearly all the Greek and Latin included in the terms of admission, as well as the studies of the Freshman and Sophomore years. Those who are curious to see the amount of study that this included are referred to the terms of admission to Williams in 1854-55, and the full course of instruction, which will be found in the catalogue. The simple facts tell their own story, and no commentary is needed.

President H. W. Everest, of Butler University, Indiana, who was a student with Garfield in Chester, as well as a student and teacher with him in Hiram, thus speaks in a late private communication: —

"I met him first at Chester. Rooming in the same building, and working for a while at the same carpenter's bench, we soon became intimate. He was a noticeable student, both on the play-ground and in the class-room. We recited Robinson's algebra together, and belonged to a literary society of our own getting-up, called the 'Mystic Ten.' At Hiram I was not classed with him, yet knew much of him as a student, but more of him as a teacher. My estimate is briefly as follows; and for many of the items I remember distinct illustrations: —

"1. His intellections were clear, vigorous, and easy in all directions, but especially so in the languages.

"2. He did not study merely to *recite* well, but to *know*, and for the pleasure of learning and knowing.

"3. It was his main object to master the thought, but the language was retained with the thought.

"4. As study was the easy play of his mind, so to recount and to review his lessons and reading was a frequent pleasure.

"5. He was a master at condensed classifications, so that his memory easily held and reproduced what he had learned.

"6. He had a wide-awake curiosity, which seemed never to be satiated. A new thing, however unimportant, always attracted his attention.

"7. He had a great desire and settled purpose to conquer, to master the lesson, to prove superior to every difficulty, to excel all competitors, to conquer and surpass himself.

"8. With this desire to conquer, there was found the most generous and exultant admiration at the success of another.

"9. Over all his study he shed the glory of a happy disposition, — of youth, hope, and manly courage."

All of these points are well taken, but several of them deserve especial emphasis. He studied to *know*, and for the pleasure of learning and knowing. With this may be connected President Everest's seventh point, Garfield's settled purpose to conquer, to prove superior to every difficulty. His love of victory, over men or things, was the strongest; but it was a love born of the noblest elements. He took no pleasure in a merely personal triumph; but a triumph that was a test of honorable superiority, he keenly enjoyed. Here, too, may be mentioned his full appreciation and generous recognition of all men, even though competitors or opponents. His determination to master whatever he undertook, especially to subdue his own nature, is well illustrated by an anecdote. Sitting on a log in the edge of the woods, back of the college building in Hiram, he once said to the companion of his walk, —

"I have made a painful discovery. I have found that my mind needs interest in a subject to incite it to continuous action. The other day I tried to read through a long bill in which I had no interest: it was merely my duty to read it. My attention wandered, thus revealing a defect in my training. If I cannot otherwise overcome this defect," he said, "I will give up my work, renounce public life, go to Germany, and take a full course in one of the universities. I must be full master of my powers at any cost."

At this time he had been in Congress several years.

His mastery of condensed classification not only aided retention and reproduction, and thus greatly facilitated the process of thorough acquisition, but was of incalculable value to him as a teacher and a public speaker. All members of his classes who appreciated him, and even those students who simply heard his lectures, cannot fail to remember the advantage that they received from his blackboard classifications. They were a capital feature of all his teaching. Probably, too, some will remember the effective use that he made of the blackboard at Chagrin Falls (in the debate soon to be mentioned), in showing up Mr. Denton's "law of the planetary distances." Besides, in his oratory classification is an element equally important with strength of statement and aptness of illustration. His curiosity could never be satisfied. No matter what he touched, he *must* understand it. When he went as commissioner to the Flat-Heads, he studied up all the Flat-Head literature that he could find. He got hold of Lewis and Clarke's report of their expedition to Oregon: he carried it with him, and read it with the utmost avidity as he rolled over the hills of Montana in the stage-coach. No doubt, too, Captain Douglass Ottinger, the other officers, and the crew of the cutter "Commodore Perry," will remember the eager interest that he took in every thing pertaining to their ship and service, when he made a trip with them down Lake Erie in 1878, to inspect the Life-Saving Service. The glow of his happy social disposition, his joyous nature, his faith, hope, and courage, and even his tendency to optimism, was an indispensable condition of his success as a student, as a teacher, and as a public man.

Finally, President Everest says Garfield did not study merely to recite well, but to know, and for the pleasure of learning and knowing. But Garfield did study to recite well, all the same. He was never indifferent to a recitation, or to any other appearance of his before a class or an audience. Consciousness that he had made a good recitation never failed to give him much satisfaction. Still, he perfectly appreciated that knowledge and training are the ends of study: nay, he recognized no antagonism between good reciting, in the proper sense, and thorough knowledge. The one is an end in itself, and is the necessary condition of the other. He once said, " If at any time I began to flag in my effort to master a subject, as working out a problem, I was stimulated to further effort by the thought, 'Some other fellow in the class will probably master it.'" In summing up the forces that acted in President Garfield's life, what he thought "the other fellow" was likely to do must never be overlooked. He was always generous in his emulations, but his eye never wandered from the "other fellow." At the same time, full recognition of noble achievement for its own sake, and faithfulness to the heavenly vision as revealed in his own heart, ran parallel with the spirit of emulation.

Although Mr. Garfield had made but slight progress in mathematics and classics when he came to Hiram, before the end of the first year he ranked well up with the best scholars. His masterful mind immediately asserted itself. All soon acknowledged that he was the peer of any: many held him superior to all his compeers. His mind was now reaching out in all directions. He was a vast elemental force, and nothing was so essential to him as room and opportunity. Hiram was now forming her future teachers, as well as creating her own culture. Naturally, therefore, he was given a place in the corps of teachers. So in the catalogue of 1853-54 his name appears twice, — "James A. Garfield, Cuyahoga County," pupil; and "J. A. Garfield, Teacher in the English Department, and of the Ancient Languages." His early engagement as a teacher may point to a certain rawness in the school. However that may be, the pupils lost nothing, but gained much. That the engagement was of great value to him, all will admit who hold with the ancients, and with the founders of the European universities, that teaching is essential to the progress and perfection of the scholar. In this respect Hiram gave him an advantage that an older school, with a higher standard and more conventionality, could not have given. The two years following he taught arithmetic, grammar, algebra, penmanship, geometry, and classes in classics. He handled large classes in the English studies with conspicuous power. He took captive the members of his classes. He won the students as a body. His pupils and fellow-students had a great deal to say about him, as well as much to write in their letters; and the result was, that he made a deep impression, both directly and indirectly, upon the patrons of the school generally. The managers of the Institute saw that his further services would be most desirable when he had finished his own studies. He and Miss Booth left for college at the same time. As they took their leave, — he to return in two years, and she in one, — the Board adopted this resolution : —

"In view of the faithfulness and service to the institution of James A. Garfield and Almeda A. Booth, we recommend to appropriate to each fifty dollars in addition to their salaries."

In that day of small things, fifty dollars was a large sum to the Hiram Board, and to these faithful teachers as well.

It was in the winter of 1853-54 that Garfield preached his first sermon in Hiram, and made his first chapel lecture. One who was so fortunate as to hear both, says the sermon was a parallel between the history of Napoleon Bonaparte and Jesus Christ. The lecture was upon the origin of the English language, a topic then beginning to attract much attention in academical and collegiate schools. He came to the stand with a book in his hand, afterwards discovered to be Fowler's English Grammar. From Part II. of this work, "Historical Elements of the English Language," he mainly drew his materials. There will be found these lines, that he quoted with much effect: —

> "Then sad relief, from that bleak coast that hears
> The German Ocean roar, deep-blooming, strong,
> And yellow-haired, the blue-eyed Saxon came."

The lecture was full of instruction, and opened up to one mind at least that inviting field, the origin, history, and nature of our noble mother-tongue.

But his studies and teaching did not exhaust his activities. He entered into the literary work of the school with great interest and enthusiasm. He was a leading spirit, first in the Eclectic Society, and later in the Philomathean. He turned his hand with equal readiness and ability to the essay, the oration, and the debate. No student's voice was more potent than his in shaping the general polity and tone of the school.

III. — THE WILLIAMS COLLEGE INTERREGNUM.

By the close of the spring term, 1854, Mr. Garfield was ready for college, and was looking about for an *alma mater*. He thought of Bethany, then presided over by Alexander Campbell, whom he greatly reverenced. He decided against Bethany

on three grounds, that he thus stated at the time:
"The course of study is not so extensive or thorough as in Eastern colleges." "Bethany leans too heavily towards slavery." "I am the son of Disciple parents, am one myself, and have had but little acquaintance with people of other views; and, having lived always in the West, I think it will make me more liberal, both in my religious and general views and sentiments, to go into a new circle, where I shall be under new influence." So he wrote to Brown, Yale, and Williams, stating what he had done, and asking how long it would take him to finish their courses.

Says Garfield, in the letter just quoted from,—

"Their answers are now before me. All tell me I can graduate in two years. They are all brief business notes; but President Hopkins concludes with this sentence: 'If you come here, we shall be glad to do what we can for you.' Other things being so nearly equal, this sentence — which seems to be a kind of friendly grasp of the hand — has settled the question for me. I shall start for Williams next week."

Upon what small pivots do great matters turn! In due time this sentence of Dr. Hopkins's will appear in somebody's book upon turning-points in life. So our Hiram student went away to Williamstown, feeling, perhaps, with Milton, —

"How soon hath time, the subtle thief of youth,
Stolen on his wing my three and twentieth year!"

But to Williamstown we cannot follow him. Our story begins again at his return to Hiram in 1856. However, the narrative may be interrupted to set down in this place some facts and reflections that force themselves upon the mind.

Garfield's three years in Hiram had been successful to an extraordinary degree. They had been years of wonderful growth to him. He had gotten out of the school all that he could get: he left much of himself behind. He had fitted himself for the junior class of an Eastern college. Indeed, he felt confident of his ability to finish the course in one year; but, feeling the need of longer and more thorough training, he wisely determined to take two years. He had demonstrated his great ability as a teacher. He had also given evidence of superior power as a public speaker. Accordingly, he was pretty well known at the age of twenty-three to that large circle of which Hiram was the centre; and the question of his future — more commonly shaping itself thus: the pulpit, or the law? was often debated with no little interest in many an Ohio home.

As he turned his face eastward, Mr. Garfield probably did not pause to answer, or even ask, the question, "What has Hiram done for me?" He always became so much a part of every place, and every place so much a part of him, that he was never well fitted for such a bit of self-analysis. First, there is the large question of nature and nurture. He held that every character is the joint product of these two causes. But how difficult to assign to each its proper share of the product! Besides, who can tell the effect of nature in determining nurture? Next comes up the question, "Which would have been better for Garfield, — young Hiram, or old Exeter or Andover?" At Hiram was freedom, a large society of opening minds, instructors learned enough to start him well in his studies, and large room for ability and force of character, of which he had a superabundance. He could do as much as he wanted to do, in pretty much his own way; and he wanted to do a great deal. The especial advantages at Exeter or Andover readily suggest themselves.

Garfield always had a warm side for the small

schools in out-of-the-way places. He thought that the personal elements in education, which he mainly prized, acted in them with more power. Late in life, replying to what had been somewhere said about necessary physical appliances, he said, —

"To all that has been said, I most heartily assent. No words of mine shall in any way detract from the importance of every thing that has been urged; but I am not willing that this discussion should close without mention of the value of a true teacher. Give me a log hut, with only a simple bench, Mark Hopkins on one end and I on the other, and you may have all the buildings, apparatus, and libraries without him."

Miss Booth was the strong individual force that acted upon him in Hiram, as President Hopkins was at Williamstown. Of his indebtedness to the one, he eloquently testified in his address; of his indebtedness to the other, he spoke on numerous occasions. He has been heard to say, "I am surprised to meet President Hopkins — some thought or word of his — so often along the path of my life." All of this is most appreciative and generous, — in a sense, both true and just: nevertheless, it may well be doubted whether, to such a nature as Garfield's, teachers, after he reached his twentieth year, were so important as he thought. It may well be questioned, now that he had got his bent, whether any school was or could be much more to him than a place to spread his tent while he surveyed the kingdom of knowledge. Probably the Hiram students, as a body, did more for him than the Hiram faculty; and the same may be true of the Williams students and faculty. Mr. Rhodes justly said of him in his Cleveland speech, "All men were foils for his own swift blades." He was one of the few who do really

"Find tongues in trees, books in the running brooks,
Sermons in stones, and good in every thing."

However these questions touching the growth of this choice spirit are settled, it was well for Garfield that he took his Ohio training to a New-England college. He never regretted, either his coming to Hiram, or his going to Williamstown. He always retained an unswerving affection for both schools. It was well, too, that on his graduation he returned to his native State. According to Professor C. D. Wilber, he was strongly tempted by a twenty-five-hundred-dollar salary not to return to Hiram. He discussed the subject with himself, and finally said, " They want me at Hiram.

They cannot pay me much, but I ought to go." And so he came back, to receive a salary not more than one-fourth of the sum named. Sense of duty inspired his choice, and the end vindicated his wisdom.

The two years at Williams College lie across the track of my story. That was an epoch of peculiar interest in his life. From 1850 to 1860 President Garfield was in the formative stage, — a period in a man's life that he always regarded with peculiar interest. He said, at the Hiram commencement in 1880, "Oh, these hours of building! If the Superior Being of the Universe would look down upon the world to find the most interesting object, it would be the unfinished, unformed character of young men and of young women." Still, interesting as those two years are, and notwithstanding that they cut the formative period of his life in two, they do not lie within the topic, " President Garfield in Hiram."

He graduated with honor Aug. 6, 1856. President Hopkins's baccalaureate sermon had for its subject, "Self-denial," and closed thus: "Go to your posts; take unto you the whole armor of God; watch the signals and follow the footsteps of your Leader. That leader is not now in the form of the Man of Sorrows; not now does the sweat of agony rain from him. Him the armies of heaven follow; and he hath on his vesture and on his thigh a name written, 'King of kings and Lord of lords.' The conflict may be long, but its issue is not doubtful. You may fall upon the field before the final peal of victory; but be ye faithful unto death, and ye shall receive a crown of life." These sentences now read like a prophecy.

IV.—GARFIELD PRESIDENT OF HIRAM.

In the fall of 1856 Mr. Garfield returned to the Eclectic Institute as teacher of ancient languages. He was now nearly twenty-five years old. He entered upon his work with his wonted enthusiasm and ability, and with greatly enlarged mind and resources. At the end of the school year, Principal Hayden, after seven years of service, resigned. The School Board now took this action as recorded in the minutes: —

"It was resolved, that the present teachers of the institution be constituted a Board of Education, to conduct the educational concerns of the school, subject to the counsel and advice of the Board."

This board of instruction[1] made Mr. Garfield its chairman, and he was so published in the catalogue for the year 1856–57. There appears to have been some hesitancy in making him the principal in name, but he was principal in fact. The next year he became principal in name as well. His style now was, "Principal, and Teacher of Ancient Languages." Thus it continued until August, 1861, when he went to the army, and his *de facto* connection with the Institute ceased. But the Board thought he might return, — at least, they were not ready to part with his name: so he was announced as principal, both in 1862 and 1863. He does not appear in the catalogue for 1864, but re-appears in 1865 and 1866 as advisory principal and lecturer. From this time on, he stands only among the trustees. Within the foregoing chronological limits, lie the life and services that are now to be described. As a matter of course, the heart of the story will be found in the five years reaching from 1856 to 1861.

A good preface to this account of Garfield's life and service as a teacher will be furnished by

[1] This Board consisted of J. A. Garfield, Norman Dunshee, H. W. Everest, J. H. Rhodes, and Almeda A. Booth.

two anecdotes that he related, at widely separated intervals, concerning his experience as a teacher in the district schools. They are also invaluable illustrations of his life and character. The first he told to two or three friends but a short time before he left Mentor for Washington, to be inaugurated President of the United States. The subject under discussion at the time was "office-seeking" in general, and the "second term" in particular.

"The fall that I was eighteen years old, I travelled a considerable circuit round about Orange in quest of a district school to teach. I was refused in one place after another for different reasons; so that at last I came home tired and discouraged. I had made up my mind that seeking positions was not in harmony with my nature; that I never should succeed in life if I hunted places; and that I would make no further effort in that direction, but would wait and see what would come to me. An hour or two after reaching home with these conclusions fully wrought out in my mind, a man from an adjoining neighborhood called at my mother's house, and said he was 'huntin' widow Gaffield's [1] Jimmie.' He wanted a teacher for his district, and he ''lowed that Jimmie would do.' I was called in," said the President-elect, "and a bargain was soon concluded. The coming of this man confirmed me in the opinion that place-

[1] A local corruption of Garfield.

seeking was not in my line; and I have never asked anybody for a place from that day to this."

The reader can reflect upon this story at his leisure. Here it suffices to say, that, in consequence of this contract, the future President of the United States taught his first school. The place was the "Ledge," in Solon, Cuyahoga County, O.; the time, the winter of 1849–50. Afterwards he taught two other district schools, each one term, — one near Zanesville, Muskingum County; and the other in Warrensville, Cuyahoga County.

Years after Garfield had ceased to teach, and when he had already acquired a national reputation as a statesman, he one day gave a lecture to the teachers' class in Hiram College. It was in this lecture that he related the second anecdote : —

"When I first taught a district school, I formed and carried out this plan: After I had gone to bed at night, I threw back the bedclothes from one side of the bed. Then I smoothed out the sheet with my hand. Next, I mentally constructed on this smooth surface my schoolroom. First I drew the aisles; here I put the stove, there the teacher's desk; in this place the water-pail and cup, in that the open space at the head of the room. Then I put in the seats, and placed the scholars upon them in their proper order. I said, Here is John, with Samuel by his side; there Jane and Eliza; and so on, until they were all placed. Then I took them up in order, beginning next my desk in this manner: This is Johnny Smith. What kind of boy is he? What is his mind, and what his temper? How is he doing? What is he now as compared with a week ago? Can I do any thing more for him? And so I went on from seat to seat, and from pupil to pupil, until I had made the circuit of the room. I found this study and review of my pupils of great benefit to them and to me. Besides, my ideal construction, made on the bed-sheet in the dark, aided me materially in the work."

The reader can reflect upon this narrative also at his leisure. Here it suffices to say, that a young man who had the ingenuity, patience, and thoughtfulness to carry on such work as this, night after night, could not but succeed as a district-school teacher, not to speak of higher capacities.

Now we will go on with the Hiram story.

The field of instruction in the Institute was regularly allotted to the different teachers. But the published scheme was never fully carried out in practice. The majority of the students were pursuing selected studies. Calls for classes were more or less irregular. Hence the teachers were compelled to accommodate themselves to the wants of the students. Then their desire to shun ruts and narrowness, to gain breadth and to preserve freshness, as well as the desire to carry their individual methods and personal force through the whole school, tended in the same direction. Still, each teacher generally worked within certain lines, though the lines were not very straight or rigid. Accordingly, it must not be thought that Mr. Garfield taught all the Latin and Greek, or that he taught nothing else. He taught classes in classics and mathematics, history, philosophy, criticism, English literature, rhetoric, English analysis, and geology. Certainly his knowledge of these subjects was not that of the specialist, but it was sufficient for present demands. Nor must it be thought that the demands were small. The standard had been greatly raised since the day that young Garfield looked with such wonder upon a class in geometry. Many young men and women were then fitting for college in Hiram,—some for the Freshman class, but more for the higher classes. Then there were many young men and women of age, ability, and character, who had no thought of going to college, but wanted the "best studies;" and these sometimes tasked the powers of the teachers quite as fully as any others. Principal Garfield took more interest in some studies than in others; but upon the whole it was hard to see that he did not teach all the studies named equally well. At some time all the studies taught in colleges, and more besides, engaged his particular attention, and aroused his special enthusiasm. He introduced Shaw's "English Literature," and Kames's "Elements of Criticism," and awakened a special interest in them. He always taught the class in English analysis. This study was a special favorite with him, and nowhere else did he more shine as a teacher. Through this class most of the better scholars at some time passed, even if they considered themselves thorough in it before. Probably no other of his classes is to-day remembered with equal interest by so many persons. Then his geology class, that recited at five o'clock in the morning, cannot be forgotten by a single surviving member. His method of teaching combined the technical question, the general question, the topic, and the teacher's own discussion of the question in hand. A critic might have said that the last element was too prominent, that he did too much himself, that he did not so much excel as a drill-master and a disciplinarian; but, if fruit is the test of method, it would be hard to sustain the criticism. He strove to awaken the student's faculties. He sought to energize or vitalize him. He revealed the world to the student, and the student to himself. He stimulated thought, created the habit of observation and reflection, aroused courage, widened the field of mental vision, and furnished inspiration in unlimited measures. If his regimen was somewhat deficient in the forces that *push* the student, it was strong in the forces that *draw* him. His associate teachers had more than ordinary ability, and were thoroughly respected by the school; but those scholars who had reached his zone always made an effort, if necessary, to be in at least one of his classes.

In the communication already quoted from, President Everest of Butler University sets these down as Garfield's striking characteristics as a teacher : —

"1. He was always clear and certain.

"2. He impressed the main things, but passed perhaps too lightly over the subordinate portions.

"3. He had rare ability at illustration.

"4. He gave more attention to the boy than to the book. He strove to develop the student, not the lesson or science.

"5. He was abundant in praise of success, but sparing of blame.

"6. He inspired his students with a spirit of investigation and conquest.

"7. By frequent and rapid reviews he kept the whole work in hand, and gave it completeness."

Principal Garfield's chapel lectures were a great source of instruction and influence. Of these he gave many hundreds, ranging over education, teaching, studies, books, methods of study and reading, physical geography, geology, history, the Bible, morals, current topics, and life questions. These lectures were full of fresh facts, new thoughts, striking illustrations, and were warm with the glow of his own life. His two years in Williams College had given his mind some new facets. He brought back the best thoughts of Dr. Hopkins, and sowed them in Hiram soil. His mind was growing every day, and the studies that nourished him nourished his pupils as well. He generally spoke from notes that he had carefully prepared, and that he carefully preserved. If these notes should be brought forth from their hiding-place and published, men would be astonished at the sweep of his thought, the versatility of his mind, and the fertility of his resources.

He appeared frequently as a preacher, both in the pulpit of the Hiram church and in the chapel. His sermons, of which more by and by, added much to his influence over his students. Here it should be said, when he came to the front in 1857, the character of the school somewhat changed. Its genius was less theological or biblical, and more secular or human. The ecclesiastical way of looking at things somewhat receded with the retirement of Principal Hayden. But morals, religion, and Bible study were by no means forgotten. Noble ideals of life and character, ideals of manliness, courage, reverence, and truth, were constantly kept in view. What Arnold of Rugby called "moral thoughtfulness" — the inquiring love of truth and practical love of goodness — was made prominent. Charles Kingsley and Thomas Hughes were a great deal read in Hiram in those days, and the Hiram type of Christianity became somewhat "muscular." Withal, such of the students as could receive it were filled with the Principal's own largeness of nature.

His rhetorical class — known in those days as "Garfield's division" — was a great theatre of interest and improvement. He had great skill in conducting such a class; especially was he a helpful critic. This class will not be forgotten by its members, nor did he forget it. One of his reminiscences in his re-union speech, June 10, 1880, was this: —

"Some may remember the time that I had an exercise which I remember with great pleasure, — when I called a young lad to the rostrum, and said, 'Now, in the next two minutes, you will speak to the best of your ability on the following subject;' and gave him the subject, and let him wrestle with it. It was a trying thing for the young lads, but they very seldom got thrown."

Strong as was Mr. Garfield's intellectual side, his moral side was even stronger. He was full of appreciation and generosity. He was keenly alive to the rights of men, even the lowest and the least worthy. He respected human nature. Tenderness, compassion, and sympathy abounded in him. His sense of justice to others was keen, no matter whether he always insisted upon its being rendered to himself or not. It hurt him to hurt others. He interested himself in the young and in the weak. He often joined the boys in their sports on the campus. Once two of his special friends were "choosing sides" for the game.

Two small boys appeared, and asked to be chosen. The choosers objected to them that they were small, and would spoil the play. "If they cannot play, I will not," said Garfield. They were chosen, and the play went on. In his address on "The Elements of Success" will be found this paragraph: —

"I feel a profounder reverence for a boy than for a man. I never meet a ragged boy of the street without feeling that I may owe him a salute, for I know not what possibilities may be buttoned up under his shabby coat. When I meet you in the full flush of mature life, I see nearly all there is of you; but among these boys are the great men of the future, — the heroes of the next generation, the philosophers, the statesmen, the philanthropists, the great reformers and moulders of the next age. Therefore, I say, there is a peculiar charm to me in the exhibitions of young people engaged in the business of education."

General Garfield once told some Hiram students, that no man is ever loved simply because he has a great or brilliant mind. He may be much respected, or greatly admired, but not loved. The intellectual ray is powerful, but also fierce and pitiless. It is not until the heart ray blends with the mental, and tempers it, as the heat ray the light ray of the sunbeam, that the emotive nature is touched. Feeling lies deeper than logic can penetrate. Only the heart can speak to the heart. In harmony with this law so beautifully formulated, the students respected and admired his ability; but the force that won them was the heart force. Garfield's great, tender heart, his all-embracing sympathy, his nice delicacy of feeling, his quick appreciation of every thing ethically good or spiritually beautiful, will be remembered farther and longer than his powerful logical faculties or his ample knowledge. He called out the demonstrativeness and affections of men in a way almost unprecedented. His heart, none but the utterly obdurate could resist. To him the phlegmatic would stir, the cold warm, the icy melt. When he put his great brotherly arm around a discouraged or fainting boy,—poor, homesick, or blind to the way before him,—the boy very likely shed tears; but somehow the mists began to clear away from his vision, and his heart grew strong. Said one years ago, "Then began to grow up in me an admiration and love for Garfield that has never abated, and the like of which I have never known. A bow of recognition, or a single word, from him, was to me an inspiration."

Those who have witnessed the marvellous drawing-out of men's hearts towards General Garfield in the last year, have simply seen on a vast scale what was seen in Hiram school more than a score of years ago. The revelations of Washington and Elberon have caused little or no surprise to the Hiram fellowship: only the lamentable occasion that brought out the revelations has been a surprise to them. The faith and fortitude, the constancy and courage, the patience and piety, that shone so bright in the White House and in Mr. Francklyn's cottage by the sea, are just what this fellowship, the occasion being given, would have expected. It was said that the eyes of the wife of William the Silent were full of unwept tears: similarly the heart of the late President was full of unshed goodness, gentleness, and tenderness.

Perhaps the foregoing paragraphs taken alone will create a false impression. Let it not be supposed that the Hiram regimen was only soft and winning. The Principal's hand was as firm as his heart was tender; and on due occasion he could be exceedingly severe. He never scolded, never became angry; but his reproofs were all the sterner because of the large background of feeling.

Boys of ability and promise came to Hiram in the period of 1856-61, as they still do, having meagre ideas of studies and of themselves. They expected, possibly because they had given the matter small thought, to study two or three terms, and then to go back to the farm or the shop. In time many of these were touched by Garfield's energizing power. Their minds began to open; new aspirations began to stir in their hearts; and they longed to carry their studies beyond the limits first set. Often these boys had troubles peculiarly their own. Some were poor; some were tethered to home; some wanted courage and self-reliance; some tended to despondency. Mr. Garfield found them out. He remembered his own experience. He seemed to read by intuition a mind that teemed with new facts, ideas, and impressions; that was stirred by a new spirit and power; that sighed for wider and higher activity. These students he aided with his counsel and encouragement. He advised and sometimes expostulated with parents. He took great pleasure in "capturing boys," as he called it; and more than one was saved to himself and to the world by his friendly mediation. A boy who wanted to study, and was poor, called out his full interest. The following letter, written to a district-school teacher who was struggling with the hard questions of life, — a letter already often published, — will illustrate the bent of his nature : —

"HIRAM, Jan. 15, 1857.

"MY DEAR BROTHER, — I was made very glad, a few days since, by the receipt of your letter. It was a very acceptable New Year's present, and I take great pleasure in responding. You have given a vivid picture of a community in which intelligence and morality have been neglected, and I am glad you are disseminating the light. Certainly men must have some knowledge in order to do right. God first said, 'Let there be light:' afterwards he said, 'It is very good.' I am glad to hear of your success in teaching, but I approach with much more interest the consideration of the question you have proposed. Brother mine, it is not a question to be discussed in the spirit of debate, but to be thought over and prayed over as a question 'out of which are the issues of life.' You will agree with me, that every one must decide and direct his own course in life; and the only service friends can afford is to give us the data from which we must draw our own conclusion and decide our course. Allow me, then, to sit beside you, and look over the field of life, and see what are its aspects. I am not one of those who advise every one to undertake the work of a liberal education: indeed, I believe that in two-thirds of the cases such advice would be unwise. The great body of the people will be, and ought to be, (intelligent) farmers and mechanics; and, in many respects, these pass the most independent and happy lives. But God has endowed some of his children with desires and capabilities for a more extended field of labor and influence; and so every life should be shaped according to 'what the man hath.' Now, in reference to yourself, *I know* you have capabilities for occupying positions of high and important trust in the scenes of active life; and I am sure you will not call it flattery in me, nor egotism in yourself, to say so. Tell me: do you not feel a spirit stirring within you that longs *to know, to do, and to dare*, — to hold converse with the great world of thought; that holds before you some high and noble object to which the vigor of your mind and the strength of your arm may be given? Do you not have longings like these, which you breathe to no one, and which you feel must be heeded, or you will pass through life unsatisfied and regretful? I am sure you have them, and they will forever cling round your heart till you obey their mandate. They are the voices of that nature which God has given you, and which, when obeyed, will bless you and your fellow-men. Now, all this might be true, and yet it might be your duty not to follow that course. If your duty to your father or your mother demands that you take another, I shall rejoice to see you taking that other course. The path of duty is where we all ought to walk, be that where it may. But I sincerely hope you will not, without an earnest struggle, give up a course of liberal study. Suppose you could not begin your study again till after your majority. It will not be too late then: but you will gain in many respects; you will have more maturity of mind to appreciate whatever you may study. You may say you will be too old to begin the course; but how could you better spend the earlier days of life? We should not measure life by the days and moments that we pass on earth.

'The life is measured by the soul's advance;
The enlargement of its powers; the expanded field
Wherein it ranges, till it burns and glows
With heavenly joy, with high and heavenly hope.'

"It need be no discouragement that you be obliged to hew your own way, and pay your own charges. You can go to school two terms every year, and pay your own way. I know this, for I did so when teachers' wages were much lower than they are now. It is a great truth, that 'where there is a will, there is a way.' It may be that by and by your father could assist you. It may be that even now he could let you commence on your own resources, so that you could begin immediately. Of this you know, and I do not. I need not tell you how glad I should be to assist you in your work; but, if you cannot come to Hiram while I am here, I shall still hope to hear that you are determined to go on as soon as the time will permit. Will you not write me your thoughts on this whole subject, and tell me your prospects? We are having a very good time in the school this winter. Give my love to Rolden and Louise, and believe me always your friend and brother, J. A. GARFIELD.

"P. S. — Miss Booth and Mr. Rhodes send their love to you. Henry James was here, and made me a good visit a few days ago. He is doing well. He and I have talked of going to see you this winter. I fear we cannot do it. How far is it from here? Was it prophetic that my last word to you ended on the picture of Congress Capitol?"[1]

He seemed always to say and do the right thing at the right time. His wit never came too late. Even trivial things became potent because *he* did them. One student points with affectionate pride to the words, "*carpe diem*," in Garfield's hand, on the fly-leaf of his Horace. Another has shown me this page of autobiography, that he wrote many years ago. The scene lies in the fall term of 1856, the first after the return from Williamstown: —

"I had to leave school at the close of the term for financial and home reasons. I was exceedingly anxious to go on. My faculties were pretty fully worked up; the kingdom of knowledge stretched away before me on every hand; my mind was opening on many questions. Life on the farm, or any life that ignored study, became more and more painful to me. My state of mind became known to a few friends, who did what they could with their sympathy. Garfield tried to steady me and give me courage. At last the end came. After participating in some public literary exercises, I withdrew from the chapel. A few friends, Garfield among them, went with me to the lower hall, where we said good-by. They returned to the chapel; and I started

[1] The letter is written on "Congress" paper. The last word of the previous sentence is on the picture of the Capitol.

homeward, fearing that I should go to school no more. When I had gone many miles, I discovered under the thread of my hat-lining a note that ran thus: —

"'You need to guard against a tone, for I see that you are a little inclined to fall into a measured rhythm. You say *sense* instead of *since*. JAMES.'

"How much influence that note has had upon my life," the page reads, "I do not know; but I feel sure that it was not small."

Perhaps it is needless to say that such a teacher and such a man was very successful as a school administrator. He had nothing of the regulation schoolmaster about him, and he put red tape to small use. He never spent his force on little things. He understood what *was*, and what was *not*, essential to discipline and good order; and he secured the first all the more readily because he was indifferent to the second. He always had a code of printed rules that he expounded each term; he exacted weekly reports of conduct: but his own personality was worth far more than both rules and reports. His management of disciplinary cases was skilful. On one occasion, after morning prayers, he read impressively selections from Prov. vii. He added, " . . . [naming three young men] are expelled from this school." Not another word was said, but the whole made a profound impression. He had unusual power in controlling and influencing bad boys. He did not always make them good; far from it: but he had so much heart and nature, was so free from cant and affectation, that rough fellows who despised a religious profession respected and loved him. Many a boy was thus inclined towards goodness, whom austerity and pretension would have driven to evil.

President Garfield left the academy for the field and the forum at the age of thirty years. But this was not until he had demonstrated his capacity for the highest educational work and honor. He had taught twenty-four terms: viz., three in the district school, six in Hiram before going to college, and fifteen afterwards, — eight years in all. Had he remained an educator, which he had not intended to do more than he had intended to preach, he would have proved himself worthy of the highest position in the land. Other things being equal, he was never greater than in Hiram in the years 1856 to 1861. He came in contact with from one hundred and seventy-five to three hundred students a term, of all ages from fifteen to twenty-five, and of all grades of ability. These students he fired with enthusiasm. The ordinary terms of respect and affection do not meet the case. Their idea of him was the largest that they were capable of forming. They could think of nothing more. It is common for students to form exaggerated opinions of their teachers, — opinions that larger knowledge of men generally shatters. But not so in this case. As their minds grew with years, he grew too; and they never had occasion to measure him over again. As these young hero-worshippers went out from Hiram, some to college and some to business, Mr. Garfield was the standard by whom they measured men. As, with rapturous devotion, they told men of his qualities, they were met sometimes with incredulity, sometimes with a pitying smile, sometimes with a sneer. They were told that Mr. Garfield might answer very well for a little place like Hiram, but that they must not expect to see men accept their estimate of him. But they continued to insist that time would show him equal to the highest honors. The very title by which they had been accustomed to call him at school clung to their lips. Hiram was not then a college, and the teachers were not commonly called professors. He became colonel, general, representative, senator, and president; but plain "Mr. Garfield" always seemed to best befit Hiram students. Still further, his home was in Hiram for many years after he ceased to teach. His relations to the school and to the community in those years will soon be described. Here it suffices to say, his influence was largely felt by the students, even when he did not know their names or faces. What is more, to gain his approval in school, or to be worthy of it afterwards, was an ideal that many a young man or woman carried out into life. These things Mr. Garfield did naturally, and almost unconsciously. His method was spontaneity. However, as years went by, his Hiram friends were able to render him substantial service in his public career. And this they were always glad to do. To serve him, some of them hardly counted their lives dear unto themselves.

Perhaps people outside the Hiram fellowship should make some allowance for the enthusiasm of youth, and for the illusions that time works. However that may be, I cannot refrain from making quotations from two private communications recently received. Both are from old Hiram students; one is an alumnus of Williams, and the other of Oberlin: —

"One day in reading the eleventh ode of Horace, Book I., he had my book; and when it came back to me he had written on a fly-leaf the phrase '*carpe diem*,' as a kind of motto. I have the book still; and, though the pencil-marks are somewhat dim, I shall keep this book. When we wanted a motto for the Delphic, he gave us 'Possunt quia posse videntur,' and translated it for us, 'They are strong because they *think* they are strong.' Both of these are real Garfield mottoes; and I have thought, that, while he was wonderfully gifted by nature, few men ever improved their opportunities as he did. He not only had courage and inspiration for himself, but he filled every one who approached him with much of his own spirit. Now that he is gone, and the vision has fled, I feel like using the words of the disciples who came from Emmaus, 'Did not our heart burn within us while he talked with us by the way?'

"I have been thinking that some one should write a paper or lecture about Garfield as a teacher. I really feel that he was one of the greatest teachers who have appeared in this country. What wisdom, what power, what inspiration, there was in him! It has been my fortune to enjoy the acquaintance of some very distinguished teachers; but even Dr. Hopkins seems to me far inferior to 'Mr. Garfield.' He *taught* all his life, — in the pulpit, on the platform, and in the halls of Congress. Instead of laboring for brilliant periods and high-sounding perorations, he endeavored to make his subjects understood, and to teach the people the science of government."

Too much prominence cannot be given to the fact that Gen. Garfield taught all his life. Nor is it easy to over-estimate the influence of his teacher-life upon his whole public career. No doubt he would have taken a strong interest in public education, had he never taught; but his experience as a teacher greatly widened and deepened his interest. Besides, that experience profoundly influenced his manner of thought and discussion. To instruct his hearers, to throw light upon his subject, was always his supreme ambition in public speaking. An old Hiram student, who often heard him on the stump, once said, "The General never succeeds so well in dealing with a great audience as when he handles it just as he handled his class." Naturally, the educators of the land took great pride in him as a statesman; and, now that he is dead, some affectionately call him "our teacher President."

A lady who has contributed other valuable *memorabilia* to this sketch thus writes of Garfield's student and teacher days: —

"I have often thought a complete conduct of life might be made from his apt quotations and happy generalizations. His studious habits never gave him a pre-occupied air. He seemed so to command his time that leisure belonged to him as much as study.

"I was never his classmate, but was once a fellow-member of a vacation lyceum that met in the lower chapel. The lyceum had night sessions; and the darkness was made apparent by the tallow candles, whose tendency to drip was a constant menace. When any one read an essay, a marshal accompanied him to the rostrum, and illuminated the face, if not the paper, of the reader. Mr. Garfield read a paper, 'The Millennium.' He was a firm believer in a swift-coming millennium; he cited authorities to prove that it was surely coming; proved its desirability, and quoted some very good poetry; but wound up with, 'Let us, therefore, do all that we can to hasten the millennium.' A student who had actually printed some of his own poetry was critic. He criticised the 'Let us.' General Garfield was accustomed to say that this criticism was of great value to him, and that then and there he dropped the hortatory 'Let us.'

"'I am a part of all that I have met,' was one of his favorite quotations. In his class-room his personality was as beneficent, as all-pervasive, as the air we breathe. Each student was etched upon his memory so that he never forgot a name, face, or initial. Often this remembrance brought tears of joy to the eyes of his former pupils after the teacher was lost in the statesman. He once said of himself, 'Of two courses, the one offering improvement, and the other pecuniary reward, I have always sought to choose the one that offered improvement.'"

Mr. Garfield's administration lifted the Eclectic Institute into new prominence. The attendance of students did not indeed increase, owing to the growing competition of other schools, especially within the Disciple pale; but its character was raised, and its influence was enlarged. There was a higher standard of scholarship. Hiram culture became more mature. Students outside of the church were drawn into the school in increasing numbers. Educators became familiar with the name of Hiram and its head. The scope of the work done is pretty fully shown by the Principal's report to the State Commissioner of Common Schools, for the year 1858. It is here somewhat condensed: —

"Students since the founding of the Institute, counting by terms, 5,045; males 2,881, females 2,164. Twenty-five students have graduated from regular colleges, and ten are now in college. The Board of Instruction consists of a principal and seven associate teachers, four male and three female. The number of students enrolled for the year ending Aug. 31, 1858, by terms, as before, 520. Two have entered college during the year, and eight now here are one year advanced in the college course. Number of students studying common branches, 250; ancient languages, 75; modern, eight; higher English branches, 190.

"The aim of the school is to hold the rank of a first-class

collegiate seminary; to train teachers for their duty in the public schools, and to prepare students for an advanced standing in college. One of the peculiarities of the Eclectic is a clause in its charter providing for the introduction of the Bible as a text-book. It is introduced in no sectarian attitude; but the sacred literature, history, and morals of the Bible are regarded as legitimate theme for academic instruction. The Institute is constantly increasing in influence and number of students, and is now more prosperous than ever."

V.—GARFIELD'S OUTSIDE WORK.

But teaching and lecturing did not exhaust Mr. Garfield's activity. He was all the time carrying on important outside work in several fields. This must now be sketched, not indeed fully, but for illustration.

First, may be mentioned his labors at teachers' institutes. His ability as a teacher, and especially as a lecturer, strongly recommended him to the institute committees as well as to the teachers who attended them. Frequent calls for lectures came to him from the various lecture associations round about. Admirable lectures on "Sir Walter Scott" and "Germany," as well as other topics, lie to-day among his unpublished papers.

He preached more or less before he went to

college. At college he preached frequently to two or three small churches of Disciples within reach of Williamstown. After his return to Hiram, he continued to preach until he went into the army. For five full years, he preached somewhere nearly every Sunday. A number of churches can be named to which he preached "one-half his time" for several years. He appeared occasionally in the pulpits of churches where he had no regular engagements. At the great "yearly meetings," where thousands gathered under the old "Bedford tent" or under the shade, he was a favorite preacher. His sermons live only in the hearts of those who heard them. They were strong in the ethical rather than in the distinctively evangelical element. He had small interest in purely theological or ecclesiastical topics. He inclined to Coleridge's canon, "That is truth which finds me." His stricter brethren found much fault with him because he was not more denominational; some said he lacked "unction:" but the people, wherever he went, would turn out to hear Garfield preach. He greatly admired the life and character of Paul the apostle; and one of his ablest sermons, remembered by many to this day,. was upon that subject. In

August, 1860, Mr. Campbell and Mr. Garfield attended the Stark County Yearly Meeting at Alliance, O. The old preacher preached Sunday morning, the young one Sunday afternoon. Mr. Robert Moffet, now of Cleveland, O., has just reproduced from his "sketch-book" a report of Garfield's sermon, written at the time. No doubt many readers will be glad to see the framework of a Garfield sermon.

"He took for his text the following passages: 'In him was life, and the life was the light of men' (John i. 4). 'Let your light so shine before men that they may see your good works, and glorify your Father which is in heaven' (Matt. v. 16).

"In the exordium he drew a contrast between the giving of the old law, and the giving of the law of the spirit of life in Christ Jesus. The one was given amid the awful thunder and smoke of Sinai; the other, amid the quiet and glory of nature's mountain scenery in Judea. The one was given in a manner to terrify the people; the other, in circumstances which invited the multitude to draw near to Jesus. The one was the awful voice of the unseen God; the other, the voice of God in a Friend and Brother.

"He then took up the subject of life and light as found in the texts.

"I. THE LAW OF ITS BEING: constitutional law, — the law by which this life must be in us.

"1. *We must be in him.* Spiritual life is spiritual union with Christ.

"2. *The union must be intimate.* When a scion is grafted into the stock, care is taken to establish a very close and intimate union, so that the life of the tree or vine may be imparted to it. So our union with Christ must be very intimate. External forms do not constitute an intimate union. There must be the faith and love of the heart. There must be a complete surrender of the will to Christ.

"3. As the scion grafted into the stock *must be capable of receiving life,* — must not be dead, — so the man grafted into Christ must not be totally dead, but must be capable of receiving life from the fountain of life, — Christ Jesus. 'If any man be in Christ, he is a new creature.' He has been quickened from his 'death in trespasses and in sins.'

"II. THE LAW OF ITS ACTION: —

"1. The *life* of Christ transferred becomes *light.* When we take Christ for our example, when we draw our inspiration from him, when his life is in us as a controlling inspiration and power, then do we become the light of the world.

"2. 'Let your light so shine.' We cannot dim the light which comes from Christ, but we can

"(*a*) Bring something between us and Jesus Christ, and prevent his shining upon us. We can fail to maintain that intimate union with Christ, who is the source of life, — that life which is the light of men.

"(*b*) We can place something between us and others, and thus hinder our light from shining before men. We need to let our light shine out into all the dark places. What for?

"(c) To induce men to glorify God our Father. The world demands a lived gospel as well as a preached gospel. Christians need to be living epistles, known and read of all men. A dying world is calling for that life which is the light of men."

President Garfield's connection with the ministry has been the theme of much curious inquiry. Hence it may be well to state some general facts connected therewith.

He was never a minister in the commonly accepted sense. The Disciples' Church originated in a revolt from the old standards of doctrine and polity, and thus gave more room to personal force and inspiration than the older and more conservative bodies. "To exercise his gifts," was each brother's privilege. Such exercise was directly encouraged. Hence "the liberty of prophesying" took a wide range. What is more, even the brethren who were known as preachers passed into the ministerial body, and out of it, with comparative ease. It must be remembered that the Disciples were a young body thirty years ago, and that they had not then attained to their present degree of order and discipline. Mr. Garfield had no other ordination than the approval and encouragement of the churches. Whether at any time he intended to devote his life to preaching, must perhaps remain in doubt. If he did, it must have been before he went to college. The probability is, that from the time when he began to preach he held it an unsettled question, until he decided it in the negative. To a few persons in his confidence, he definitely announced, as early as 1857 or 1858, that he should not be a preacher. His action was in harmony with this announcement. While preaching week by week, he was taking an active part in politics, and was carrying on a course of reading in the law. That the pulpit took a strong hold of his mind, cannot be questioned. Once he was called to the pulpit of what is now the Central Church of Cincinnati, but declined. No doubt he would have achieved high distinction as a preacher, but he did not feel that he had the inward vocation for the work. His genius drew him to the State by its very bent, as any one who has followed his history can see. Ceasing to preach at the same time that he ceased to teach (save an occasional later discourse), his preaching had been not only the source of much good to others, but a source of great strength to him, both as a man and as a public servant.

Here are presented all the facts needed to

answer the question of Garfield's having been a preacher, that occupied so much attention the last Presidential campaign. Sometimes he was made the victim of violent attacks; sometimes, of ill-considered defences. On the one hand it was said he had "abandoned the ministry;" and on the other replied, that he did not preach much or long, that he was only a "lay preacher," and things of that sort. The history now given shows that there was no room for the attack, and no need of the apology.

One incident of peculiar interest rose out of Mr. Garfield's short ministry. He was preaching in Chagrin Falls, Cuyahoga County, where infidelity had long had a strong grasp. Spiritualism had also taken a strong hold of the community. Mr. William Denton, an itinerant Spiritualistic and scientific lecturer and debater, occasionally visited the village, in which he gained a large following. So he did in other similar centres in the Western Reserve. His particular effort was to overthrow the Bible. He sometimes followed the line of argument marked out by Paine one hundred years ago, and pursued by Col. Ingersoll to-day. But his favorite weapon was the discoveries of science, especially geology. These he so interpreted as to sap faith in the Mosaic history. More narrowly, he advocated the development theory. Mr. Denton was a man of considerable discursive reading: he made pretensions to being a practical geologist, and was a public speaker of much fluency and force. According to his custom, he threw out a challenge in Chagrin Falls, to all comers, to meet him in debate upon his favorite ground. The Hiram teacher and preacher took up the glove. At the time he had no special knowledge of the subject. He had studied geology at college, and had perhaps read a few books on the science since. He made his preparation with his usual thoroughness. Instead of "two days," as one historian has glibly said, he devoted weeks and even months to the study of the subject. In the holidays of 1858 the debate came on. Mr. Denton's friends expected an easy victory, so did Mr. Denton himself; and even Mr. Garfield's friends looked forward with much fear and trembling. The roads and weather could hardly have been worse. Nevertheless, public interest and even excitement ran high; and the largest audience-room in the town was packed with eager listeners day after day and night after night, for nearly a week. The contest need not here be followed point by point. Suffice it to say, that was before Mr. Darwin, in "The Origin of Species," gave evolution its present shaping; and the proposition in dispute stated the doctrine as it had been left by Lamarck and the author of "The Vestiges of Creation." Mr. Garfield's strength and resources proved ample. He rose to the level of the occasion, and surpassed expectations. The Christian portion of the community claimed a decided triumph; the irreligious either admitted it, or called it a "drawn battle;" while Mr. Denton said that his antagonist was the ablest and the noblest that he had ever met. His influence in all the country round about immediately waned, and never regained its former height.

This debate was coincident with a dawning of popular interest in scientific subjects in Mr. Garfield's constituency, and in much wider circles. Many important results followed the debate. First, the defences of the Christian faith were strengthened in a considerable region of country. In the second place, it added much to the defender's power and influence. Third, it led at once to a great quickening of interest in science among Hiram students. Fourth, the interest reached out into the larger community of which Hiram was the centre; and more invitations to lecture on scientific topics than he could possibly accept flowed in upon the debater.

At the very time of his return from Williams College, President Garfield was drawn into politics. This was due to several causes. First may be named the bent of his mind already mentioned. Next the inspiring Presidential campaign of 1856. Now the Republican party, born in a day, first came into national prominence. The attempt to limit the extension of slavery took full possession of his soul, and Gen. Fremont's candidacy fired his imagination. Mr. Garfield made several speeches that campaign in Hiram and adjoining towns. The next year he took a more prominent part in the canvass. Year by year, both the number and the geographical range of his speeches increased. He soon became a recognized political force in Portage County. In 1859 he was chosen State Senator from the Portage-Summit district. He was now twenty-eight years old. That campaign he appeared in Akron on the same platform with Mr. Chase, then candidate for Governor; and one good judge said the Senatorial candidate made the better speech. He served in the Senate one term, and at the close entered a still wider field of activity and influence. Nothing more need be said of his entry into politics than that his rise was rapid, almost instantaneous. As early as 1859, in which campaign he took an active part, he had become a favorite speaker in a considerable section of the State; and in the Senate he immediately came to the front.

As a matter of course, Hiram school received only a part of its Principal's energies, particularly after 1859. Preaching, lecturing, politics, and his law-reading made heavy and constant draughts upon him; but he was so full of faculties, of strength, and resources, that he did not seem weakened thereby. In 1859 or 1860 this was a common day's work for him: a chapel lecture in the morning; five solid hours of teaching, perhaps six; attention to administrative details; a speech ten miles away in the evening; home to bed at midnight. If the next day was Sunday, he would give two sermons, perhaps fifteen miles off. Of course no man who covers such a field as this can be called a specialist. Still, he always kept abreast of his school-work. The range of his ability, and the great strength that he put into whatever he undertook, attracted public attention, gave prominence to the school, and increased the pride that his pupils felt in him.

Only the most vigorous and wide-reaching intellectual life could sustain such labors as these. Garfield's mind was ever fresh, his ·thoughts ever new. His reading lay, first, along the lines of his work, — teaching, lecturing, preaching, and politics; second, in 1858, he entered his name as a student-at-law with a Cleveland firm. His legal studies he carried on at home, and with such thoroughness and zeal, that he fitted for the Ohio bar in the time usually required by students who have nothing else on hand. But, third, he read widely outside of his work, both present and prospective. He read "hard reading," but fiction and poetry as well. He naturalized Tennyson, of whom he became a profound student, in Hiram. In later years he read everywhere, — on the cars, in the omnibus, and after retiring at night. He rarely, or never, went away from home, even for a few hours, but he took his book. He made special efforts to procure out-of-the-way reading. If he was leaving Washington for a few days, and had nothing requiring immediate attention on hand, he would go to the great Library of Congress, and say to the librarian, " Mr. Spofford, give me something that I don't know any thing about." A stray book coming to him in this way would often lead to a special study of the subject. In this way he kept his mind full and fresh.

But, with all his reading, he could not have done the work that he did, but for the ready and powerful grasp with which he took hold of a subject, and for the wondrous ease and quickness with which he could organize the material that he needed. He seemed to see at a glance the relations of things. In his studies he strove to get hold of the underlying principle, and was never satisfied until he could reduce facts to order. Once he said, "I could not stay in politics unless I found some philosophy." Hence the breadth of his views of all subjects. Here is also the explanation of Judge Cooley's remark in his Ann Arbor oration: "He always discussed large subjects in a large way." His powers, the whole mass of his being, came to be under the control of his will.

General Garfield was always absorbed and happy in his work, in studies, in teaching, in arms, in legislation. But he ever looked back to his teacher-life with peculiar satisfaction. Addressing the National Association of School Superintendents, in 1879, he said, —

"I feel at home among teachers; and, I may say, I look back with more satisfaction upon my work as a teacher than upon any other work I have done. It gives me a pleasant home feeling to sit among you, and revive old memories."

In the Hiram period he was full of ambition and strength; he had plenty of work and plenty of leisure; his friends and fellow-workers were congenial; and his joyous nature ran full and free. To all who beheld it, his teacher-life must remain a thing of beauty and a joy forever. Again let the reader substitute his name for Miss Booth's in this passage: —

"As the earlier teachers were called away to other fields of duty, their places were supplied by selection from those who had been Eclectic students; and thus Miss Booth found herself associated with teachers whose culture she had guided, and who were attached to her by the strongest ties of friendship. I know how apt we are to exaggerate the merits of those we love; but, making due allowance for this tendency, as I look back upon the little circle of teachers who labored here, under the leadership of our honored and venerable friend Mr. Hayden, during the first six years of the Eclectic, and upon the younger group, associated with me from 1856 until the breaking-out of the war, I think I wrong no one of them by saying, that for generous friendship and united, earnest work, I have never seen and never expect to see their like again. Enough new members were added to the corps of teachers from year to year to keep alive the freshness of young enthusiasm; and yet

enough experience and maturity of judgment were left to hold the school in a steady course of prosperity."

VI.—GARFIELD'S LATER HIRAM LIFE.

In 1861 Mr. Garfield went to the army, and in 1863 to Congress. His services as a soldier and statesman do not lie within the scope of this sketch. But Hiram continued his Ohio home until he removed to Mentor in 1877. Some phases of his later Hiram life must be here described.

In November, 1858, he married Miss Lucretia Rudolph, whose mental gifts, both native and acquired, well fitted her for his wife and companion. She had been a pupil with him, both in Chester and in Hiram, as well as a pupil of his in Hiram. Now she became both his fellow-student and co-worker. His obligations to her in the wifely relation he strongly and beautifully recognized on all fitting occasions. Her great strength of character, long before known to private friends, was fully revealed to the world in the long tragedy that closed at Elberon, Sept. 19, 1881. Mr. and Mrs. Garfield's domestic life was eminently happy and beautiful. After the war Grandma Garfield, now known so pleasantly to the world as "the little white-haired mother," was generally a member of the family. They were a happy trio, — a fond mother, a dutiful son and husband, a faithful daughter and wife. Both General and Mrs. Garfield were always conspicuous for private and domestic virtues, "filial affection, unbroken troth, and parental love."

At first they did not set up housekeeping, but boarded. In the month of April, 1863, the General — then on a visit home from the army — purchased for eight hundred and twenty-five dollars the only home that they ever owned in Hiram, — the small two-story frame house that so many friends remember. This house Mrs. Garfield refitted and enlarged in the fall of 1863, at an expense of one thousand dollars. Here they made their happy home until, in 1872, the family having outgrown it, he sold it to its present owner and occupant. Henceforth the Garfields spent more time in Washington; but whenever in Hiram, — as they always were each summer until the removal to Mentor in 1877, — they made their home at father Rudolph's. Their Hiram life was perfectly simple and natural, as became their estate, their nature, and their surroundings. Save the constantly-used and ever-growing library, nothing in or about General Garfield's home stood in contrast to the homes of his neighbors. His house was a place for "plain living and high thinking." If the old walls could speak, what thoughts would they not voice, what emotions utter, what joyousness describe! He never kept a carriage, and save for two short intervals, — one just before and one just after the war, — never a horse and buggy. To get to and from the railroad, he depended upon the hack, or some neighbor's vehicle, or walked. It may be added, that it was from the old house that little Trot was buried in December, 1863, just as her father reached Hiram on his way to Washington from the Army of the Cumberland; and that it was to father Rudolph's that the body of little Eddie was brought for burial in the autumn of 1876. The two children — the eldest and the youngest born — sleep side by side in the Hiram graveyard.

Talking of walking to and from the railroad, let me say that more of it was done twenty years ago than now. As I write, there comes to me a vision of an autumn evening in the year 1858. Mr. Garfield, Miss Booth, Henry Newcomb, and the writer — all of whom, save the last, have passed over, and "joined the majority" — alighted from the same train at the "Jeddo" platform. The two teachers had been to Cleveland; and Mr. Garfield had brought home with him a copy of "The Atlantic Monthly" for the current month. Here let me say that no man or woman less than forty years old can well appreciate the advent of this magazine. Such people *found* "The Atlantic" when they began to read. But in 1857 — "The Atlantic's" natal year — a great many minds were waiting for "something of the kind;" and the magazine *came* to them. Thus it came to Mr. and Mrs. Garfield, Miss Booth, and others in the Hiram fellowship. He thought Dr. Holmes the strongest of the early contributors, and much appreciated, both his prose and his verse. He followed the successive numbers of "The Autocrat" with great interest. As the quartet before mentioned walked to Hiram that beautiful autumn evening, he read to them the twelfth number of this serial. I seem to hear again the intonations and to see the gestures with which he read the professor's "Prelude:" —

> "I'm the fellah that tole one day
> The tale of the won'erful one-hoss shay."

This little incident gives an opportunity to say that the scope of General Garfield's intellectual

My Dear Friend —

I shall be sorry if the time comes when you can stop writing. Through his friends the General still seems to speak to me, and your words help me to feel that he does indeed live somewhere in the great Universe.

I quite approve of your plan in regard to the Memorial Volume. It would be most appropriate that the speeches to which you refer should appear in such a volume.

Your friend
Lucretia R. Garfield.

Prof. B. A. Hinsdale

tastes and likes was singularly wide. He took equal though a very different interest in Tooke's "History of Prices," and in the "Biglow Papers." He grew wise over the grave and weighty page of Bacon, and laughed over "Pickwick" until it seemed that his own prediction, "I believe Dickens will kill me yet," would be realized. He delighted in the knightly tales of Scott, and in both the tragedy and comedy of Shakspeare. He was as rich in humor as he was strong in logic. He abounded in delightful fancies and in pleasant conceits. The election to the Presidency, indeed, laid its hand heavily upon him, repressing somewhat his early spirits; but in Hiram he was full of "jest and youthful jollity," of "quips and cranks." At the same time he never lost his propriety, or surrendered the dignity of his carriage. The over-grave might, indeed, have taken offence at his mirth and flow of spirits; but he who could "unbend" with a boy could instantly rise to the level of the grave and the serious.

Few men ever saw clear around General Garfield, he was so many-sided. He became the "sage of Mentor,"—the man to whom the people looked for counsel and wisdom; but he was much more than a sage. He was full of human nature. Mr. Lowell read him aright when he said in Exeter Hall, London, "He was so *human*." He could ever give the one touch of nature that makes the whole world kin. He had read books; he "talked like a book;" but he was not a book. Men spoke admiringly of his great attainments; but he was never a recluse, never seemed bookish. He gathered the metal from which he forged his armor and his weapons from all mines; but they were always forged in his own fires. He generally seemed to have abundant leisure. His delight in conversation was equalled only by his excellence as a converser. He was at home to all men, and at home with them. He would leave on the mind of the Montana stage-driver, on whose box he rode, the impression that he was an extraordinary man; and he met the courtly Sir Edward Thornton, on the latter's departure for England, with an equal dignity and grace.

Astonishment has often been expressed by those familiar with intellectual work, that Representative Garfield performed such a great amount of work the nine Congresses that he sat in the House of Representatives. At the same time, a fuller appreciation of what he did, which is sure to follow the gathering-up of his literary work, and the publication of an adequate life, will add to this astonishment. No man in this country contributed so much that is valuable to the public discussion of serious questions, between 1870 and 1880. This was profoundly felt by the managers of the Republican campaign last year. A note addressed to the Hon. Edward McPherson, secretary of the Republican Congressional Committee, brought this reply: —

"GETTYSBURG, PENN., Oct. 3, 1881.

"DEAR SIR, — I have found the statement of the issues [of documents] made by the Republican Congressional Committee of 1880. The total number of copies issued by us was 12,973,000. Of this the reprint of General Garfield's speeches reached the large aggregate of 3,881,000 copies, or more than one-fourth of the whole. The same proportion, no doubt, applies to the National Committee.

"No candidate ever so powerfully impressed himself upon the country as General Garfield; and he, more truly than any one else, elected himself. Usually candidates are a burden. He was a help almost to the extent of carrying the campaign. This I felt daily as the months rolled on.

"Respectfully yours,
"EDW. McPHERSON.
"PRESIDENT HINSDALE."

Here it may be added, that Mr. McPherson's committee published fifteen Garfield documents; that one exceeded a circulation of half a million copies, and several others approached that number.

Now, the explanation of General Garfield's work, so great and so valuable, lies in these facts, — his great abilities, his thorough mental training and sound habits of study, his powerful physical constitution, his just conception of public life and public duty, his noble ambition to fill out that conception, and the favorable surroundings of his Ohio home. He devoted himself to his proper work. His comparative retirement and freedom from interruption gave him one of the conditions for that work which he needed.

What is more, his constituency did not greatly annoy him with calls for offices or clamor for patronage. Much surprise has been expressed that so great a man as General Garfield lived in so small a place as Hiram. The surprise is ill-founded. It is more than doubtful whether he ever could have done so much, had he lived in a great social and business centre. Macaulay expressed the opinion that a great work on political science, like Adam Smith's "Wealth of Nations," is more likely to come from a humble clergyman in the Hebrides than from an active member of the British Parliament; and there was equally good cause for looking to Hiram for a great statesman, rather than to New York or Philadelphia.

General Garfield's readiness on all occasions has often been remarked. Probably some have attributed this readiness to the inspiration of genius. The explanation lies partly in his genius, but much more in his indefatigable work. He treasured up knowledge of all kinds. "You never know," he would say, "how soon you will need it." Then he forecasted occasions, and got ready to meet them. One hot day in July, 1876, he brought to his Washington house an old copy of "The Congressional Globe." Questioned he said, "I have been told confidentially that Mr. Lamar is going to make a speech in the House on general politics, to influence the Presidential canvass. If he does, I shall reply to him. Mr. Lamar was a member of the House before the war; and I am going to read some of his old speeches, and get into his mind." Mr. Lamar made his speech Aug. 2, and Mr. Garfield replied the 4th. Men expressed surprise at the fulness and completeness of the reply delivered on such short notice. But to one knowing his habits of mind, especially to the one who had the aforesaid conversation with him, the whole matter was as light as day. His genius was emphatically the genius of preparation. How apposite here is this paragraph from his address on "College Education:" —

"Men look with admiring wonder upon a great intellectual effort, like Webster's reply to Hayne, and seem to think that it leaped into life by the inspiration of the moment. But if, by some intellectual chemistry, we could resolve that masterly speech into its several elements of power, and trace each to its source, we should find that every constituent force had been elaborated twenty years before, it may be in some hour of earnest intellectual labor. Occasion may be the bugle-call that summons an army to battle; but the blast of a bugle cannot ever make soldiers, or win victories."

Mr. Garfield excelled almost all men in comprehensive generalizations; also in the patient, untiring labor with which he would hunt down special facts. Some loose leaves found the other day in an old memorandum-book, probably not opened before for a dozen years, happily illustrate this latter point. They will also call attention to a little thing long since forgotten.

Senator Sumner published in "The Atlantic Monthly" for December, 1866, an article entitled "Clemency and Common Sense." Upon one feature of this article General Garfield wrote this criticism, which appeared in "The New-York Evening Post:" —

"In Senator Sumner's very learned and interesting article in the December number of 'The Atlantic Monthly,' he has minutely analyzed the Homeric fable of Scylla and Charybdis, and has located the Sirens near by, and made them a party to the dangers of, Scylla.

"He says, 'For the fable Homer is our highest authority,' and he represents the Sirens as playing their part to tempt their victims. . . . 'Charybdis was a whirlpool in which ships were often sucked to destruction. Scylla was a rock on which ships were often dashed to pieces.' 'Ulysses in his wanderings encountered these terrors; but, by prudence and the counsels of Circe, he was enabled to steer clear between them, *although the Sirens strove to lure him onto the rock.*'

"Again, after quoting from the 'Odyssey' the descriptions of the whirlpool and the rock, the Senator says, '*Near by* were the Sirens, who strove by their music to draw the navigator on to certain doom.'

"He then represents Ulysses as stuffing the ears of his companions with wax to shut out the ravishing melody of the Sirens, causing himself to be lashed to the mast like another Farragut, and steering clear between Scylla and Charybdis, beyond the Sirens, 'Till dying off the distant sounds decay.'

"Now, the island, or rather promontory, of the Sirens is on the Italian coast, more than a hundred miles north of Scylla and Charybdis. Surrentum is generally believed to have been their home, and is set down in Bohn's 'Classical Atlas' at 40° 38' north latitude, while Scylla is 38° 15'.

"Homer, who, as the Senator says, 'is our highest authority' for this fable, does not associate the Sirens with the dangers of the narrow passage.

"They lived in a verdant meadow strewn with the bones of victims, who had been lured to the shore by the irresistible charm of their music.

"Circe having described their abode, and taught Ulysses how to escape them, says, —

"'When their companions shall have sailed beyond them, then I cannot tell thee which will afterward be thy way,' and then proceeded to point out the dangers of Scylla and Charybdis.

"Let us believe that the honorable Senator's mistake in regard to the Sirens arises from the fact that he has never been lured by their charms to an intimate acquaintance."

The loose leaves mentioned above are Garfield's original draught of this note. It may not read here just as it does in the "The Evening Post."

Those were grand years in Garfield's life that lay between 1865 and 1877. At the first date he was well started upon his great legislative career: at the second, he had not become so absorbed in public affairs as he afterwards became. They were years of reading, study, thinking, and communion with friends and family. He was happy in his family, in his friends, and in his work. To live by his side those years, to be welcome to his house, to walk with him through field and wood, to hear him discuss books, men, and questions, with him "to outwatch the Bear,"—was a privilege such as the gods of high Olympus never granted to their greatest favorites.

General Garfield retained his Hiram interest and affection to the last. This can be shown by short notices of his relations to the church, the College Board, the students, and the Hiram fellowship.

He early became a member of the Hiram church, and never removed his proper membership to another congregation,—neither to Mentor nor Washington. His interest in both the congregation and the pulpit continued. In the church he frequently participated in the social services. The last time that he did so, he spoke feelingly of the gloom and chill cast over life by unbelief in the central Christian doctrines. A letter just received speaks of another of these occasions: "A little talk that he gave one Sunday afternoon near twilight, in the blessed Hiram church, has come into my mind again and again, these last days. It was five or six years ago; and I cannot recall what he said, except that he quoted these words of Christ to his disciples, perhaps for a text: 'It is expedient for you that I go away: for if I go not away, the Comforter will not come unto you; but if I depart, I will send him to you.'"

He conscientiously performed his duties as a member of the Board of Trustees. No member was more useful, or made more sacrifice to be present at the meetings. June 7, 1881, in a letter to the President of the College, he wrote: "I feel a sense of positive loss in not being able to attend the commencement at Hiram, but of course it is impossible. . . . Express to the Board my regret that I am not able to be with them." Record should also be made of the fact that he always stood with the most liberal in his contributions to the treasury.

So long as Hiram was his home, he gave the students occasional lectures; and, even after he moved away, on his flying visits he would visit the chapel, if possible, and make a "talk." In the spring of 1871 he gave a course of ten lectures on Social Science. In 1869 and 1870, he had made a special study of the census and its related subjects, and had attempted to get an improved census law enacted. He read widely the literature of statistics, English, French, and Belgian. His lectures were an outgrowth of these studies. Professor I. N. Demmon, then of Hiram, now of Michigan University, who heard these lectures, thus speaks of them under date of Oct. 17, 1881: —

"On consulting my diary for that year, I find that the first lecture was given on Friday afternoon, May 26. The subject was 'The Methods of Thought.' The second, given on the following day, attempted a classification of the sciences. During the next week, at least four more lectures were given, as follows: 'Practical Value of Social Science;' 'Preservation and Extension of Life;' 'Society and Government, their Nature and Origin;' 'Reign of Law.' I took rough notes of the lectures, which I have since regretted that I did not write out and elaborate at the time. The lectures were full of suggestive thought and happy illustration, and were delivered in the General's engaging manner, greatly to the delight and instruction of us all. They were given off-hand, apparently from rough notes. A rational, and at the same time devout, spirit ran through them all."

But it must not be supposed that these lectures flowed spontaneously out of their author's general reading upon the subjects discussed: he devoted to them much labor and time, — more, probably, than he ever gave to a case in the Supreme Court. All of which he did on account of his interest in the subjects themselves, and his desire to aid the students and college.

Soon after President Garfield's election to the Senate in the winter of 1879–80, a letter of congratulation was sent to him in the name of the faculty and students. The letter spoke of his election, and particularly of the honorable manner in which it had been accomplished. Soon came back this graceful reply: —

"WASHINGTON, D.C., Jan. 28, 1880.

"PROF. G. H. COLTON, LOUIS HOFFMAN, AND C. P. WILSON, *Hiram, Portage Co., Ohio.*

"GENTLEMEN, — I owe you an apology for so long neglecting to acknowledge your very kind letter of the 17th inst. I have been so constantly engaged since it came, that it has been really impossible to answer it sooner.

"I thank you with all my heart for the kind congratulations with which the faculty and students of Hiram College have honored me. So much of my life was identified with the educational work of Hiram, that I could not be true to myself should I ever cease to cherish with the utmost affection, not only the memories of the place, but its dearest interests.

"I concur with you in esteeming more highly than the office itself the manner in which the Senatorship was conferred upon me; and I may add that I prize still more highly the approval of thoughtful, cultivated men, and especially those who know me so well as the faculty and students of Hiram College. I beg you to express to them my heartfelt thanks for their kind remembrance.

"Very truly yours,
"J. A. GARFIELD."

Of his relations to the community, a word suffices. He discharged to the full his duties as a citizen. His democratic manner and spirit levelled all barriers to approach. All his neighbors knew that he was approachable and generous; and all had the most unbounded confidence in his probity and honor.

The great day of every year in Hiram is Commencement. It is a day very like what Commencement was to the smaller New-England colleges before the railroads so mixed up the city and the country. It is a day looked forward to with great interest by a large number of persons. General Garfield always made it a point to attend, if consistent. As the time drew near, the question, "Will Mr. Garfield [or, "the General"] be there?" was often asked in the regions round about. It is, perhaps, needless to say, that to the "old students" (as they are now called) he was always the centre of interest. To Hiram he came,

June 10, 1880, two days after his nomination at Chicago, partly to attend the Commencement, but more to be present at the great re-union that is held every five years. How different his coming from that of 1851! Then he came unobserved, a student poor and plain: now he comes with flags, and bands of music, powerful friends and a huzzaing multitude, and a troop of correspondents to tell it all to the world. At the close of the exercises he made this, his last Commencement speech: —

"It always has given me pleasure to come here, and look upon these faces. It has always given me new courage and new strength. It has brought back a large share of that richness that belongs to those things out of which come the joys of life. While I have been sitting here this afternoon, watching your faces, and listening to the very interesting address just delivered, it occurred to me that the best thing you have that all men envy — I mean, all men who have reached the meridian of life — is perhaps the thing you care for least, and that is your leisure, — the leisure you have to think in, and to be let alone; the leisure you have to throw the plummet with your hands, and sound the depths, and find what is below; the leisure you have to walk about the towers of yourselves, and find how strong or how weak they are, and determine which need building up, and how to shape them, that you may be made the final being that you are to be. Oh, these hours of building! If the Superior Being of the universe would look down upon the world, to find the most interesting object, it would be the unfinished and unformed character of young men and young women. Those behind me have probably, in the main, settled such questions. Those who have passed middle manhood and middle womanhood are about what they will always be, and there is little left of interest or curiosity as to their development; but in your young, unformed natures, no man knows the possibilities that lie treasured up. While you are working up those possibilities with that splendid leisure, you are the most envied of all classes of men and women in the world. I congratulate you on your leisure. I commend you to keep it as your gold, as your wealth, as your means, out of which you can demand all possible treasures that God laid down when he formed your nature, and unveiled and developed the possibilities of your future. This place is too full of memories for me to trust myself to speak more, and I will not; but I draw again to-day, as I have drawn for a quarter of a century, evidences of strength and affection from the people who gather in this place, and I thank you for the permission to see you and meet you and greet you as I have done to-day." [1]

[1] Soon after Garfield's graduation, President Hopkins preached a Baccalaureate Sermon on "Leisure," from the text, "Gather up the fragments that remain, that nothing be lost." This sermon, which he either heard or read, was a seed-thought in Garfield's mind. He struck the "leisure" chord again in his inimitable Chautauqua speech delivered at sunrise, Aug. 9, 1881.

The next day he presided in the Tabernacle, and made his last re-union speech. This has been once given in this sketch, and need not be here repeated. Feb. 4, 1881, he made his last visit to Hiram. He came primarily to attend a funeral; but he met and greeted the faculty and students in the chapel, as was his wont. As noted down by one of the latter, these were his last public words in that place: —

"To-day is a sort of burial-day in many ways. I have often been in Hiram, and have often left it; but, with the exception of when I went to the war, I have never felt that I was leaving it in quite so definite a way as I do to-day. It was so long a work-shop, so long a home, that all absences have been temporary, and involved always a return. I cannot speak of all the ties that bind me to this place. There are other things buried beneath this snow besides dead people. The trees, the rocks, the fences, and the grass are all reminders of things connected with my Hiram life.

"It is a revival of youth to me to be in this place, to see its bright young life. I see before me just such a set of students as I saw here twenty-four, twenty-six, yes, twenty-eight years ago,—just as young, just as bright, just as hopeful of the future. It is pleasing to know that Hiram life is ever the same. A few days ago I saw a girl in the full bloom of early womanhood, who is the daughter of a woman who was my pupil here twenty-four years ago. She was the picture of her mother, whom I have never seen since, but I am told that she has become a gray-haired matron. As the daughter stood before me, the likeness of what the mother was then, what thoughts and feelings came over me of the years that are gone! There is an idea of immortality in this, — life is reproduced in things that follow. A fountain of perpetual youth is in this old chapel: there are no wrinkles in its walls. It is a very comforting thought, that though the ancients sought the fountain of perpetual youth, and found it not, it can be found in the associations of a place like this.

"It is pitiful that we often do not appreciate good things until they are gone. Emerson has said, 'To-day is a king in disguise.' He passes among us; and, if we heed not, he leaves us, and we are none the wiser. Get acquainted with what there is in to-day; take what it contains, and appropriate it to yourself. The strong friendships and deep impressions that you are forming now will live in time to come. The other day a man came to me whom I had known here twenty-five years ago, but he was changed: he was fat and whiskered and half bald; and when I took him by the hand, and called him by name with 'W. D.' for his initials, he cried like a man to be remembered. I believe he is richer, fuller, more of a man, for what he gained here at Hiram. If I thought the time would ever come when I should live the Hiram life out of me, I should hope to die just before it came.

"Never despise the days of Hiram life and childhood. The associations that you are now forming, your lessons, your thoughts, and your deeds from day to day, are what go to make up your life here; and this is the foundation of your after-life. Be wise now; and, when you live over again the life you lived here, may it be such as you could wish!

"I cannot see what lies beyond. I may be going on an Arctic voyage; but, be that as it may, I know that years ago I builded upon this promontory a cairn, from which, wherever my wanderings may lead me, I can draw some sustenance for life and strength. May the time never come when I cannot find some food for mind and heart on Hiram Hill!"

At the close of his remarks he greeted those who were present, one by one. Many of the students were the children of his old scholars, and his greetings were often accompanied by pleasant reminiscences. As he stepped into the sleigh that stood at the door, where years before he had watched his "star in the east," he said to one of his early friends, "We have come to the parting of the ways, but I hope it will not be for long." These were his last words to her, for they never met again. Then he was driven away from Hiram forever, over the snow that covered so many other things than dead people. How little, indeed, did he know of the sea upon whose shore he stood! The inauguration, the struggle for the dignity of his office, Mrs. Garfield's illness, the assassin's shot, the brave fight for life, his heroic and tender death, soon followed in quick succession. These things can only be mentioned; but how fitting the phrase of Minister Lowell in Exeter Hall: "In the presence of that death-scene, so homely, so human, so august in its unostentatious heroism, the commonplaces of ordinary eulogy stammer with the sudden shame of their own ineptitude."

Here ends the story. Save in one or two minor instances, it has been wholly impersonal, as was fit. But, before he lays down the pen that falteringly has drawn this sketch, surely the writer's personality may for one moment come into view.

I have now discharged, as best I could within my space, what seemed a sacred duty, both to the dead and to the living. I hope this outline has been so drawn, and so filled in with the "little history" in which President Garfield always took so much interest, as to form a sketch of his Hiram life not altogether unworthy of the theme. Garfield the student and teacher rises before us vast and mountain-like. If the common student or teacher cannot encompass the mountain, he can at least grasp the shrubs that root upon its sides.

My personal obligations to General Garfield are the strongest possible. It was in the winter of 1853–54 that our acquaintance began. But the vision that now rises before my mind begins with the autumn of 1856. Then it was, that on his return to Hiram, with the honors of Williams upon his head, and the light of the future in his eye, he sought me out in the sore doubts and troubles of my closing boyhood, and drew me closer to himself. Then began the friendship that grew stronger and closer until his untimely fall at the post of duty. In those twenty-five years I was permitted to share much of his life, his work, his love. I followed him as a son his father, though it was with very unequal steps. In all the greater labors, and especially in the crises of my life, he endowed me with his knowledge and his wisdom. The measures of instruction, sympathy, and friendship, that he poured into my mind and heart, were not, indeed, all that he could impart, but they were all that I could receive. To testify to his worth and greatness while he lived, in evil as well as in good report, was always a glad office; as it is to pay even this poor tribute to his memory, now that he is no more.

Now that he is no more! Men tell me that he

is dead. They say he died in the audience-chamber of the world. The funeral-car that glided past me at Pittsburg in the gray mist of the morning contained, they said, his coffin. They called a hearse behind which I rode, his hearse. They termed some words that I uttered at an open grave, a benediction at his burial. Are, then, God and nature so at strife? Does nature indeed lend such evil dreams? There comes to me a passage that pleased him three and twenty years ago. Dr. Holmes speaks of the "sweet illusions" that mingled with the fancies of his youth, — illusions which he loved so well that he would not outgrow them.

"The firing of the great guns at the Navy Yard," he says, "is easily heard at the place where I was born and lived. 'There is a ship-of-war come in,' they used to say when they heard them. Of course I supposed that such vessels came in unexpectedly, after indefinite years of absence, — suddenly as falling stones; and that the great guns roared in their astonishment and delight at the sight of the old war-ship splitting the bay with her cutwater. Now, the sloop-of-war 'The Wasp,' Captain Blakely, after gloriously capturing 'The Reindeer' and 'The Avon,' had disappeared from the face of the ocean, and was supposed to be lost. But there was no proof of it; and, of course, for a time hopes were entertained that she might be heard from. Long after the

112 PRESIDENT GARFIELD AND EDUCATION.

last real chance had utterly vanished, I pleased myself with the fond illusion that somewhere on the waste of waters she was still floating; and there were *years* during which I never heard the sound of the great guns booming inland from the Navy Yard without saying to myself, '"The Wasp" has come!' and almost thinking I could see her as she rolled in, crumpling the water before her, weather-beaten, barnacled, with shattered spars and threadbare canvas, welcomed by the shouts and tears of thousands. This was one of those dreams that I nursed and never told. Let me make a clean breast of it now, and say that, so late as to have outgrown childhood, perhaps to have got far on towards manhood, when the roar of the cannon has struck suddenly on my ears, I have started with a thrill of vague expectation and tremulous delight; and the long-unspoken words have articulated themselves in the mind's dumb whisper, '" *The Wasp*' *has come!*'"[1]

Let no one call me boyish if I tell a like dream that I nurse. It is that my teacher, friend, and President is not really dead, but that he has gone on some distant journey from which he will return richer and wiser than before. Surely some day, as I sit musing in the old college, or abstractedly pace the floor, there will come without a footfall, and then at the door a knock, that shall startle me with a thrill of vague expectation and tremulous delight, and the long-unspoken words shall

[1] Autocrat of the Breakfast Table, p. 239.

articulate themselves in the mind's dumb whisper, "Garfield has come!"

"I cannot think he wished so soon to die
With all his senses full of eager heat,
And rosy years that stood expectant by
To buckle the winged sandals on their feet.

. . . .

"The shape erect is prone: forever stilled
The winning tongue; the forehead's high-piled heap,
A cairn which every science helped to build,
Unvalued will its golden secrets keep:
He knows at last if Life or Death be best:
Wherever he be flown, whatever vest
The being hath put on which lately here
So many-friended was, so full of cheer
To make men feel the Seeker's noble zest,
We have not lost him all; he is not gone
To the dumb herd of them that wholly die;
The beauty of his better self lives on
In minds he touched with fire, in many an eye
He trained to Truth's exact severity:
He was a Teacher: why be grieved for him
Whose loving word still stimulates the air?
In endless file shall loving scholars come
The glow of his transmitted touch to share,
And trace his features with an eye less dim
Than ours whose sense familiar wont makes numb." [1]

[1] "Agassiz:" J. R. Lowell.

II.

ADDRESSES AT HIRAM COLLEGE MEMORIAL SERVICE.

SUNDAY afternoon, Sept. 25, 1881, while the remains of President Garfield lay in state in Cleveland, a Hiram College memorial service was held in the First Presbyterian Church. The church was crowded; and the exercises were marked by deep feeling, as well as great interest and solemnity. Isaac Errett of Cincinnati made the opening prayer, and President Pendleton of Bethany College gave the benediction. The regular choir of the church discoursed beautiful music. The following are the addresses made, in their proper order: —

I.— B. A. HINSDALE, PRESIDENT OF HIRAM COLLEGE.

BRETHREN IN THE HIRAM FELLOWSHIP, — There was never but one man who could fitly preside at a Hiram re-union. And he was the man whom we have gathered, not to honor, but to remember. With what felicity did he always open the service! with what aptness guide all our thoughts and feelings! Can you think of Garfield as presiding at his own obsequies, not knowing that they are his own? If you can, please to consider that I have resigned the chair, and that he is present and presiding in our midst.

James Abram Garfield: born Nov. 19, 1831; a student at Hiram in August, 1851, at Williamstown in 1854; President of the Eclectic Institute in 1857; an Ohio Senator in 1859; a soldier in 1861; elected a Representative in Congress in 1862, and re-elected each two years succeeding until 1878; chosen United-States Senator in January, 1880; nominated by the Republican party for the Presidency in June of the same year; elected to that high office in November following; inaugurated Chief Magistrate of the Republic, March 4, 1881; shot by the assassin, July 2; died at Elberon, Sept. 19: these dates mark the salient points of a career that, in respect to high character, noble achievement, lofty promise not yet fulfilled, beautiful romance, generous enthusiasm, pure ambition, and a final euthanasia, has no parallel in all the tides of time.

Were I limited to one phrase in which to describe James A. Garfield, I should say, "Greatness of nature." With what wealth of noble faculties was he endowed! Close observation, high analytical and generalizing ability, solidity of judgment, depth and purity of feeling, strength of will, power of rhetorical exposition, artistic sense, poetic sentiment, reverence of spirit, and noble courage, — these are only a few of his great gifts. Were I allowed a second phrase of description, I should add, "Richness of culture." Fulness of knowledge, breadth of attainment, discipline of all the great faculties of the mind, ripeness of experience, — these are phrases that describe but imperfectly what study and the friction of life had done for him. Greatness of nature, and richness of culture, together fitly describe his life and character. And this is in perfect harmony with his own maxim, "Every character is the joint product of nature and nurture."

One of the most striking features of this noble product of nature and nurture was his many-sidedness. Tennyson says of the Duke of Wellington, —

"He stood four-square to all the winds that blew."

This is a bold figure, and it admirably expresses the poet's thought. But General Garfield had many more sides than four. You can hardly take up a point of observation where you will not discover something in him both interesting and striking. He seemed to face in all directions. He faced to law and politics, to science and to literature, to arms and the camp, to religion and the Christian ministry, to the Senate and the forum, to the farm and the arts, to the social circle and domestic life, and in as many more directions as the diamond from its polished facets flashes its lustrous beauty.

But we are not come together to remember the late President in all the phases of his great life and character. To-day we leave the soldier to soldiers, the lawyer to lawyers, the statesman to statesmen. Mr. Garfield faced towards Hiram; and to us this will always be his most engaging side. Here we recall the sound scholar, great teacher, discreet administrator, wise counsellor, sure guide, faithful friend, and noble man. Under circumstances that make the world weep, are we gathered to hold a memorial service for him whose fourfold connection with our college, as pupil, teacher, president, and trustee, has made the humble name of Hiram known all over the land.

Rapid as was General Garfield's march upon the nation, still the public, as a whole, were slow in finding him out. They never did fully find him out until his life was ebbing away to the music made by the Atlantic's sobs. But the students of Hiram had discovered his greatness long before the year 1860. They were, in fact, the original discoverers of James A. Garfield. Years ago a Hiram student sang at one of our re-unions, —

> "Right proud are we the world should know
> As hero him we long ago
> Found truest helper, friend."

Young Mr. Garfield first came to Hiram in August, 1851. The next school year he became one of the teachers, and continued such until 1854, when he went to college. On his graduation in 1856, he returned as teacher, and the next year became the Principal. From this time to August, 1861, when he left his class-room for the camp, he was the head of Hiram. Within these years lies the service that we should remember. I can only say, in general, that it was fully marked by all the great qualities of his later life, — wealth of knowledge, buoyancy of spirits, dignity of carriage, wisdom in counsel, kindness and justice, faithfulness of friendship. I draw the outline, and leave it for you to fill in the picture.

Of my own obligations to him, first as a pupil, next as a co-teacher, then as friend, nay, as a brother, I cannot trust myself to speak. Only he who chanted the elegy over the slain Saul, and Jonathan his son, can voice my grief: "How are the mighty fallen in the midst of the battle! O Jonathan, thou wast slain in thine high places! I am distressed for thee, my brother Jonathan: very pleasant hast thou been unto me: thy love to me was wonderful, passing the love of women. How are the mighty fallen, and the weapons of war perished!"

One of the very grandest phases of this grand man was his great simplicity of character. This he retained unsullied to the end. Nothing could corrode or taint his native honest fibre. Principalities and powers, dignities and dominion, were nothing to him in comparison with the fellowship of his early friends. His love for the old school continued to the very end. His last visit was made not long before his final departure for Washington. He made one of his beautiful speeches in the chapel. He spoke of the memories that lay under the snow; said, never since he went to the army had he left Hiram with similar feelings; said he was about to sail out into unknown, perhaps Arctic seas, but that he felt, that, on the Hiram promontory, he had built a cairn from which he could draw supplies throughout the voyage. He called for "Ho, Reapers of Life's Harvest," joined heartily in the song, shook hands with all present, and drove away homeward. The last autograph letter that he wrote me, in the midst of the great political tempest that burst so soon after his inauguration, contained these words:—

"I throw you a line across the storm, to let you know that I think, when I have a moment between breaths, of the dear old quiet and peace of Hiram and Mentor."

How he longed for this "dear old quiet and peace" in all storms, was well known to all his closer friends; and how he sighed for it as he lay upon his bed of pain in the heats of Washington and by the shore of the far-resounding sea, history has recorded.

There is one person living whom to-day we must not forget. And who is this? You all anticipate my answer. She is a Hiram student, one of our fellowship, the lamented President's noble wife. Many of Hiram's two thousand daughters have done nobly; but thou, Lucretia, excellest them all. Wheresoever his story shall go in all the world, there shall also this that you have done be told for a memorial of you. In behalf of all who are in the Hiram fellowship, I wish to thank you for your heroic devotion, unfaltering courage, and immortal hope in the sick-chamber of your husband. It was not for yourself and your children alone that you wrought: you wrought for the nation, for the world, and for us. We recognize the deep debt of obligation that we can never pay.

But it is all over. Black Care, that perched like the night-raven in our homes the evening of July 2, sits in them still. April 28, 1865, I stood with General Garfield in the pouring rain, on Dr. Robison's doorsteps on Superior Street, when the hearse of President Lincoln passed by to the Public Square. Yesterday I passed the same place as I followed Garfield's hearse to the same destination. To-day his remains lie where Lincoln's lay. And it is left for us to adjust ourselves to a world that contains no living Garfield.

He has left us his life and his spirit. Storm and war and strife are all over, and he has entered upon a quiet and a peace that neither Hiram nor Mentor knew. He is thrice happy, and doubly immortal, — immortal in life and immortal in death.

Let me ask, why was all this permitted? Why was the assassin allowed to strike him down? Why were not the prayers of the people granted? Why did the night-raven never lift his wings, and fly away? Why was the Most High deaf? and why did the heavens give no sign? What a strange providence! How can it fit into any plan of divine wisdom and love? Thus far I have scarcely tried to answer these questions, though they have pressed upon me many an hour. It is a great test of faith in God. But Garfield believed in God. He thought that an increasing purpose runs through the ages, and comprehends the lives of men; and I think so too. Still, hitherto I have been able to do little more than say, "Lord, I believe: help thou mine unbelief!" For myself, I must leave the problem to the future. History will no doubt discover and disclose what passes my power to comprehend.

I have dwelt upon the dark side of the great tragedy. True, there are great elements of good in the story. These I hope will be duly emphasized, for we must not dwell too much under the cypress. In Garfield's young days at Hiram, when he was full of joyous life, this saying of Emerson's was a great favorite with him: "To-day is a king in disguise. Strip off his robes, and enjoy him while he is here." And I think I hear him who presides over us, in spirit, say, "Be not so carried away with grief, so paralyzed with sorrow, so blind with weeping, that you cannot discover the good that is in it all." Still, for one, —

>"I falter where I firmly trod,
>   And falling with my weight of cares
>   Upon the great world's altar-stairs
>That slope through darkness up to God,
>
>"I stretch lame hands of faith, and grope,
>   And gather dust and chaff, and call
>   To what I feel is Lord of all,
>And faintly trust the larger hope."

II.—J. H. RHODES, ESQ., OF CLEVELAND.

To thousands of men and women the words "Garfield at Hiram" bring swift and happy visions of the golden age the world over, when memory is not busy with the dead past, but life is eager, joyous, standing on tiptoe to catch each new, bright morning. Then surely it was true, as he often said, "Each day is a king in disguise."

It always seems to me now that from boyhood he was almost conscious of his high destiny in life. He was born to lead and command. He captured all hearts as naturally as he breathed. He could not help winning them if he would.

It is not now the time for critical analysis or historic preciseness. We see him only through the mist of tears. We cry out in our despair, like

> "An infant crying in the night,
> An infant crying for the light,
> And with no language but a cry."

But generations hence his memory and his life, hallowed by the lapse of years, and looked at through a long line of succeeding events, like some grand mountain-peak viewed from afar, will not be less grand, will rise into the heavens with equal glory as now.

To many who are here to-day, visions come again of Garfield in the class-room or the chapel at Hiram. They see a fair-faced, blue-eyed young man, in the robust vigor of early manhood, overflowing with animal spirits, and breezy, cheerful good-nature, standing before a class, and irradiating the room with his grand enthusiasms for knowledge and ideas which made each pupil feel as if he were in an atmosphere highly electrified, out of which he passed feeling that life had new meanings to him, and longing for the return of the next lesson. The crayon often became a magic wand with which new worlds were disclosed to the young explorer in search of new continents.

"Observe all things," and "Question all men," were maxims that he daily illustrated. No man was so humble, he often remarked, but something new can be learned by talking with him. With all men he was, therefore, social. If he did not learn any thing from another, young Garfield had already learned that ideas can only be clearly held when they can be clearly clothed in words; and, as long as he could find a good listener, he delighted to pour forth his own thoughts, thus crystallizing ideas and opinions already formed. Many a man wondered at the wealth of conversation with which he was flooded. Many a small audience thought it strange he should speak as abundantly and as eloquently to them as if there were thousands to be moved. All men were foils for his own swift blades, and so he grew daily in strength and breadth.

He died young, but he was born at the right time. His young manhood began with the great stir in modern thought which had already revolutionized the world. The age of invention and discovery had just begun to usher into our modern life the triumphs of electricity and steam. The ferment of scientific research had opened up a thousand new fields of inquiry. The great conflict between old decays and new creations in the world of politics was at hand. Literature had just had a new birth, and the modern period of books and newspapers had been inaugurated. I can remember how, in the years 1855–1860, the very air seemed surcharged with the new life that already threatened storms and hurricanes. I never heard him wish that he had been born in another age. He did not sigh that his lot had not been cast amid the stirring scenes of ancient Rome or modern Europe. He was born in America, and for America; and he lived long enough to see the sun of the modern life and thought full-orbed and high advanced in the day. He went away from Hiram at twenty-three to Williamstown, to return in the fall of 1856 with the baptism of fire from that new heaven on his heart and head. For two years after his graduation at Williams, we roomed together at Hiram. The old office in "the Orchard" is more hallowed to me by that two years of companionship than any other temple made by human hands. It was both an education and an inspiration to hear him at this period.

It was after his return from Williams College that he began to preach. Preaching was a vent for the overflow of his energies and activity. In preaching he had a greater range of thought than in the schoolroom. The effect upon him of two years at the feet of that great teacher, Mark Hopkins, was very marked. His thought ranged through wider circles. Whilst the dogmas of the church at Williamstown did not seem to have attached themselves strongly, the philosophic and metaphysical methods of President Hopkins became a part of his own methods. The result of this was, that his preaching had a new charm for the people who heard him.

It was during the years that followed his return from Williamstown that he found so much inspiration and strength from companionship with that remarkable woman, Almeda A. Booth, whose intellectual grasp, and range of thought, were only second in Hiram to his own. He owed much to her; and he has made public acknowledgment in a beautiful tribute to that woman, whom he compared to Margaret Fuller.

Whilst teaching at Hiram, and preaching in various places in Northern Ohio, his mind had turned to the law as a life profession; and among the legacies I have of this period are synopses made by us of the first two volumes of Bouvier's "Institutes." The law in its great principles, its broad generalizations, its sacred regard for life and property, its conservative influence and power in maintaining order and peace in society, had a great charm for his mind; and I distinctly remember that he would synopsize the "Institutes" so thoroughly as to cover every doctrine laid down. In subsequent years he achieved distinction in the law. But politics, in the higher and almost forgotten meaning of the word, had become a subject of great interest to him. The great struggle in the land, which ended in the downfall of American slavery, had already begun. He was intensely absorbed in this great controversy, and soon entered as State Senator upon that public career with which the world is so familiar. Into this he poured his energies, as he had formerly into teaching and preaching. Here, too, in Hiram began his devotion to the little woman whose name is revered in every home in the civilized world. Their acquaintance began a few years earlier at Chester. Writing to me in 1871, in the midst of his public life, and nearly thirteen years after his marriage, he said, "There is not a day when I do not inly fear such completeness will not be allowed to last long on this earth." Verily, she was "the rainbow on his storm of life, the anchor on its sea." His mind was imaginative, and his temper poetical. The fresh beauties of "In Memoriam" were his delight; and thousands of times did I hear him recite, in those early days, the passage beginning, —

> "The tide flows down, the wave again
>   Is vocal in its wooded walls:
>   My deeper sorrow also falls,
> And I can speak a little then."

The Cuyahoga River, above the Rapids, will forever be associated with him in my mind: there once we stopped our carriage on the old bridge, and looked up the stream, and saw in the tall trees on either side what Tennyson means by "wooded walls."

It is hard to find any reconciliation to the fact that he is dead, and that his bodily form will be visible on earth no more. It may be that his outward frame will be resolved again to dust, and become, in the long processes of Nature, flowers and fruit, cloud or frost; but I never can conceive of him as dead. I do not believe he is dead. Death has no definition or limitations which can include so great a soul. Immortality was no myth with him. His voice, I think, is still heard to-day, in this beautiful poem, "After Death in Arabia," by Edwin Arnold, which, with a slight paraphrase, I will read: —

> "*He who died at Elberon sends*
> *This to comfort all his friends.*
>
> "Faithful friends! *It* lies, I know,
> Pale and white and cold as snow;
> And ye say, 'Our Garfield's dead!'
> Weeping at the feet and head,

I can see your falling tears,
I can hear your sighs and prayers;
Yet I smile, and whisper this, —
' *I* am not the thing you kiss;
Cease your tears, and let it lie;
It *was* mine, it is not I.'

"Sweet friends! what the women lave,
For its last bed of the grave,
Is but a hut which I am quitting,
Is a garment no more fitting,
Is a cage from which, at last,
Like a hawk my soul hath passed.
Love the inmate, not the room, —
The wearer, not the garb, — the plume
Of the falcon, not the bars
Which kept him from those splendid stars.

"Loving friends! Be wise and dry
Straightway every weeping eye, —
What ye lift upon the bier
Is not worth a wistful tear.
'Tis an empty sea-shell, — one
Out of which the pearl has gone;
The shell is broken, — it lies there;
The pearl, the all, the soul, is here.
'Tis an earthen jar, whose lid
Allah sealed, the while it hid
That treasure of his treasury,
A mind that loved him; let it lie!

Let the shard be earth's once more,
Since the gold shines in his store.

" Allah glorious! Allah good!
Now thy world is understood;
Now the long, long wonder ends;
Yet ye weep, my erring friends,
While the man whom ye call dead,
In unspoken bliss, instead,
Lives and loves you; lost, 'tis true,
By such light as shines for you;
But in the light ye cannot see
Of unfulfilled felicity, —
In enlarging paradise,
Lives a life that never dies.

" Farewell, friends! Yet not farewell;
Where I am, ye, too, shall dwell.
I am gone before your face,
A moment's time, a little space.
When ye come where I have stepped
Ye will wonder why ye wept;
Ye will know, by wise love taught,
That here is all, and there is naught.
Weep awhile, if ye are fain, —
Sunshine still must follow rain;
Only not at death, — for death,
Now I know, is that first breath
Which our souls draw when we enter
Life, which is of all life centre.

"Be ye certain all seems love,
Viewed from Allah's throne above;
Be ye stout of heart, and come
Bravely onward to your home!
La Allah illa Allah! yea!
Thou love divine! Thou love alway!

"*He that died at Elberon gave
This to those who made his grave.*"

III.—HON. C. B. LOCKWOOD OF CLEVELAND.

I have always thought that General Garfield was greater than any of his works, wiser than any of his words; and I think this is the general impression of all those who knew him well.

I remember, in his early manhood, his coming into the pulpit one morning, and relating this circumstance: He said that as he walked to church he met a boy by the way, who called him, and said, "Mr. Garfield, explain to me why this thistle-seed is covered with down. You see that it is just fitted to be blown by the winds of heaven, to be scattered broadly over the earth, and to do great harm. Why is it so?" He commenced with that narration a sermon that I shall never forget; and I will relate its salient points, because I believe they were the groundwork of all that he was in life. General Garfield, more than any other man that I ever knew, believed in God. His belief was most implicit. Not always in the God of tradition, but in the God who is the Father of this race of ours. His reply to the young man was, that the earth was cursed for our sake; and his only explanation was, that this was a part of the curse. He said the fall made it absolutely necessary, if we would be any thing in the world, that we should be men of business. I remember, and I shall never forget, the wonderful picture he drew of the providence of God in the world. He said, "The time will come when this race of ours shall be relieved from the burdens that now seem to bear it downward; and that time will come just as soon as we are fitted for it. The great Father waits and longs to give us leisure; but in his great love for us, and in his great wisdom, he is compelled to hold us to this work — to this drudgery — day by day. This is because in his love he is determined to make the most of us." He said, further, that in his view the knowledge and use of the great powers of nature were only withheld from us because it was unsafe to put them in our hands. "Ah!" he said, "controlled by passion, see how unsafe it would be." But he said further,

"Watch it, if you will. The progress of civilization and Christianity, the labor-saving machines that are being invented, shall go on step by step. Measured by our ability to use the new powers, the revelation of them shall come to us. Oh!" he said, "I look forward to the time when the promised millennium shall come to us; and it seems to me this is the direction in which it is to come. It is to follow in the wake of civilization; and so fast as we are prepared and fitted to take these powers, and use them for the glory of God and men, they will be given to us." I have often said to myself, as this wonderful knowledge was coming to us, the knowledge of these inventions and labor-saving machines that has come in the past few years, "Is it a measure of our growth in purity?" If the theory that he then announced, nearly twenty-five years ago, be true, then surely it must be·evidence of some growth toward safety, at least, to have these things within our power. General Garfield recognized in all the movements of earth this Father, God. He felt that this nation — and this accounts for his wonderful love for it, and his willingness to make great sacrifices for it — was a nation through which was to be organized into law and into institutions the will of that Father, — the divine principles which were to make for the happiness of our race in the future. It is only a few days since I heard him discoursing on this subject; and he said this about it: "The time is very near at hand when this nation shall be the power in all the world that shall say, 'No more war;' when its voice will be heard in favor of peace, and when no civilized government in all this world will dare to provoke a war against the wishes, the advice, and the counsel of this great land of ours." He looked forward, and he thought he saw in its movements that it was to be the instrumentality of great good in the world: and when he left the pulpit, when he went into the field, wherever he went, he felt that he was doing this great work, — that he was an instrument in the hands of that God, who, by some means, communicated still with all those who sought to do his will. He struggled to open the avenues, that that influence might come in, and make him a manly, powerful man, that he might be of use to his time. He said to me the night after the election, nearly at the break of day, "This has been to me a strange scene. I have passed through it, with the excitement of all the people and of all my friends; and I have lain down upon my pillow at night without an anxiety. I could not have believed it a few years since, but I have passed through it all without an anxious thought."

I said, " General, that illustrates your faith in God."—"Ah!" he said, " I was sure that the best would be true, and, if the highest was to be subserved, success would be upon our side; if not, upon the other: and I have been literally without anxiety."

Oh! my dear friends, if there is one thought that I would leave with you it is this one; and I think his view of life would include all that we mourn to-day. I think, if his voice could be heard, he would say to us, " Be not anxious. God reigns. He is infinite in his wisdom and his love." And he would thank God for his power and his willingness to take control of and so manage the great affairs of this nation and of the race that the highest good should be accomplished. I think that this is the secret of the great life of General Garfield, — that which brought him a peace amid all the struggles of life, that flowed like a river.

IV.—PROFESSOR C. D. WILBUR, WILBUR, NEB.

I am mindful that my time is necessarily short, and have only one idea to present in behalf of our lamented friend. It is this: that, in all the story of my long intercourse and friendship with him, there was one principle at the foundation of his movements, and that was his love of duty. I noticed, that, in the references made to him by those who belong to the Hiram alumni, his labors after he came to Hiram from Williams College were eloquently mentioned. But let me tell you all, that there was a time when he was somewhat tempted not to come back to Hiram; and the temptation came to him in the shape of an offer of a twenty-five-hundred-dollar salary to go and teach school somewhere else. I remember how he discussed that with himself; he and I being in the same room, No. 12, Old South College. He said, "They want me back at Hiram: they cannot pay me much, but I ought to go there." He followed the word *ought;* and thither he bent his willing footsteps, and did all that work. It was simply his love of duty; and, wherever you find him, you find him acting up to that standard.

In it will be found that courage which made

him do or dare. We were both co-workers and teachers in Hiram more than twenty-five years ago; and this was his thought then : " I can," said he, " smell the coming battle afar off. There is a great amount of work to do in this world, and I must get ready for it." How this came to him, no matter. It was probably through the wonderful impressiveness that separated him from all the social world around. " And where shall I go to get ready?" To use his own expression, " I want to go where I can get the irons forged for the conflict; and where shall I go?" So we made a careful survey of all the colleges in the land. We wrote letters to all the presidents of Eastern colleges. " I turn my face toward the East," he said, "because there is the accumulation of vast libraries, science, history, veteran professors who have grown gray in teaching; and I would go and counsel with them." There came a letter from that wonderful man, that sage, teacher, and counsellor, Mark Hopkins; and the statement in the letter, " If you come to us, we will do you all the good we can," led him there; and he always regarded it as the wisest step in his intellectual life, that he did so. He preceded me there by three months, and prepared a room, and got every thing ready. Having wrought together in Hiram, we worked together, studied together, and roomed together, in old Williams.

He very soon cleared the amphitheatre, laid out his work, and declared his purposes. "Here is this vast library of so many thousand volumes: I must know what it contains. Here is this realm of study in history and science: I must go through this, — I must know about it." I want to say to you that he did not seem to have one leisure hour there. It was work, work, work, early and late; and one condition of his great success was his great physical endurance to go through it all. I want to say to you, that at Hiram every one seemed to love one another, that it was a school of brotherly love. I have walked in it all the days since I was there, although my lot has been cast far beyond. But when he went to Williams College he found an atmosphere essentially different. If he stood or fell, he would stand or fall on his own merits. There was no favoritism. When we from Ohio went there, we went from the West, — the wilderness of the West, although it was Ohio. It was almost a barbarous West.

We found that we were in a focus of not unfriendly, but unrelenting, criticism. If we could not stand the test, we could not pass. So Garfield had to meet this test; and let me say that in six months, although the criticism was formidable, he had broken down all the college walls so completely, that, though every class seemed to be bound by its traditions and its peculiar style of selfishness, all seemed to be laid low, and he was one with all the college, and the hero of all. From this you may know the style of the man and his heart: speaking kind words, doing all those things that were just right, remembering the Golden Rule, and in every intellectual contest coming off the victor; and this he did by the hardest study. He never chose or sought for a college honor in his life: they all came to him from his fellows without his solicitation. I have watched his career from that day until this, and I know that never did he seek an honor, or an office, in his life; and yet, when they came to him, he wrought so faithfully and so well, that he dignified and honored the place he occupied. And as the days go on, in the very light of this great fact we shall require of the occupant of the great office of President of the United States, hereafter, higher qualifications than we have ever demanded before, just because this worthy man has occupied and honored it, and made .it sacred by his presence.

Our college life was of this sort. It was continual work. Garfield used to say, "I must so comprehend all these studies that I can analyze them at night, and put them in shape." And so he did. While he gathered in those rich harvests from those grand old men who were teachers, every day or every night before midnight saw the postings of them, which you will find among his papers now. He put them in that finished shape, so that any hour he could bring them to his hand, and use them. He used to say to me that he wrote down these thoughts at the time so that they would be complete; for, he said, "There come to every one at times expressions that he will forget, and never have, unless they are treasured at the time." So he acted, so he wrought, and so he managed to accumulate those vast possessions that are the wonderment and the marvel of his friends to-day.

I will close by detailing an incident of our interior room-life. Every thing was in perfect order; and when the sunset came, there came with it the oft-repeated, never-forgotten circumstance. It was an hour and a moment that was deemed by him sacred to his mother. It seemed to be in accordance with a promise: "Whenever the sun is setting, read in the Bible, for I will read with you then." That was his mother's word to him, and he never forgot it. No matter what the press was, he always had time for that. We all know, that, when he went up Greylock, he drew forth the Testament in the sunset upon the mountain, before his companions, and said, "Such is my habit." But down in the old room at the college it was an every-evening occurrence.

Sometimes we would post the books; that is to say, repeat to one another passages, not of Scripture, but of philosophy or of poetry, — Shakespeare or any other author, according to our liking. Sometimes hours were delightfully passed in that way. It was discipline, at the same time. His memory was prodigious, — far beyond mine. I had hardly thought of it until one day last fall, when I was visiting him at his own home, he said to me, "Can you repeat to me that little poem that was the epitome of life? It was done up, perhaps, in five stanzas; but the roll of it, the style of it, the measure of it, has kept with me all the days since." It was a short view of life. He had some such view as Lincoln had when he would insist on the reading of that poem, "Oh! why should the spirit of mortal be proud?" But this poem was more condensed, more to the point, more practical, as Garfield himself was. So I tried to remember and repeat it to him. It fits so well here, seeing that now he lies yonder, that I will venture to give it, and, with it, close. It is by Barry Cornwall: —

> "Day dawned. Within a curtained room,
> Filled to faintness with perfume,
> A lady lay at point of doom.
>
> Day closed. A child had seen the light;
> But for the lady, fair and bright,
> She rested in undreaming night.
>
> Spring rose. The lady's grave was green;
> And near it oftentimes was seen
> A gentle boy, of thoughtful mien.
>
> Years fled. He wore a manly face,
> And struggled in the world's rough race,
> And gained at last a lofty place.
>
> And then he died. Behold before ye
> Humanity's poor sum and story, —
> Life, death, and all that is of glory."

V.—J. W. ROBBINS OF OMAHA, NEB.

At the Chicago Convention a motion was made one day that three members should be expelled from their seats. It was a tumultuous body, surrounded, in the high galleries encircling the vast room, by ten thousand people. The delegates had sat there until worn out. It was, at that moment, a gathering which seemed to be ruled more by passion than by reason. At any rate, this extraordinary resolution which had been read was about to be passed with a storm of approval. At that moment a form, familiar to so many here, rose upon a chair; and I never can forget the first words that he spoke. I wish that I could repeat them as he did. It was only necessary for him to appear before that Convention, to attract, in the midst of the greatest tumult, universal attention. He said, "Gentlemen, I fear that we are about to commit a great error." A great hush fell upon that body of men, and they commenced to think. He talked there perhaps ten minutes. He talked long enough for them to have time to think, and to weigh the words of wisdom that he spoke; and, when he sat down, the purpose and the temper of that great body of seven hundred delegates were changed as I never saw a change wrought before or since. It was to General Garfield, owing to the peculiar circumstances which it would not be proper for me to mention here, the greatest personal triumph, I believe, that ever came to him in all his life. At that moment, when the congratulations of some of the most eminent men of the nation were being showered upon him, I happened to pass along where he was; and not thinking that my congratulations would be aught to him, but filled as I was at that moment with pride and with such emotions at the grand spectacle that I had seen, I reached out my hand to him. He took it, and with his other pulled me clear down to him, put his lips to my ear, and whispered this: "How many Hiram boys do you think there are in the gallery?" That needs no comment. In that moment of supreme exultation, in that moment when he had won, as I have said, the grandest personal triumph that ever came to him, his first thought was to know whether, in all that vast gathering, there were any, and, if so, how many, of the Hiram circle, to feel pride in his achievement, and to share with him the victory.

VI.—HON. A. H. PETTIBONE OF GREENVILLE, TENN.

Standing to-day before an audience of Hiram students, with all the sad associations and thrilling memories that come up to me, I am reminded impressively of the past. I come from the battlefield of Chickamauga, where, in the last few days, we have had a re-union of our Garfield's old comrades of the Army of the Cumberland; and, when we heard that finally his spirit had winged its everlasting flight, we turned what we intended to be a season of rejoicing and festivity into a solemn requiem occasion. Speaking to you with those associations at Chickamauga fresh upon me, I can but think of the sweet lines of "Miles O'Reilly:"—

> "There are bonds of all sorts in this world of ours, —
> Fetters of friendship, and ties of flowers,
> And true-lover's knots, I ween:
> The girl and the boy are bound by a kiss;
> But there's never a tie, old friend, like this: —
> 'We have drunk from the same canteen.'"

And in that spirit, coming to this stand on this occasion, and in the presence of all these Hiram students, — recollecting the old associations that used to bind us in the early days, — I feel that we have all of us "drunk from the same canteen."

But it is not for me to occupy time in reminiscence. There are others here better prepared and better fitted to do that than I am. I come here for another purpose. I have been wont to be belligerent in life, and for sixteen years I have differed most fearfully and bitterly from the men whom we used to meet in gray along the Tennessee; but only the other day, under the shadow of old Lookout, while the plain of Chickamauga lay before us, and the old heights of Missionary Ridge frowned down upon us, I saw a scene that I would that all of you could see. I must preface my account of it by saying that the last time I ever took our old friend by the hand was just a week before the assassin fired the fatal pistol. I was going home; and he said to me in his peculiar way, giving me not his hand, but both hands, " Good-by. Tell all the boys they must meet me at Chattanooga, at the re-union of the Army of the Cumberland." And, when I told him that the ex-Confederates were going to meet us and to greet us, it seemed to put new animation into his face, and new fire into his eye, and he said, "Oh, won't we have a jolly time!" It was not to be; but the Confederate soldiers met us there. For some years I have felt down yonder as if every man's hand was against me: but I know now that a touch of real, genuine feeling makes all the world akin; and I say to this audience in Cleveland, that nowhere in the world, and among no class of people, is James A. Garfield more mourned and honored and loved than among the stalwart followers of Stonewall Jackson and Lee and Cheatham, — the nameless, unnumbered host who are now stretching out their hands to us from all the land between us and the Gulf. I saw old Frank Cheatham, who fought him at Chickamauga, sitting upon the stand; and again and again the tears unbidden would start from his eyes while the minute-guns were firing, reminding us that Garfield was no more. I speak, then, for that people. All Tennessee is in mourning. The good women and the good men of the South, the poor men and rich men, are mourning to-day, literally mingling their tears with ours. For long weeks, day after day, they would come to my home at Greenville, early in the morning and late in the evening, and ask me, "Major, how is *our* President?"

From the colored people and the mountaineers, from the glorious old boys in gray, and from those I love still better, — the Union soldiers of Tennessee, — there came that question; and I noticed always an accent was laid upon the pronoun *our*, — "How is *our* President?"

I cannot take longer time. I shall bear back to that people your feeling. I only come to give you their greeting.

VII. — H. C. WHITE, ESQ., OF CLEVELAND.

The composite pillar of a great life stands broken. The blow of the inhuman iconoclast has fallen. But the ruined shaft still reaches to the heavens, and for its capital bears the martyr's thorny crown.

We are here to-day with aching hearts, but tender hands, to garland with blooming memories the pedestal of this masterpiece. We are here to open

> "That book of memory
> Which is to grieving hearts like the sweet shower
> To the parched meadow or the dying tree;
> Which fills with elegy the craving mouth
> Of sorrow, slakes with song the piteous drought,
> And leaves us calm, but weeping silently."

The lessons of the·life here closed, like its own history, are easily clustered in chapters. These chapters unfold in harmonious development, and are merged in logical gradations. Yet there is a marked completeness in each chapter. His life, thus stratified, illustrates the unyielding grasp of purpose which runs through its entire plan and tenor. Holding on to this single clew, running through all the labyrinth of circumstances, he marched with steady step through all the wildering mazes of life. It is given us here to-day to open a chapter of this history, completed now a quarter of a century.

James A. Garfield never ceased to be a teacher, because he never ceased to be a learner. Many of us here knew him when he wielded the upbuilding forces of education with the arm of a Titan and the hand of a master. A peculiar tone was given to his career as teacher by the fact that during the whole of it he was at once teacher and learner. Scattering light with wonderful effulgence, his light was clear and far-reaching, because he was simultaneously filling and trimming his own lamp of knowledge. Thus, in God's economy, he was enabled to bless us out of that inheritance of poverty which was his. The blending of these forces aided his native endowment of mind and heart in the production of those grand qualities which he possessed in such full measure as a teacher: —

First, In that all-compassing love and sympathy.

Secondly, In that exhaustless enthusiasm which sent the rippling and unseen waves of inspiration into the dullest and deadest soul.

Not entirely to the progress of this self-development must we attribute his great power as an intellectual and moral builder. Such power was inborn and native to him. He won many, because he loved much. By the sheer force of the spirit he breathed, he lifted all who touched the circle of his influence to a higher, purer life. Thus the best edifying force with which he wrought was his own noble self. His whole life was a constantly increasing offering-up of himself. He began the sacrifice, in no small measure, while he was a teacher. His best text-book was his own great heart, mind, and life. Broadly and deeply learned, he venerated classic learning, and bowed to its authority. In the choice of methods, he gave it its due office as a disciplining force. More than that, in the alembic of his mind, in the very process of mental assimilation, the dead tongue and the dead past took on the glow and form of living beauty. But, after all, the value and currency of this coinage came largely from the mould and impress of his mind and heart, rather than from the intrinsic preciousness of the native metal. He never wore the perfunctory mental habit of the professor. He was not merely equipped with the intellectual weapons of the scholastic trainingmaster, to be thrown down at the end of the hour of drill. He never lost an opportunity to mould *moral* impressions. Better than the iron of the Latin thought and tongue he taught so skilfully, was the *love* that he poured out with it. Better than the philosophy of the subtle Greek, was the grace of his life. Better than the great systems of science that he opened, was the sincerity of character irradiating his every-day life. Better than his expositions of mathematics, was his example of manliness.

Another source of his power lay in his constant and unwearied lifting into view of great life purposes. How, by wisest precept and loftiest example, he bent up the angle of our aims to high and worthy objects! These aims were not theoretical and unattainable: their binding, guiding force lay in their practicability. Upon these grand harmonies which burst upon our enraptured ears in the olden time, his whole life was tuned. They were not mere erratic ideals, wandering darkly in his heavens: they were the fixed stars to which his moral vision ever turned, on whatever stormy sea he rode.

I have found these grand tenets of his life crystallized in forms of beauty by the poetic soul of another, now dead. Let me read them. This was his summary: these are the rules he always accepted: —

"First, *labor*. Nothing can be had for nothing. Whatever a man achieves, he must pay for; and no favor of fortune can absolve him from his duty.

"Secondly, *patience and forbearance*, which are simply dependent on the slow justice of time.

"Thirdly, and most important, *faith*. Unless a man believes in something far higher than himself, something infinitely purer and grander than he can ever become, — unless he has an instinct of an order beyond his dreams, of laws beyond his comprehension, of beauty, goodness, and justice beside which his own ideals are dark, — he will fail in every loftier form of ambition, and ought to fail."

As a teacher, he possessed in wonderful degree another excellence: upon whomsoever he laid hold, he never let go. The seeds of truth, once implanted by his hand, he watched to see germinate, grow, and yield fruit. His manner of dealing with immortal elements rendered, in his view, his work immortal. Hence those who had received the impress of his moulding hand, he bore with him in the casket of his memory, enshrined in his heart, up the toilsome steeps of his glorious career; and, while standing upon "the perilous heights," he still bore the obscurest to the end.

Thus transient pupilage, with some of us, became enduring discipleship. He fashioned his work and life as a teacher after the highest model. In the harmonious development of the whole being, — the only true culture, — in the impartation of himself in loving sympathy, in the unyielding love encircling all beneath him, he exhibits the pattern of the Great Teacher.

I know these are dead leaves, rather than living flowers, from the field of memory. These are but the superficial, abstract impressions, left after the lapse of years. To me the sweet savor and memory of his kindly aid as a teacher is the richest of all legacies. A thousand bright memories springing out of this blessed relationship of teacher and pupil come thronging around me; but they swim and glint upon the floods which choke the utterance. To many of you was vouchsafed the blessing of other and later relationships: to me the older one never ended. God grant that it may never end to any of us!

He taught lessons to all people, out of all events. His great grasp of mind and wonderful power of generalization made it easy for him to evoke great lessons out of all situations and junctures; and while in him we had unbounded faith, and trusted him as equal to all trials and burdens, yet his own humility and better wisdom never allowed him to close his eyes to perils.

His own prophetic spirit has given us the best lesson that we can get out of the awful mystery of the hour. Standing on the sloping heights of Arlington, over the graves of fifteen thousand men, he spoke these words, now suggestive and full of peace to us all:—

"For the noblest man that lives, there still remains a conflict. He must still withstand the assaults of time and fortune, must still be assailed with temptations before which lofty natures have fallen. But with *these* the conflict ended, the victory was won, when death stamped on them the great seal of heroic character, and closed a record which years can never blot."

VIII. — COLONEL H. N. ELDRIDGE OF CHICAGO.[1]

The lengthening shadows remind me and you that you have a right to be impatient. What I have to say, then, shall have one virtue, — brevity.

You have gathered at this place of prayer, not to recount the glories of the soldier, not to tell the story of the statesman. It is for another, a higher, a holier purpose. These upturned faces — strangers to me individually, for the most part — I know are the faces of those who have sat at the same seat of learning, and who have drank draughts of knowledge from the same source. Of all the relationships of life, so far as my knowledge and observation go, the relationships which spring from college association are the purest, the holiest, the best. For, after all, my friends, what are all these grand attainments of genius without a heart? You will bear me out in saying, that, above and beyond all men that you ever met, James Abram Garfield had the power of making himself a part of your life. College days, of all others, are the days of sentiment; and the recollection of college life comes as a sweet memory in the bustling cares that come after, and, like

[1] Colonel Eldridge was a classmate of Garfield's at Williams.

glints of sunshine through the rifted cloud, they are a glory and a beauty forever. It is his generous impulses, and the greatness of his heart, that you and I have come here to think of, to remember, and to dream over again, this September afternoon.

Wherever Garfield went, he carried with him that which could never be forgotten. I recollect an incident that occurred soon after General Hancock was nominated for the Presidency, when there was an appearance of the tide turning that way. I dined with a pronounced and prominent politician; and the remark was made by me, "Should the election take place to-day, I fear that my old friend Garfield would be in the minority."— "Yes," said he; "but the election don't take place to-day, and that is what troubles me. I fear that betwixt now and next November the great people of the North will learn to know your friend as you know him." My friends, the millions of this land and the millions of other lands are beginning to know him as you and I know him; and as the days shall come, and as the time of this solemn pageant shall become the past, the light of his memory shall be as the torch in the fisherman's boat, that distance frees from all smoke, and that only gleams the brighter, the farther it recedes from view.

PART II.

President Garfield's Speeches and Addresses

ON

EDUCATION AND EDUCATORS.

INTRODUCTION TO SPEECHES.

THE phrase "Education and Educators" does not fully describe this collection of addresses and speeches. Still they form a distinct group, having a centre of unity, and so may properly be brought together. Nor has any better description than the one used occurred to their collector.

The great interest that President Garfield always took in education, even after he ceased to teach, and grew to influence as a statesman, is well known to those who have only a general acquaintance with his life. Still the extent of his interest, and the value of his contributions to educational discussions and literature, is known to very few. Even this collection, in which are brought together all of the speeches that he himself published, and more besides, is an inadequate witness to his interest and activity. He made many lectures and addresses at institutes, at college commencements, and to schools that he casually visited, which were either never published, or were meagrely reported in the local press. He was always a generous respondent on such occasions, and always said something worth remembering. Many a teacher did he thus cheer, many a student stimulate, many a parent arouse to his duties to his children, many a citizen awaken to his relations to public education. He was always keenly alive to politics, and to party politics; but never, even in the most exciting times, did he lose his interest in the progress of knowledge and the education of the people. This collection shows the range and the value of his contributions to the discussions of these subjects, though it by no means exhausts them. It shows as well the range of his reading upon educational subjects.

His efforts to advance the educational interests of the country, as they are here revealed, may be grouped under four heads.

I.—THE STATE AND EDUCATION.

Here his influence was felt along several lines of educational enterprise. These will be mentioned in order.

1. *The National Bureau of Education.*— Feb. 14, 1866, Mr. Garfield presented to the House of

INTRODUCTION TO SPEECHES. 163

Representatives a memorial of the National Association of School Superintendents, recently held in Washington, asking for the establishment of a National Bureau of Education; also a bill that accompanied said memorial. This bill was read twice, referred to a select committee of seven, and ordered printed. This committee consisted of the following gentlemen: Garfield of Ohio, Patterson of New Hampshire, Boutwell of Massachusetts, Donnelly of Minnesota, Moulton of Illinois, Goodyear of New York, and Randall of Pennsylvania.

April 3, following, Mr. Garfield reported from the Committee a substitute for the original bill. This bill, known as House Bill No. 276, was wider in its scope than the bill submitted with the memorial. Made a law, it would establish a Department of Education. June 5 and 8 it was debated by the House at considerable length. It was supported by Messrs. Donnelly, Banks, Beaman, and others, and opposed by Messrs. Rogers and Pike. In its favor, it was argued that the department proposed would be of great service in gathering and publishing statistics and other information concerning education; also, that education in the South needed particular attention, that the States were not likely to give. It was urged against the bill, that such a department was unnecessary and unconstitutional, and that it would be expensive. Mr. Garfield closed the debate. He had granted to other members so much of the hour allowed by the rules, that his own speech was cut short by the Speaker's hammer. However, in obedience to the earnest request of friends of education, he wrote out his speech in full, and published it as found in this volume. The bill was lost, 59 yeas to 61 nays. June 19 a reconsideration was carried by a vote of 76 to 44. On this question, Mr. Garfield said that the measure was framed "at the earnest request of the School Commissioners of several of the States." He added, "It is an interest that has no lobby to press its claims. It is the voice of the children of the land, asking us to give them all the blessings of our civilization. I hope that the interest which has moved the other side of the House to vote solidly against this liberal and progressive measure will at least induce this side to save it from defeat." The expressions "other side" and "this side" need no comment. Without the argument implied in these terms, it is doubtful whether the bill would have carried. It now passed, 80 yeas to 44 nays. Immediately

INTRODUCTION TO SPEECHES. 165

the bill went to the Senate, and was referred to the Judiciary Committee. At the next session, Jan. 30, 1867, Mr. Trumbull reported it back to the Senate. After brief discussion it passed, Feb. 27. The President's approval, March 2, made it a law.

That this beneficent law was peculiarly Mr. Garfield's work, is shown by the facts recited. He introduced the subject to the House, was chairman of the special committee, drew up the bill, and was its principal champion on the floor. The bill as reported by him was not changed in any particular in either house. What is more, the great change wrought in the temper of the House, as shown by the votes (June 8, 49 to 51; June 19, 80 to 44), was almost wholly due to the persistent zeal with which he urged the measure in private.

Apparently the Department of Education was in advance of public sentiment: certainly it was in advance of Congressional sentiment. No sooner was it created, than it was attacked. In these later debates the measure was accredited to Garfield's "persuasive eloquence." One member said it was carried by "dint of personal entreaty." The author of the Department defended it point by point. He protested time and again against "putting out the eyes of the government." But, in spite of his efforts, the Department was reduced to a Bureau in the Interior Department, the appropriations were cut down, and the Bureau was for a time thoroughly crippled. By and by Congress began to deal more generously with this child of his; and the appropriation for the fiscal year ending June 30, 1882, is more than fifty thousand dollars,[1] the largest ever made.

The Bureau immediately attracted the attention of friends of education in the Old World. John Bright wrote this letter concerning it: —

"ROCHDALE, Jan. 4, 1868.

"DEAR SIR, — I write to thank you for sending me a copy of General Garfield's speech on education. I have read it with much interest.

"The Department now to be constituted at Washington will doubtless prepare statistics which will inform the world of what is doing in the United States on the education question; and the volume it will publish will have a great effect in this country, and, indeed, in all civilized countries.

"You will have observed the increased interest in education shown in England since the extension of the suffrage.

[1] These are the yearly appropriations: 1867, $1,678.67; 1868, $11,757.17; 1869, $23,151.82; 1870, $5,842.50; 1871, $14,606.00; 1872, $26,669.89; 1873, $34,835.79; 1874, $34,771.07; 1875, $35,562.53; 1876, $35,561.00; 1877, $32,061.70; 1878, $30,340.00; 1879, $31,220.00; 1880, $36,720.00; 1881, $45,580.00; 1882, $50,155.00.

I hope some great and good measure may be passed at an early period.
"I am very truly yours,
"JOHN BRIGHT.
"GEORGE J. ABBOT, ESQ., United States Consul, Sheffield."

This is the Act as drawn by him, and as originally passed: —

"AN ACT TO ESTABLISH A DEPARTMENT OF EDUCATION.

"*Be it enacted by the Senate and House of Representatives of the United States of America, in Congress assembled*, That there shall be established, at the city of Washington, a Department of Education for the purpose of collecting such statistics and facts as shall show the condition and progress of education in the several States and Territories, and of diffusing such information respecting the organization and management of schools and school systems, and methods of teaching, as shall aid the people of the United States in the establishment and maintenance of efficient school systems, and otherwise promote the cause of education throughout the country.

"SECT. 2. *And be it further enacted*, That there shall be appointed by the President, by and with the advice and consent of the Senate, a Commissioner of Education, who shall be intrusted with the management of the department herein established, and who shall receive a salary of four thousand dollars per annum, and who shall have authority to appoint one chief clerk of his department, who shall receive a salary of two thousand dollars per annum, one clerk who shall receive a salary of eighteen hundred dollars per annum, and one clerk who shall receive a salary of sixteen hundred dollars per annum, which said clerk shall be subject to the appointing and removing power of the Commissioner of Education.

"SECT. 3. *And be it further enacted,* That it shall be the duty of the Commissioner of Education to present annually to Congress a report embodying the results of his investigations and labors, together with a statement of such facts and recommendations as will, in his judgment, subserve the purpose for which this department was established. In the first report made by the Commissioner of Education under this Act, there shall be presented a statement of the several grants of land made by Congress to promote education, and the manner in which these several trusts have been managed, the amount of funds arising therefrom, and the annual proceeds of the same, as far as the same can be determined.

"SECT. 4. *And be it further enacted,* That the Commissioner of Public Buildings is hereby authorized and directed to furnish proper offices for the use of the department herein established."

July 28, 1868, this provision was attached to the Legislative Appropriation Bill: —

"After the thirtieth day of June, 1869, the Department of Education shall cease; and there shall be established and attached to the Department of the Interior an office to be denominated the office of education, the chief officer of which shall be Commissioner of Education, at a salary of three thousand dollars per annum, who shall, under the direction of the Secretary of the Interior, discharge all such duties, and superintend, execute, and perform all such acts and things, touching and respecting the said office of education, as are devolved by law upon said Commissioner."

2. *The Army Post Schools.* — In the year 1866 General Garfield brought forward another educational measure that has already yielded fruit, and that promises to yield still more in the future. May 2 he moved a new section to the Army Bill then pending, as follows : —

"*And be it further enacted*, That whenever troops are serving at any post, garrison, or permanent camp, there shall be established a school where all enlisted men may be provided with instruction in the common English branches of education, and especially in the history of the United States; and the Secretary of War is authorized and directed to detail such commissioned and non-commissioned officers as may be necessary to carry out the provisions of this section."

He supported the proposition in this short speech : —

"Mr. Speaker, I only ask a word on that subject. One of the greatest evils known in standing armies is the evil of idleness, the parent of all wickedness, and especially the ignorance connected with it. I hope we shall be able to do something to eradicate that evil from our army, and to do something to make it a patriotic army. In the wearisome months spent in camp and at posts and garrisons, there is nothing for the soldiers to do but to indulge in some deviltry. It is a great evil in the army. I want the enlisted men to have opportunities for culture; and I ask that the Secretary of War shall detail officers fitted for that purpose. I think such a section will relieve the army from this evil. It has been drawn hastily, but I think will commend itself to the country.

"One word more. If it were in my power, I would make a law that every man and woman in the United States should study American history through the period of their minority. We cannot do that throughout the United States generally, but we can enforce it to some extent upon the privates in our army."

The proposed section was added to the bill: it became law, and forms now the substance of Section 1,231 of the Revised Statutes, thus:—

"Schools shall be established at all posts, garrisons, and permanent camps at which troops are stationed, in which the enlisted men may be instructed in the common English branches of education, and especially in the history of the United States; and the Secretary of War may detail such officers and enlisted men as may be necessary to carry out this provision. It shall be the duty of the post or garrison commander to set apart a suitable room or building for school and religious purposes."

Little or no attempt to carry out this provision appears to have been made until the end of the year 1877. In December of that year the Secretary of War, "believing this to be an important provision of law, from the full enforcement of which much benefit would accrue, not only to the service, but to the enlisted men, — many of whom sadly needed the contemplated instruction," — convened a board of officers to consider what steps should be taken to fully carry it out. This board, — consisting of the Quartermaster-General, the Adjutant-General, and the Judge-Advocate-General, — after full inquiry, reported an elaborate code of rules for the government of post schools, libraries, and reading-rooms. The report was approved by the Secretary, and announced to the army in General Order No. 24. Col. A. McD. McCook was detailed as visitor and inspector of the various post-schools, with all the necessary powers and authority.[1] The results, up to November, 1879, are thus summed up by Gen. Eaton, the head of the National Bureau: —

"Immediate measures were taken at nearly all the permanent military posts toward the establishment of schools for promoting the intelligence of soldiers and affording educa-

[1] Report of Secretary of War, 1878.

tion to their children, as well as to those of officers and civilians at the remote frontier-posts. Requisitions for the construction of suitable buildings for chapel, school, and library were soon forwarded by post-commanders, and approved by the War Department, whenever funds for the purpose were available. At twenty-nine posts such buildings, at a cost of $33,708, were erected; and, at others, existing rooms were put to service. In all, sixty-nine posts were thus provided with schools in 1878-79, and an average of seven hundred and fifty-four enlisted men and one thousand and thirty-nine children received instruction in them.

"A letter from the officer who was put in general charge of this education in the army (Gen. A. McD. McCook) says that great difficulty has been experienced in the selection of enlisted men suitable for teachers, and that, at numerous posts, schools could not be established (or, if established, had to be discontinued) on account of the want of men that could be trusted to do the teaching.

"Enlisted men detailed as teachers receive thirty-five cents a day extra pay. They are subject to military discipline, as other soldiers, and are liable to be called on to perform active service at any time. Normal schools, to prepare for teachers enlisted men possessing the qualifications and inclination to become such, have been established at Columbus Barracks, O., and David's Island, N.Y., depots of the general recruiting-service, and thus a better class of teachers will probably be soon provided. They are expected to understand the rudiments of a common-school education; to be conversant with reading, writing, and arithmetic; and to possess a fair knowledge of geography, grammar, and history. They must also be able to demonstrate clearly, and in plain language, the subjects before them.

"School-books for these schools are furnished by the Quartermaster's Department, on the application of postcommanders, in lieu of, or in connection with, the newspapers and periodicals which it has been the custom to furnish to each post in proportion to its strength of garrison."

Since 1879 the post-schools have made laudable progress; and there can be no doubt that they will do much for the intelligence and *morale* of the army in the future.[1]

3. *The "Hoar Bill."* — The speech on "National Aid to Education," Feb. 6, 1872, was in support of the proposition to dedicate the public lands to education. The subject under immediate consideration was House Bill No. 1,043, "To establish an educational fund, and to apply the proceeds of the public lands to the education of the people," — what is known as the "Hoar Bill." Unfortunately this beneficent measure has not yet become a law, though steadily growing in public favor; but, when it has finally triumphed, General Garfield's early and able advocacy will not be forgotten.

4. *Education and the South.* — President Gar-

[1] See Appendix for fuller information touching these schools.

field studied "the Southern question" profoundly. That he saw the radical trouble in the South, and knew the remedy, is shown by his short speech to the delegation of colored men that visited him at Mentor, Jan. 14, 1881. In a private letter dated Dec. 30, 1880, he wrote, "I have no doubt that the final cure for the 'Solid South' will be found in the education of its youth and in the development of its business interests; but both these things require time." No part of his Inaugural is more eloquent than that in which he presented this subject. What is more, in the last private conversation the writer ever had with him (the evening of March 6, 1881), he said, "I am going to keep that subject before me all the time, and shall see that something is done in that direction if possible." His plan was not worked out, probably, when he was stricken by the assassin's bullet; but his heart was fixed upon this as a prominent feature of his administration,—national aid to public, and especially to Southern, education.

II.—THE STATE AND SCIENCE.

His views touching this question were always liberal and progressive. In the Ohio Senate he strove to secure the enacting of a law authorizing a geological survey of the State. He submitted a bill for that purpose, and supported it in a lengthy and able report. He also made a similar report upon weights and measures. At Washington he supported every intelligent and practical scheme touching the extension of scientific knowledge, or its reduction to practical uses, — the coast-survey, the light-houses, the signal-service, the life-saving service, Arctic exploration, and the geological and other surveys.

Every man who went to him with a well-considered proposition pointing in such directions as these found him an eager and appreciative listener. The scientific men of the country, especially those who were in any way serving the government, as well as the public, — geologists, botanists, astronomers, engineers, and explorers, — came to rely greatly upon him for securing the appropriations that they needed to carry on or enlarge their work. Nor was this solely because he was for some time the head of the Appropriations Committee. For many years he was a regent of the Smithsonian Institution. Here he was brought into official relations with Agassiz and Henry, both of whom became his intimate friends. His general views touching the sphere of the National Government as respects science, he stated in his speech upon that subject.

Besides, he made a strenuous attempt, in 1869, to secure a more rational and efficient census law. After months of labor enthusiastically devoted to the subject, he carried his bill through the House; but it failed in the Senate. The law of 1880, under which our only real census has been taken, is little more than his bill of ten years before reproduced.

Here it may be remarked, that no man in either house of Congress, from 1863 to 1880, was more constantly on the outlook for opportunities to do something, by way of legislation, for science, education, and general knowledge. The man who cares to go through the Congressional proceedings will probably be surprised to find how often he came forward with an amendment to a bill, or with an original measure, professing to reach some such end that he thought valuable. Some of these failed, but many succeeded.

III.—STUDIES AND METHODS.

President Garfield graduated in the traditionary college course. In 1854–56 the modern courses of study had not been established, at least fully, in any American college. He was an excellent classical student and teacher. Probably he did not so much excel as a grammarian; but few students or teachers equalled him in reading thoughts out of (or into?) Latin or Greek. After he became absorbed in public affairs, he kept alive his classical reading, more particularly the Latin poets. Once he said, "Early in life men read Virgil; later, Horace." Certainly Horace grew upon him with the flight of years. Since his death, it has been said that his collection of editions of the poet is one of the finest in the country. The last summer Hon. W. M. Evarts brought him a new and choice edition that he had found in Europe. This was presented to the President on his sick-bed, and gave him much pleasure. But, while thus drawn to the old literatures by taste, appreciation, and association, he could not help seeing that the new conditions — the enormous extension of knowledge, the growth of modern literature, and the development of industry — called imperatively for a widely differentiated education. The "new education" took a strong hold upon his mind. He believed in the new courses of study. He favored a revision of the classical course. He said Greek and Latin must somewhat give way, but confessed at the time that the proposition was like putting his brothers and sisters out of doors. His views on these subjects matured as early as 1867. That year the Eclectic Institute became Hiram College. Naturally he was called upon to start the old school upon her new course. This he did in the address entitled "College Education," in which he stated his conclusions both fully and strongly. In one direction they are also developed in "Elements of Success in Life." Even at the time when he spoke at Hiram (1867), and before, the era of change in college study had begun. Since that day, the new spirit has reached and influenced nearly every college in the land. Attention may also be called to the short speech before the Washington Convention of School Superintendents in 1879. This shows that he thought the public schools open to much criticism and amendment. Perhaps it is proper to add that his private utterances upon this point were even stronger than those made in public.

IV.—TRIBUTES TO EDUCATORS.

In the three addresses thus grouped, General Garfield gives expression to his estimate of the scientific and educational character. Dr. Morse he did not know personally; and so his short speech at the Morse Commemoration was wholly historical. But the other two addresses are full of interesting biographical detail. It is true that Morse, and even Henry, in later years, was not an educator in the sense of being a teacher; but knowledge is so related to instruction, science to education proper, that the admirable commemorative addresses upon them may be fitly put into this collection. There is a peculiar fitness in the other addresses appearing here. Miss Booth and Mr. Garfield were fellow-students and fellow-teachers, and her name will be linked with his in the memories of hundreds of their joint disciples to their latest day. The Hiram fellowship justly regard this as an admirable discourse, and one of the noblest products of his eloquence. With it the volume fitly closes.

I.

The National Bureau of Education.

SPEECH IN THE HOUSE OF REPRESENTATIVES,
JUNE 8, 1866.

I.

THE NATIONAL BUREAU OF EDUCATION.

MR. SPEAKER,—I did intend to make a somewhat elaborate statement of the reasons why the select committee recommend the passage of this bill; but I know the anxiety that many gentlemen feel to have this debate concluded, and to allow the private bills now on the calendar, and set for this day, to be disposed of, and to complete as soon as possible the work of this session. I will therefore abandon my original purpose, and restrict myself to a brief statement of a few leading points in the argument, and leave the decision with the House. I hope this waiving of a full discussion of the bill will not be construed into a confession that it is inferior in importance to any measure before the House; for I know of none that has a nobler object, or that more vitally affects the future of this nation.

I first ask the House to consider the magnitude of the interests involved in this bill. The very attempt to discover the amount of pecuniary and personal interest we have in our schools shows the necessity of such a law as is here proposed. I have searched in vain for any complete or reliable statistics showing the educational condition of the whole country.

The estimates I have made are gathered from various sources, and can be only approximately correct. I am satisfied, however, that they are far below the truth.

Even from the incomplete and imperfect educational statistics of the Census Bureau, it appears that in 1860 there were in the United States 115,224 common schools, 500,000 school officers, 150,241 teachers, and 5,477,037 scholars; thus showing that more than 6,000,000 of the people of the United States are directly engaged in the work of education.

Not only has this large proportion of our population been thus engaged, but the Congress of the United States has given 53,000,000 acres of public lands to fourteen States and Territories of the Union for the support of schools. In the old ordinance of 1785, it was provided that one section of every township — one thirty-sixth of all the public lands of the United States — should be set apart, and held forever sacred to the support of the schools of the country. In the ordinance of 1787, it was declared that, "religion, morality, and knowledge being necessary to good government and the happiness of mankind, schools and the means of education shall forever be encouraged."

It is estimated that at least $50,000,000 have been given in the United States by private individuals for the support of schools. We have thus an interest, even pecuniarily considered, hardly second to any other. We have school statistics tolerably complete from only seventeen States of the Union.

Our Congressional Library contains no educational reports whatever from the remaining nineteen. In those seventeen States, there are 90,835 schools, 129,000 teachers, 5,107,285 pupils; and $34,000,000 are annually appropriated by the Legislatures for the support and maintenance of common schools. Notwithstanding the great expenditures entailed upon them during four years of war, they raised by taxation $34,000,000 annually for the support of common schools. In several States of the Union, more than fifty per cent of all the tax imposed for State purposes is for the support of the common schools. And yet gentlemen are impatient because we wish to occupy a short time in considering this bill.

I will not trouble the House by repeating commonplaces so familiar to every gentleman here, as that our system of government is based upon the intelligence of the people. But I wish to suggest that there never has been a time when all our educational forces should be in such perfect activity as at the present day.

Ignorance — stolid ignorance — is not our most dangerous enemy. There is very little of that kind of ignorance among the white population of this country.

In the Old World, among the despotic governments of Europe, the great disfranchised class — the pariahs of political and social life — are indeed ignorant, mere inert masses, moved upon and controlled by the intelligent and cultivated aristocracy. Any unrepresented and hopelessly disfranchised class in a government will inevitably be struck with intellectual paralysis. Our late slaves afford a sad illustration.

But among the represented and voting classes of this country, where all are equal before the law, and every man is a political power for good or evil, there is but little of the inertia of ignorance. The alternatives are not education or no education; but shall the power of the citizen be directed aright towards industry, liberty,. and patriotism? or, under the baneful influence of false theories and evil influences, shall it lead him continually downward, and work out anarchy and ruin, both to him and the government?

If he is not educated in the school of virtue and integrity, he will be educated in the school of vice and iniquity. We are, therefore, afloat on the sweeping current: we must make head against it, or we shall go down with it to the saddest of destinies.

According to the census of 1860, there were 1,218,311 inhabitants of the United States over twenty-one years of age who could not read or write; and 871,418 of these were American-born citizens. One-third of a million of people are being annually thrown upon our shores from the Old World, a large per cent of whom are uneducated; and the gloomy total has been swelled by the 4,000,000 slaves admitted to citizenship by the events of the war.

Such, sir, is the immense force which we must now confront by the genius of our institutions, and the light of our civilization. How shall it be done? An American citizen can give but one answer. We must pour upon them all the light of our public schools. We must make them intelligent, industrious, patriotic citizens, or they will drag us and our children down to their level. Does not this question rise to the full height of national importance, and demand the best efforts of statesmanship to adjust it?

Horace Mann has well said that —

"Legislators and rulers are responsible. In our country and in our times, no man is worthy the honored name of a statesman who does not include the highest practicable education of the people in all his plans of administration.

"He may have eloquence, he may have a knowledge of all history, diplomacy, jurisprudence, and by these he may claim, in other countries, the elevated rank of a statesman; but unless he speaks, plans, labors, at all times and in all places, for the culture and edification of the whole people, he is not, he cannot be, an American statesman."

Gentlemen who have discussed the bill this morning tell us that it will result in great expense to the government. Whether an enterprise is expensive, or not, is altogether a relative question, to be determined by the importance of the object in view.

Now, what have we done as a nation in the way of expenses? In 1832 we organized a Coast Survey Bureau, and have expended millions upon it. Its officers have triangulated thousands of miles of our coasts, have made soundings of all our bays and harbors, and carefully mapped the shoals, breakers, and coast-lines from our northern boundary on the Atlantic to the extreme northern boundary on the Pacific coast. They have established eight hundred tidal stations to observe the fluctuations of the tides. We have expended vast sums in order perfectly to know the topography of our coasts, lakes, and rivers, that we might make navigation more safe. Is it of no consequence that we explore the boundaries of that wonderful intellectual empire which encloses within its domain the fate of succeeding generations and of this Republic? The children of to-day will be the architects of our country's destiny in 1900.

We have established an Astronomical Observatory, where the movements of the stars are watched, latitude and longitude calculated, and chronometers regulated for the benefit of navigation. For this observatory we pay one-third of a million per annum. Is it of no consequence that you observe the movements of those stars which shall, in the time to come, be guiding stars in our national firmament?

We have established a Light House Board, that is employing all the aids of science to discover the best modes of regulating the beacons upon our shores: it is placing buoys as way-marks to guide ships safely into our harbors. Will you not create a light-house board to set up beacons for the coming generation, not as lights to the eye, but to the mind and heart, that shall guide them safely in the perilous voyage of life, and enable them to transmit the blessings of liberty to those who shall come after them?

We have set on foot a score of expeditions to explore the mountains and valleys, the lakes and rivers, of this and other countries. We have expended money without stint to explore the Amazon and the Jordan, Chili and Japan, the gold shores of Colorado and the copper cliffs of Lake Superior, to gather and publish the great facts of science, and to exhibit the material resources of physical nature. Will you refuse the pitiful sum of $13,000 to collect and record the intellectual resources of this country, the elements that lie behind all material wealth, and make it either a curse or a blessing?

We have paid three-quarters of a million dollars for the survey of the route for the Pacific Railroad, and have published the results, at a great cost, in thirteen quarto volumes, with accompanying maps and charts. The money for these purposes was freely expended. And now, when it is proposed to appropriate $13,000 to aid in increasing the intelligence of those who will use that great continental highway when it is completed, we are reminded of our debts, and warned against increasing our expenditures. It is difficult to treat such an objection with the respect that is always due in this hall of legislation.

We have established a Patent Office, where are annually accumulated thousands of models of new machines invented by our people. Will you make no expenditure for the benefit of the intelligence that shall stand behind those machines, and be their controller? Will you bestow all your favors upon the engine, and ignore the engineer? I will not insult the intelligence of this House by waiting to prove that money paid for education is the most economical of all expenditure; that it is cheaper to prevent crime than to build jails; that schoolhouses are less expensive than rebellions. A tenth of our national debt expended in public education fifty years ago would have saved us the blood and treasure of the late war. A far less sum may save our children from a still greater calamity.

We expend hundreds of thousands annually to promote the agricultural interests of the country, — to introduce the best methods in all that pertains to husbandry. Is it not of more consequence to do something for the farmer of the future than for the farm of to-day?

As man is more precious than soil, as the immortal spirit is nobler than the clod it animates, so is the object of this bill more important than any mere pecuniary interest.

The genius of our government does not allow us to establish a compulsory system of education, as is done in some of the countries of Europe. There are States in this Union, however, which have adopted a compulsory system; and perhaps that is well. It is for each State to determine. A distinguished gentleman from Rhode Island told me lately that it is now the law in that State that every child within its borders shall attend school, and that every vagrant child shall be taken in charge by the authorities, and sent to school. It may be well for other States to pursue the same course; but probably the General Government can do nothing of the sort. Whether it has the right of compulsory control, or not, we propose none in this bill.

But we do propose to use that power, so effective in this country, of letting in light on subjects, and holding them up to the verdict of public opinion. If it could be published annually from this Capitol, through every school-district of the United States, that there are States in the Union that have no system of common schools; and if their records could be placed beside the records of such States as Massachusetts, New York, Pennsylvania, Ohio, and other States that have a common-school system, — the mere statement of the fact would rouse their energies, and compel them for shame to educate their children. It would shame all the delinquent States out of their delinquency.

Mr. Speaker, if I were called upon to-day to point to that in my own State of which I am most proud, I would not point to any of the flaming lines of her military record, to the heroic men and the brilliant officers she gave to this contest; I would not point to any of her leading men of the past or the present: but I would point to her com mon schools; I would point to the honorable fact, that in the great struggle of five years, through which we have just passed, she has expended $12,000,000 for the support of her public schools. I do not include in that amount the sums expended upon our higher institutions of learning. I would point to the fact, that fifty-two per cent of the taxation of Ohio for the last five years, aside from the war-tax and the tax for the payment of her public debt, has been for the support of her schools. I would point to the schools of Cincinnati, Cleveland, Toledo, and other cities of the State, if I desired a stranger to see the glory of Ohio. I would point to the 13,000 schoolhouses and the 700,000 pupils in the schools of Ohio. I would point to the $3,000,000 she has paid for schools during the last year alone. This, in my judgment, is the proper gauge by which to measure the progress and glory of States.

Gentlemen tell us there is no need of this bill, the States are doing well enough now. Do they know through what a struggle every State has come up, that has secured a good system of common schools? Let me illustrate this by one example. Notwithstanding the early declaration of William Penn, —

"That which makes a good constitution must keep it, namely, men of wisdom and virtue; qualities, that, because they descend not with worldly inheritance, must be carefully propagated by a virtuous education of youth, for which spare no cost, for by such parsimony all that is saved is lost;"

notwithstanding that wise master-builder incorporated this sentiment in his "framework of government," and made it the duty of the governor and council "to establish and support public schools;" notwithstanding Benjamin Franklin, from the first hour he became a citizen of Pennsylvania, inculcated the value of useful knowledge to every human being in every walk of life, and by his personal and pecuniary effort did establish schools and a college for Philadelphia; notwithstanding the Constitution of Pennsylvania made it obligatory upon the Legislature to foster the education of the citizens: notwithstanding all this, it was not till 1833-34 that a system of common schools, supported in part by taxation of the property of the State, for the common benefit of all the children of the State, was established by law; and, although the law was passed by an almost unanimous vote of both branches of the Legislature, so foreign was the idea of public schools to the habits of the people, so odious was the idea of taxation for this purpose, that even the poor who were to be specially benefited were so deluded by political demagogues as to clamor for its repeal.

Many members who voted for the law lost their nominations; and others, although nominated, lost their elections. Some were weak enough to pledge themselves to a repeal of the law; and in the session of 1835 there was an almost certain prospect of its repeal, and the adoption in its place of an odious and limited provision for educating the children of the poor by themselves. In the darkest hour of the debate, when the hearts of the original friends of the system were failing from fear, there rose on the floor of the House one of its early champions, one who, though not a native of the State, felt the disgrace which the repeal of this law would inflict, like a knife in his bosom; one who, though no kith or kin of his would be benefited by the operations of the system, and though he should share its burdens, would only partake with every citizen in its blessings; one who voted for the original law although introduced by his political opponents, and who had defended and gloried in his vote before an angry.

and unwilling constituency: this man, then in the beginning of his public career, threw himself into the conflict, and by his earnest and brave eloquence saved the law, and gave a noble system of common schools to Pennsylvania.

I doubt if at this hour, after the thirty years crowded full of successful labors at the bar, before the people, and in halls of legislation, the venerable and distinguished member [Mr. Stevens], who now represents a portion of the same State in this House, can recall any speech of his life with half the pleasure he does that, for no measure with which his name has been connected is so fraught with blessings to hundreds of thousands of children. and to homes innumerable.

I hold in my hand a copy of his brave speech, and I ask the clerk to read the passages I have marked.

"I am comparatively a stranger among you, born in another, in a distant State: no parent or kindred of mine did, does, or probably ever will, dwell within your borders. I have none of those strong cords to bind me to your honor and your interest; yet, if there is any one thing on earth which I ardently desire above all others, it is to see Pennsylvania standing up in her intellectual, as she confessedly does in her physical resources, high above all her confederate rivals. How shameful, then, would it be for these her native sons to feel less so, when the dust of their ancestors is mingled with her soil, their friends and relatives enjoy her present prosperity, and their descendants, for long ages to come, will partake of her happiness or misery, her glory or her infamy!

. . . .

"In giving this law to posterity, you act the part of the philanthropist by bestowing upon the poor, as well as the rich, the greatest earthly boon which they are capable of receiving; you act the part of the philosopher by pointing, if you do not lead them, up the hill of science; you act the part of the hero, if it be true, as you say, that popular vengeance follows close upon your footsteps. Here, then, if you wish true popularity, is a theatre on which you may acquire it.

. . . .

"Let all, therefore, who would sustain the character of the philosopher or philanthropist, sustain this law. Those who would add thereto the glory of the hero can acquire it here; for, in the present state of feeling in Pennsylvania, I am willing to admit that but little less dangerous to the public man is the war-club and battle-axe of savage ignorance than to the lion-hearted Richard was the keen cimeter of the Saracen. He who would oppose it, either through inability to comprehend the advantages of general education, or from unwillingness to bestow them on all his fellow-citizens, even to the lowest and the poorest, or from dread of popular vengeance, seems to me to want either the head of the philosopher, the heart of the philanthropist, or the nerve of the hero."

He has lived long enough to see this law, which he helped to found in 1834, and more than any other man was instrumental in saving from repeal in 1835, expanded and consolidated into a noble system of public instruction. 12,000 schools have been built by the voluntary taxation of the people, to the amount, for schoolhouses alone, of nearly $10,000,000. Many millions of children have been educated in these schools. More than 700,000 attended the public schools of Pennsylvania in 1864-65; and their annual cost provided by voluntary taxation, in the year 1864, was nearly $3,000,000, giving employment to 16,000 teachers.

It is glory enough for one man to have connected his name so honorably with the original establishment and effective defence of such a system.

But it is said that the thirst for knowledge among the young, and the pride and ambition of parents for their children, are agencies powerful enough to establish and maintain thorough and comprehensive systems of education.

This suggestion is answered by the unanimous voice of publicists and political economists. They all admit that the doctrine of "demand and supply" does not apply to educational wants. Even the most extreme advocates of the principle of *laissez-faire* as a sound maxim of political philosophy admit that governments must interfere in aid of education. We must not wait for the *wants* of the rising generation to be expressed in a *demand* for means of education. We must ourselves discover or supply their *needs*, before the time for supplying them has forever passed.

In his "Political Economy,"[1] John Stuart Mill says, —

"But there are other things, of the worth of which the demand of the market is by no means a test; things of which the utility does not consist in ministering to inclinations, nor in serving the daily uses of life, and the want of which is least felt where the need is greatest. This is peculiarly true of those things which are chiefly useful as tending to raise the character of human beings. The uncultivated cannot be competent judges of cultivation.

"Those who most need to be made wiser and better usually desire it least, and, if they desired it, would be incapable of finding the way to it by their own lights. It will continually happen, on the voluntary system, that, the end not being desired, the means will not be provided at all, or that, the persons requiring improvement having an imperfect or altogether erroneous conception of what they want, the supply

[1] Vol. ii., pp. 528, 529; American ed., pp. 573–575.

called forth by the demand of the market will be any thing but what is really required. Now, any well-intentioned and tolerably civilized government may think, without presumption, that it does, or ought to, possess a degree of cultivation above the average of the community which it rules, and that it should therefore be capable of offering better education and better instruction to the people, than the greater number of them would spontaneously demand.

"Education, therefore, is one of those things which it is admissible in principle that the government should provide for the people. The case is one to which the reasons of the non-interference principle do not necessarily or universally extend.

"With regard to elementary education, the exception to ordinary rules may, I conceive, justifiably be carried still further. There are certain primary elements and means of knowledge which it is in the highest degree desirable that all human beings born into the community should acquire during childhood. If their parents, or those on whom they depend, have the power of obtaining for them this instruction, and fail to do it, they commit a double breach of duty, — toward the children themselves, and toward the members of the community generally, who are all liable to suffer seriously from the consequences of ignorance and want of education in their fellow-citizens. It is therefore an allowable exercise of the powers of a government to impose on parents the legal obligation of giving elementary instruction to children. This, however, cannot fairly be done without taking measures to insure that such instruction shall be always accessible to them, either gratuitously or at a trifling expense."

This is the testimony of economic science. I trust the statesmen of this Congress will not think the subject of education too humble a theme for their most serious consideration. It has engaged the earnest attention of the best men of ancient and modern times, especially of modern statesmen and philanthropists.

I will fortify myself in the positions I have taken by quoting the authority of a few men who are justly regarded as teachers of the human race. If I keep in their company, I cannot wander far from the truth. I cannot greatly err while I am guided by their counsel.

In his eloquent essay entitled "Way to establish a Free Commonwealth," John Milton said, —

> "To make the people fittest to choose, and the chosen fittest to govern, will be to mend our corrupt and faulty education, to teach the people faith, not without virtue, temperance, modesty, sobriety, economy, justice; not to admire wealth or honor; to hate turbulence and ambition; to place every one his private welfare and happiness in the public peace, liberty, and safety."

England's most venerable living statesman, Lord Brougham, enforced the same truth in these noble words: —

"Lawgivers of England, I charge ye, have a care! Be well assured that the contempt lavished upon the cabals of Constantinople, when the council disputed on a text while the enemy, the derider of all their texts, was thundering at the gate, will be a token of respect compared with the loud shout of universal scorn which all mankind in all ages will send up against you if you stand still and suffer a far deadlier foe than the Turcoman — suffer the parent of all evil, all falsehood, all hypocrisy, all discharity, all self-seeking, him who covers over with pretexts of conscience the pitfalls that he digs for the souls on which he preys — to stalk about the fold, and lay waste its inmates: stand still, and make no head against him, upon the vain pretext, to soothe your indolence, that your action is obstructed by religious cabals, — upon the far more guilty speculation, that by playing a party game you can turn the hatred of conflicting professors to your selfish purposes!

"Let the soldier be abroad if he will: he can do nothing in this age. There is another personage abroad, — a person less imposing, — in the eye of some, insignificant. The schoolmaster is abroad; and I trust to him, armed with his primer, against the soldier in full uniform array."

Lord Brougham gloried in the title of Schoolmaster, and contrasted his work with that of the military conqueror in these words: —

"The conqueror stalks onward with 'the pride, pomp, and circumstance of war,' banners flying, shouts rending the air, guns thundering, and martial music pealing, to drown the shrieks of the wounded and the lamentations for the slain. Not thus the schoolmaster in his peaceful vocation. He meditates and prepares in secret the plans which are to bless mankind; he slowly gathers around him those who are to further their execution; he quietly, though firmly, advances in his humble path, laboring steadily, but calmly, till he has opened to the light all the recesses of ignorance, and torn up by the roots the weeds of vice. His is a progress not to be compared with any thing like a march; but it leads to a far more brilliant triumph, and to laurels more imperishable than the destroyer of his species, the scourge of the world, ever won."

The learned and brilliant Guizot, who regarded his work in the office of Minister of Public Instructution, in the government of France, the noblest and most valuable work of his life, has left us this valuable testimony : —

" Universal education is henceforth one of the guaranties of liberty and social stability. As every principle of our government is founded on justice and reason, to diffuse education among the people, to develop their understandings and enlighten their minds, is to strengthen their constitutional government, and secure its stability."

In his Farewell Address, Washington wrote these words of wise counsel : —

" Promote, as an object of primary importance, institutions for the general diffusion of knowledge. In proportion as the structure of a government gives force to public opinion, it is essential that public opinion should be enlightened."

In his Inaugural Address, when first taking the Presidential chair, the elder Adams said, —

"The wisdom and generosity of the legislature in making liberal appropriations in money for the benefit of schools, academies, and colleges, is an equal honor to them and to their constituents, a proof of their veneration for letters and science, and a portent of great and lasting good to North and South America and to the world. Great is truth — great is liberty — great is humanity — and they must and will prevail."

Chancellor Kent used this decided language: —

"The parent who sends his son into the world uneducated, defrauds the community of a lawful citizen, and bequeaths to it a nuisance."

I shall conclude the citation of opinions with the stirring words of Edward Everett: —

"I know not to what we can better liken the strong appetence of the mind for improvement than to a hunger and thirst after knowledge and truth, nor how we can better describe the province of education than to say, it does that for the intellect which is done for the body, when it receives the care and nourishment which are necessary for its growth, health, and strength.

"From this comparison I think I derive new views of the importance of education. It is now a solemn duty, a tender, sacred trust.

"What! feed a child's body, and let his soul hunger! pamper his limbs, and starve his faculties!

"Plant the earth, cover a thousand hills with your droves of cattle, pursue the fish to their hiding-places in the sea, and spread out your wheat-fields across the plains, in order to supply the wants of that body which will soon be as cold and senseless as their poorest clod, and let the pure spiritual essence within you, with all its glorious capacities for improvement, languish and pine! What! build factories, turn in rivers upon the water-wheels, unchain the imprisoned spirits of steam, to weave a garment for the body, and let the soul remain unadorned and naked!

"What! send out your vessels to the farthest ocean, and make battle with the monsters of the deep, in order to obtain the means of lighting up your dwellings and workshops, and prolonging the hours of labor for the meat that perisheth, and permit that vital spark which God has kindled, which he has intrusted to our care, to be fanned into a bright and heavenly flame, — permit it, I say, to languish and go out!"

It is remarkable that so many good things have been said, and so few things done, by our national statesmen, in favor of education. If we inquire what has been done by the governments of other countries to support and advance public education, we are compelled to confess with shame that every government in Christendom has given a more intelligent and effective support to schools than has our own.

The free cities of Germany organized the earliest school systems after the separation of Church and State. The present schools of Hamburg have existed more than one thousand years. The earliest school-codes were framed in the Duchy of Wurtemburg in 1565, and in the Electorate of Saxony in 1580. Under these codes were established systems of schools, more perfect, it is claimed, than the school system of any State of the American Union.

Their systems embraced the gymnasium and the university, and were designed, as their laws expressed it, "to carry youth from the elements to the degree of culture demanded for offices in Church and State."

The educational institutions of Prussia are too well known to need a comment. It is a sufficient index of their progress and high character, that a late Prussian school-officer said of his official duties, —

"I promised God that I would look upon every Prussian peasant child as a being who could complain of me before God if I did not provide for him the best education as a man and a Christian which it was possible for me to provide."

France did not think herself dishonored by learning from a nation which she had lately conquered; and when, in 1831, she began to provide more fully for the education of her people, she sent the philosopher Cousin to Holland and Prussia to study and report upon the schools of those states. Guizot was made minister of public instruction, and held the office from 1832 to 1837. In 1833 the report of Cousin was published, and the educational system of France was established on the Prussian model.

No portion of his brilliant career reflects more honor upon Guizot than his five-years' work for the schools of France. The fruits of his labors were not lost in the revolutions that followed. The present emperor is giving his best efforts to the perfection and maintenance of schools, and is endeavoring to make the profession of the teacher more honorable and desirable than it has been hitherto.

Through the courtesy of the Secretary of State, I have obtained a copy of the last annual report of the Minister of Public Instruction in France, which exhibits the present state of education in that empire.

At the last enumeration there were in France, in the colleges and lyceums, 65,832 pupils; in the secondary schools, 200,000; and in the primary or common schools, 4,720,234.

Besides the large amount raised by local taxation, the imperial government appropriated, during the year 1865, 2,349,051 francs for the support of primary schools.

Teaching is one of the regular professions in France; and the government offers prizes, and bestows honors upon the successful instructor of children. During the year 1865, 1,154 prizes were distributed to teachers in primary schools.

An order of honor, and a medal worth 250 francs, are awarded to the best teacher in each commune.

After long and faithful service in his profession, the teacher is retired on half-pay, and, if broken down in health, is pensioned for life. In 1865, there were 4,245 teachers on the pension-list of France. The minister says in his report: "The statesmen of France have determined to show that the country knows how to honor those who serve her, even in obscurity."

Since 1862, 10,243 libraries for the use of common schools have been established; and they now contain 1,117,352 volumes, more than a third of which have been furnished by the imperial government. Half a million text-books are furnished for the use of children who are too poor to buy them. It is the policy of France to afford the means of education to every child in the empire.

When we compare the conduct of other governments with our own, we cannot accuse ourselves so much of illiberality as of reckless folly in the application of our liberality to the support of schools. No government has expended so much to so little purpose. To fourteen States alone we have given for the support of schools 83,000 square miles of land, or an amount of territory nearly equal to two such States as Ohio. But how has this bountiful appropriation been applied? This chapter in our history has never been written. No member of this House or the Senate, no executive officer of the government, now knows, and no man ever did know, what disposition has been made of this immense bounty. This bill requires the Commissioner of Education to report to Congress what lands have been given to schools, and how the proceeds have been applied. If we are not willing to follow the example of our fathers in giving, let us, at least, have the evidence of the beneficial results of their liberality.

Mr. Speaker, I have thus hurriedly and imperfectly exhibited the magnitude of the interests involved in the education of American youth; the peculiar condition of affairs which demand at this time an increase of our educational forces; the failure of a majority of the States to establish school systems, the long struggles through which others have passed in achieving success; and the humiliating contrast between the action of our government and those of other nations in reference to education: but I cannot close without referring to the bearing of this measure upon the peculiar work of this Congress.

When the history of the Thirty-ninth Congress is written, it will be recorded that two great ideas inspired it, and made their impress upon all its efforts; viz., to build up free States on the ruins of slavery, and to extend to every inhabitant of the United States the rights and privileges of citizenship.

Before the Divine Architect builded order out of chaos, he said, "Let there be light." Shall we commit the fatal mistake of building up free States without first expelling the darkness in which slavery had shrouded their people? Shall we enlarge the boundaries of citizenship, and make no provision to increase the intelligence of the citizen?

I share most fully in the aspirations of this Congress, and give my most cordial support to its policy; but I believe its work will prove a disastrous failure unless it makes the schoolmaster its ally, and aids him in preparing the children of the United States to perfect the work now begun.

The stork is a sacred bird in Holland, and is protected by her laws, because it destroys those insects which would undermine the dikes, and let the sea again overwhelm the rich fields of the Netherlands. Shall this government do nothing to foster and strengthen those educational agencies which alone can shield the coming generations from ignorance and vice, and make it the impregnable bulwark of liberty and law?

I know that this is not a measure which is likely to attract the attention of those whose chief work is to watch the political movements that affect the results of nominating conventions and elections. The mere politician will see in it nothing valuable, for the millions of children to be benefited by it can give him no votes. But I appeal to those who care more for the future safety and glory of this nation than for any mere temporary advantage, to aid in giving to education the public recognition and active support of the Federal Government.

II.

National Aid to Education.

SPEECH IN THE HOUSE OF REPRESENTATIVES,
FEB. 6, 1872.

II.

NATIONAL AID TO EDUCATION.[1]

"The preservation of the means of knowledge among the lowest ranks is of more importance to the public than all the property of all the rich men in the country." — JOHN ADAMS'S WORKS, Vol. III., p. 457.

"That all education should be in the hands of a centralized authority, ... and be consequently all framed on the same model, and directed to the perpetuation of the same type, is a state of things, which, instead of becoming more acceptable, will assuredly be more repugnant to mankind, with every step of their progress, in the unfettered exercise of their highest faculties." — "*The Positive Philosophy of Auguste Comte,*" p. 92: JOHN STUART MILL.

MR. SPEAKER, — In the few minutes given me, I shall address myself to two questions. The first is: What do we propose by this bill to give to the cause of education? and the second is: How do we propose to give it? Is the gift itself wise? and is the mode in which we propose to give

---

[1] The House had under consideration House Bill No. 1,043, "To establish an Educational Fund, and to apply the Proceeds of the Public Lands to the Education of the People."

it wise? This arrangement will include all I have to say.

And, first, we propose, without any change in the present land policy, to give the net proceeds of the public lands to the cause of education. During the last fifteen years these proceeds have amounted to a little more than thirty-three million dollars, or one per cent of the entire revenues of the United States for that period. The gift is not great; but yet, in one view of the case, it is princely. To dedicate for the future a fund which is now one per cent of the revenues of the United States, to the cause of education, is, to my mind, a great thought, and I am glad to give it my indorsement. It seems to me, that, in this act of giving, we almost copy its prototype in what God himself has done on this great continent of ours. In the centre of its greatest breadth, where otherwise there might be a desert forever, he has planted a chain of the greatest lakes on the earth; and the exhalations arising from their pure waters every day come down in gracious showers, and make that a blooming garden which otherwise might be a desert waste. It is proposed that the proceeds arising from the sale of our great wilderness lands, like the dew, shall fall forever, not upon the lands but upon the minds of the children of the nation, giving them, for all time to come, all the blessing and growth and greatness that education can afford. That thought, I say it again, is a great one, worthy of a great nation; and this country will remember the man who formulated it into language, and will remember the Congress that made it law.

The other point is one of even greater practical value and significance just now than this that I have referred to. It is this: How is this great gift to be distributed? We propose to give it, Mr. Speaker, through our American system of education; and, in giving it, we do not propose to mar in the least degree the harmony and beauty of that system. If we did, I should be compelled to give my voice and vote against the measure; and here and now, when we are inaugurating this policy, I desire to state for myself, and, as I believe, for many who sit around me, that we do here solemnly protest that this gift is not to destroy or disturb, but it is rather to be used through and as a part of, and to be wholly subordinated to, what I venture to call our great American system of education. On this question

I have been compelled heretofore to differ with many friends of education, here and elsewhere, — many who have thought it might be wise for Congress, in certain contingencies, to take charge of the system of education in the States. I will not now discuss the constitutional aspects of that question; but I desire to say that all the philosophy of our educational system forbids that we should take such a course. And, in the few moments awarded to me, I wish to make an appeal for our system as a whole as against any other known to me. We look sometimes with great admiration at a government like Germany, that can command the light of its education to shine everywhere, that can enforce its school-laws everywhere throughout the empire. Under our system we do not rejoice in that, but we rather rejoice that here two forces play with all their vast power upon our system of education. The first is that of the local, municipal power under our State governments. There is the centre of responsibility. There is the chief educational power. There can be enforced Luther's great thought of placing on magistrates the duty of educating children.

Luther was the first to perceive that Christian schools were an absolute necessity. In a celebrated paper addressed to the municipal councillors of the empire in 1524, he demanded the establishment of schools in all the villages of Germany. To tolerate ignorance was, in the energetic language of the reformer, to make common cause with the Devil. The father of a family who abandoned his children to ignorance was a consummate rascal. Addressing the German authorities, he said, —

"Magistrates, remember that God formally commands you to instruct children. This divine commandment parents have transgressed by indolence, by lack of intelligence, and because of overwork.

"The duty devolves upon you, magistrates, to call fathers to their duty, and to prevent the return of these evils which we suffer to-day. Give attention to your children. Many parents are like ostriches, content to have laid an egg, but caring for it no longer.

"Now, that which constitutes the prosperity of a city is not its treasures, its strong walls, its beautiful mansions, and its brilliant decorations. The real wealth of a city, its safety and its force, is an abundance of citizens, instructed, honest, and cultivated. If in our days we rarely meet such citizens, whose fault is it, if not yours, magistrates, who have allowed our youth to grow up like neglected shrubbery in the forest?

"Ignorance is more dangerous for a people than the armies of an enemy."

After quoting this passage from Luther, Laboulaye, in his eloquent essay entitled "L'État et ses Limites,"[1] says, —

"This familiar and true eloquence was not lost. There is not a Protestant country which has not placed in the front rank of its duties the establishment and maintenance of popular schools."

The duties enjoined in these great utterances of Luther are recognized to the fullest extent by the American system. But they are recognized as belonging to the authorities of the State, the county, the township, the local communities. There these obligations may be urged with all the strength of their high sanctions. There may be brought to bear all the patriotism, all the morality, all the philanthropy, all the philosophy, of our people; and there it is brought to bear in its noblest and best forms.

But there is another force, even greater than that of the State and the local governments. It is the force of private voluntary enterprise, — that force which has built up the multitude of private schools, academies, and colleges throughout the United States, not always wisely, but always

[1] Pp. 204, 205.

with enthusiasm and wonderful energy. I say, therefore, that our local self-government, joined to and co-operating with private enterprise, has made the American system of education what it is.

In further illustration of its merits, I beg leave to allude to a few facts of great significance. The governments of Europe are now beginning to see that our system is better and more efficient than theirs. The public mind of England is now, and has been for several years, profoundly moved on the subject of education. Several commissioners have lately been sent by the British Government to examine the school systems of other countries, and lay before Parliament the results of their investigations, so as to enable that body to profit by the experience of other nations.

Rev. J. Frazier, one of the assistant commissioners appointed for this purpose, visited this country in 1865, and in the following year made his report to Parliament. While he found much to criticise in our system of education, he did not withhold his expressions of astonishment at the important part which private enterprise played in our system. In concluding his report, he speaks of the United States as "a nation of which it is no flattery or exaggeration to say, that it is, if not the most highly, yet certainly the most generally, educated and intelligent people on the globe."

But a more valuable report was delivered to Parliament in 1868, by Matthew Arnold, one of the most cultivated and profound thinkers of England. He was sent by Parliament to examine the schools and universities of the Continent; and after visiting all the leading states of Europe, and making himself thoroughly familiar with their system of education, he delivered a most searching and able report. In the concluding chapter, he discusses the wants of England on the subject of education. No one who reads that chapter can fail to admire the boldness and power with which he points out the chief obstacles to popular education in England. He exhibits the significant fact, that, while during the last half-century there has been a general transformation in the civil organization of European governments, England, with all her liberty and progress, is shackled with what he calls a civil organization, which is, from the top to the bottom of it, not modern. He says,—

"Transform she must, unless she means to come at last to the same sentence as the church of Sardis : ' Thou hast a name that thou livest, and art dead.'

" However, on no part of this immense task of transformation have I now to touch, except on that part which relates to education; but this part, no doubt, is the most important of all, and it is the part whose happy accomplishment may render that of all the rest, instead of being troubled and difficult, gradual and easy. . . .

"Obligatory instruction is talked of. But what is the capital difficulty in the way of obligatory instruction, or, indeed, any national system of instruction, in this country? It is this : that, the moment the working-class of this country have this question of instruction really brought home to them, their self-respect will make them demand, like the working-classes on the Continent, public schools, and not schools which the clergyman or the squire or the mill-owner calls 'my school!' And what is the capital difficulty in the way of giving them public schools? It is this: that the public school for the people must rest upon the municipal organization of the country. In France, Germany, Italy, Switzerland, the public elementary school has, and exists by having, the commune, and the municipal government of the commune, as its foundations; and it could not exist without them. But we, in England, have our municipal organization still to get: the country districts with us have at present only the feudal and ecclesiastical organization of the Middle Ages, or of France before the Revolution. . . .

"The real preliminary to an effective system of popular education is, in fact, to provide the country with an effective municipal organization; and here, then, is, at the outset, an illustration of what I said, — that modern societies need a civil organization which is modern."

In the early part of 1870 a report was made to the Minister of Public Instruction by Mr. C. Hippeau, a man of great learning, and who, in the previous year, had been ordered by the French Government to visit the United States, and make a careful study of our system of public education. In summing up his conclusions at the end of his report, he expresses opinions which are remarkable for their boldness, when we remember the character of the French government at that time; and his recommendations have a most significant application to the principle under consideration. I translate his concluding paragraphs: —

"What impresses me most strongly as the result of this study of public instruction in the United States is the admirable power of private enterprise in a country where the citizens early adopted the habit of foreseeing their own wants for themselves; of meeting together and acting in concert; of combining their means of action; of determining the amount of pecuniary contribution which they will impose upon themselves, and of regulating its use; and, finally, of choosing administrators who shall render them an account of the resources placed at their disposal, and of the use which they may make of their authority.

"The marvellous progress made in the United States during the last twenty years would have been impossible if the national life, instead of being manifested on all points of the surface, had been concentrated in a capital, under the pressure of a strongly organized administration, which, holding the people under constant tutelage, wholly relieved them from the care of thinking and acting by themselves and for themselves. Will France enter upon that path of decentralization, which will infallibly result in giving a scope now unknown to all her vital forces and to the admirable resources which she possesses? In what especially concerns public instruction, shall we see her multiplying, as in America, those free associations, those generous donations, which will enable us to place public instruction on the broadest foundation, and to revive in our provinces the old universities that will become more flourishing as the citizens shall interest themselves directly in their progress?

"To accomplish this, it will also be necessary that governments, appreciating the wants of their epoch, shall with good grace relinquish a part of the duties now imposed upon them, and aid the people in supporting the rigid *régime* of liberty, by enlarging the powers of the municipal councils and of the councils of the departments, by favoring associations and public meetings, by opening the freest field to the examination and discussion of national interests; in short, by deserving the eulogy addressed by a man of genius to a great minister of France: 'Monseigneur, you have labored ten years to make yourself useless.'"

I have made these citations to show how strongly the public thought of Europe is moving toward our system of public education, as better and freer than theirs. I do not now discuss the broader political question of State and municipal government as contrasted with centralized government. I am considering what is the best system of organizing the educational work of a nation, not from the political standpoint alone, but from the standpoint of the schoolhouse itself. This work of public education partakes in a peculiar way of the spirit of the human mind in its efforts for culture. The mind must be as free from extraneous control as possible, — must work under the inspiration of its own desires for knowledge; and, while instructors and books are necessary helps, the fullest and highest success must spring from the power of self-help.

So the best system of education is that which draws its chief support from the voluntary effort of the community, from the individual efforts of citizens, and from those burdens of taxation which they voluntarily impose upon themselves. The assistance proposed in this bill is to be given through the channels of this, our American system. The amount proposed is large enough to stimulate to greater effort and to general emulation the different States and the local school authorities, but not large enough to carry the system on, and to weaken all these forces by making the friends of education feel that the work is done for them without their own effort. Government shall be only a help to them, rather than a commander, in the work of education.

In conclusion, I say, that, in the pending bill, we disclaim any control over the educational system of the States. We only require reports of what they do with our bounty; and those reports, brought here and published for the information of the people, will spread abroad the light, and awaken the enthusiasm and emulation of our people. This policy is in harmony with the act of 1867 creating the Bureau of Education, and whose fruits have already been so abundant in good results. I hope that the House will set its seal of approval on our American system of education, and will adopt this mode of advancing and strengthening it.

III.

Suffrage and Schools.

EXTRACT FROM "THE FUTURE OF THE REPUBLIC: ITS DANGERS AND HOPES." AN ADDRESS DELIVERED BEFORE THE LITERARY SOCIETIES OF WESTERN RESERVE COLLEGE, HUDSON, O., JULY 2, 1873.

III.

SUFFRAGE AND SCHOOLS.

AFTER all, territory is but the body of a nation. The people who inhabit its hills and its valleys are its soul, its spirit, its life. In them dwells its hope of immortality. Among them, if anywhere, are to be found its chief elements of destruction. And this leads me to consider an alleged danger to our institutions, which, if well founded, would be radical and fatal. I refer to the allegation that universal suffrage as the supreme source of political authority is a fatal mistake. When I hear this proposition urged, I feel, as most Americans doubtless do, that it is a kind of moral treason to listen to it, and that to entertain it would be political atheism. That the consent of the governed is the only true source of national authority, and is the safest and firmest foundation on which to build a government, is the most fundamental axiom of our political faith. But we must not forget that a majority — perhaps a large majority — of the thinkers, writers, and statesmen of Christendom declare that our axiom is no axiom; indeed, is not true, but is a delusion and a snare, — a fatal heresy.

At the risk of offending our American pride, I shall quote a few paragraphs from what is probably the most formidable indictment ever penned against the democratic principle. It was written by the late Lord Macaulay, a profound student of society and government, and a man who on most subjects entertained broad and liberal views. Millions of Americans have read and admired his History and Essays; but only a few thousands have read his brief but remarkable letter of 1857, in which he discusses the future of our government. We are so confident of our position, that we seldom care to debate it.

The letter was addressed to the Hon. H. S. Randall of New York, acknowledging the receipt of a copy of that gentleman's "Life of Jefferson." I quote a few paragraphs: —

"LONDON, May 23, 1857.

"DEAR SIR, — You are surprised to learn that I have not a high opinion of Mr. Jefferson, and I am surprised at your surprise. I am certain that I never wrote a line, and that I never in parliament, in conversation, or even on the hustings, — a place where it is the fashion to court the populace, — uttered a word indicating the opinion that the supreme authority in a state ought to be intrusted to the majority of citizens told by the head; in other words, to the poorest and most ignorant part of society. I have long been convinced that institutions purely democratic must, sooner or later, destroy liberty or civilization, or both.

"In Europe, where the population is dense, the effect of such institutions would be almost instantaneous. What happened lately in France is an example. In 1848 a pure democracy was established there. During a short time there was a strong reason to expect a general spoliation, a national bankruptcy, a new partition of the soil, a maximum of prices, a ruinous load of taxation laid on the rich for the purpose of supporting the poor in idleness. Such a system would, in twenty years, have made France as poor and as barbarous as the France of the Carlovingians. Happily the danger was averted; and now there is a despotism, a silent tribune, an enslaved press, liberty is gone, but civilization has been saved. I have not the smallest doubt, that if we had a purely democratic government here the effect would be the same. Either the poor would plunder the rich, and civilization would perish, or order and property would be saved by a strong military government, and liberty would perish. You may think that your country enjoys an exemption from these evils. I will frankly own to you that I am of a very different opinion. Your fate I believe to be certain, though it is deferred by a physical cause. As long as you have a boundless extent of fertile and unoccupied land, your laboring population will be far more at ease than the laboring population of the Old World; and while that is the case the Jeffersonian policy may continue to exist without causing any fatal calamity. But the time will come when New England will be as thickly peopled as Old England. Wages will be as low, and will fluctuate as much, with you as with us. You will have your Manchesters and Birminghams. Hundreds and thousands of artisans will assuredly be sometimes out of work. Then your institutions will be fairly brought to the test. Distress everywhere makes the laborer mutinous and discontented, and inclines him to listen with eagerness to agitators, who tell him that it is a monstrous iniquity that one man should have a million while another cannot get a full meal. In bad years there is plenty of grumbling here, and sometimes a little rioting. But it matters little, for here the sufferers are not the rulers. The supreme power is in the hands of a class, numerous indeed, but select, of an educated class, of a class which is, and knows itself to be, deeply interested in the security of property and the maintenance of order. Accordingly the malcontents are firmly yet gently restrained. The bad time is got over without robbing the wealthy to relieve the indigent. The springs of national prosperity soon begin to flow again; work is plentiful; wages rise, and all is tranquillity and cheerfulness. I have seen England three or four times pass through such critical seasons as I have described. Through such seasons the United States will have to pass, in the course of the next century, if not of this. How will you pass through them? I heartily wish you a good deliverance. But my reason and my wishes are at war, and I cannot help foreboding the worst. It is quite plain that your government will never be able to restrain a distressed and discontented majority. For with you the majority is the government, and has the rich, who are always a minority, absolutely at its mercy. The day will come when, in the State of New York, a multitude of people, none of whom has had more than half a breakfast, or expects to have more than half a dinner, will choose a legislature. Is it possible to doubt what sort of legislature will be chosen? On one side is a statesman preaching patience, respect for vested rights, strict observance of public faith. On the other is a demagogue ranting about the tyranny of capitalists and usurers, and asking why anybody should be permitted to drink champagne and to ride in a carriage while thousands of honest people are in want of necessaries? Which of the two candidates is likely to be preferred by a workingman who hears his children cry for bread? I seriously apprehend that you will, in some such season of adversity as I have described, do things which will prevent prosperity from returning; that you will act like people in a year of scarcity, devour all the seed-corn, and thus make the next year a year, not of scarcity, but of absolute famine. There will be, I fear, spoliation. The spoliation will increase distress. The distress will produce fresh spoliation. There is nothing to stay you. Your Constitution is all sail and no anchor. As I said before, when society has entered on this downward progress, either civilization or liberty must perish. Either some Cæsar or Napoleon will seize the reins of government with a strong hand, or your Republic will be as fearfully plundered and laid waste by barbarians in the twentieth century as the Roman empire was in the fifth; with this difference, that the Huns and Vandals who ravaged the Roman empire came from without, and that your Huns and Vandals will have been engendered within your country by your own institutions.

"Thinking thus, of course I cannot reckon Jefferson among the benefactors of mankind."

Certainly this letter contains food for serious thought, and it would be idle to deny that the writer has pointed out what may become serious dangers in our future. But the evils he complains of are by no means confined to democratic governments, nor do they in the main grow out of popular suffrage. If they do, England herself has taken a dangerous step since Macaulay wrote. Ten years after the date of this letter, she extended the suffrage to eight hundred thousand of her workingmen,—a class hitherto ignored in politics; and still later we have extended it to an ignorant and lately enslaved population of more than four millions. Whether for weal or for woe, enlarged suffrage is the tendency of all modern nations. I venture the declaration that this opinion of Macaulay is vulnerable on several grounds.

In the first place, it is based upon a belief from which few if any British writers have been able to emancipate themselves; viz., the belief that mankind are born into permanent classes, and that in the main they must live, work, and die in the fixed class or condition in which they were born. It is hardly possible for a man reared in an aristocracy like that of England to eliminate this conviction from his mind, for the British empire is built upon it. Their theory of national stability is, that there must be a permanent class which shall hold in their own hands so much of the wealth, the privilege, and the political power of the kingdom, that they can compel the admiration and obedience of all other classes.

At several periods of English history, there have been serious encroachments upon this doctrine; but, on the whole, British phlegm has held to it sturdily, and still maintains it. The great voiceless class of day-laborers have made but little headway against the doctrine. The editor of a leading British magazine told me a few years ago, that, in twenty-five years of observation, he had never known a mere farm-laborer in England to rise above his class.[1] Some, he said, had done so

[1] This statement made a deep impression upon President Garfield's mind, and he often referred to it in speaking of the relative opportunities that England and America offer to the

in manufactures, some in trade; but in mere farm-labor, not one. The government of a country where such a fact is possible has much to answer for.

We deny the justice or the necessity of keeping ninety-nine of the population in perpetual poverty and obscurity in order that the hundredth may be rich and powerful enough to hold the ninety-nine in subjection. Where such permanent classes exist, the conflict of which Macaulay speaks is inevitable. And why? Not that men are inclined to fight the class above them; but they fight any artificial barrier which makes it impossible for them to enter that higher class, and become a part of it. We point to the fact, that in this country there are no classes in the British sense of that word, — no impassable barriers of caste. Now that slavery is

boy born of a lowly condition. His own career is an impossibility in England. Said his Grace the Archbishop of Canterbury, in his Memorial Address, delivered at the Church of St. Mary's-in-the-Fields, London, Sept. 26, —

"All this was calculated to enlist our sympathy; and then we were taught to trace a career such as England knows nothing of, and to wonder at the mode in which great men are formed in a country so like and yet so dissimilar from our own."

His Grace then gave a rapid summary of the President's career, — the scholar, master, student, preacher, soldier, legislator, and President.

abolished, we can truly say, that through our political society there run no fixed horizontal strata through which none can pass upward. Our society resembles rather the waves of the ocean, whose every drop may move freely among its fellows, and may rise toward the light, until it flashes on the crest of the highest wave.

Again, in depicting the dangers of universal suffrage, Macaulay leaves wholly out of the account the great counterbalancing force of universal education. He contemplates a government delivered over to a vast multitude of ignorant, vicious men, who have learned no self-control, who have never comprehended the national life, and who will wield the ballot solely for personal and selfish ends. If this were indeed the necessary condition of democratic communities, it would be difficult, perhaps impossible, to escape the logic of Macaulay's letter. And here is a real peril, — the danger that we shall rely upon the mere extent of the suffrage as a national safeguard. We cannot safely, even for a moment, lose sight of the *quality* of the suffrage, which is more important than its quantity.

We are apt to be deluded into false security by political catch-words, devised to flatter rather than instruct. We have happily escaped the dogma of the divine right of kings. Let us not fall into the equally pernicious error that multitude is divine because it is a multitude. The words of our great publicist — the late Dr. Lieber, whose faith in republican liberty was undaunted — should never be forgotten. In discussing the doctrine of "Vox populi, vox Dei," he said, —

"Woe to the country in which political hypocrisy first calls the people almighty, then teaches that the voice of the people is divine, then pretends to take a mere clamor for the true voice of the people, and lastly gets up the desired clamor!"[1]

This sentence ought to be read in every political caucus: it would make an interesting and significant preamble to most of our political platforms. It is only when the people speak truth and justice that their voice can be called the "voice of God." Our faith in the democratic principle rests upon the belief that intelligent men will see that their highest political good is in liberty regulated by just and equal laws, and that, in the distribution of political power, it is safe to follow the maxim, "Each for all, and all for each." We confront the dangers of the suffrage by the blessings of univer-

[1] Civil Liberty, p. 415.

sal education. We believe that the strength of the State is the aggregate strength of its individual citizens, and that the suffrage is the link that binds in a bond of mutual interest and responsibility the fortunes of the citizen to the fortunes of the State.

Hence, as popular suffrage is the broadest base, so when coupled with intelligence and virtue it becomes the strongest, the most enduring base, on which to build the superstructure of government.

Our great hope for the future, — our great safeguard against danger, — is to be found in the general and thorough education of our people, and in the virtue which accompanies such education. And all these elements depend in a large measure upon the intellectual and moral culture of the young men who go out from our higher institutions of learning. From the standpoint of this general culture we may trustfully encounter the perils that assail us. Secure against dangers from abroad; united at home by the strongest ties of common interest and patriotic pride; holding and unifying our vast territory by the most potent forces of civilization; relying upon the intelligent strength and responsibility of each citizen, and most of all upon the power of truth,

— without undue arrogance, we may hope that in the centuries to come, our Republic will continue to live, and hold its high place among the nations as

"The heir of all the ages, in the foremost files of time."

IV.

Popular Education.

EXTRACTS FROM THE LETTER OF ACCEPTANCE AND
THE INAUGURAL ADDRESS, JULY 12, 1880,
AND MARCH 4, 1881.

IV.

POPULAR EDUCATION.

NEXT in importance to freedom and justice is popular education, without which neither freedom nor justice can be permanently maintained. Its interests are intrusted to the States and to the voluntary action of the people. Whatever help the nation can justly afford should be generously given to aid the States in supporting common schools; but it would be unjust to our people, and dangerous to our institutions, to apply any portion of the revenues of the nation, or of the States, to the support of sectarian schools. The separation of the Church and the State on every thing relating to taxation should be absolute.

But the danger which arises from ignorance in the voter cannot be denied. It covers a field far wider than that of negro suffrage and the present condition of the race. It is a danger that lurks and hides in the sources and fountains of power in every State. We have no standard by which to measure the disaster that may be brought upon us by ignorance and vice in the citizen when joined to corruption and fraud in the suffrage.

The voters of the Union, who make and unmake constitutions, and upon whose will hang the destinies of our governments, can transmit their supreme authority to no successors save the coming generation of voters, who are the sole heirs of sovereign power. If that generation comes to its inheritance blinded by ignorance and corrupted by vice, the fall of the Republic will be certain and remediless. The census has already sounded the alarm in the appalling figures which mark how dangerously high the tide of illiteracy has risen among our voters and their children. To the South this question is of supreme importance. But the responsibility for the existence of slavery does not rest upon the South alone. The nation itself is responsible for the extension of the suffrage, and is under special obligations to aid in removing the illiteracy which it has added to the voting population. For the North and South alike, there is but one remedy. All the constitutional power of the Nation and of the States, and all the volunteer forces of the people, should be summoned to meet this danger by the saving influence of universal education.

It is the high privilege and sacred duty of those now living to educate their successors, and fit them, by intelligence and virtue, for the inheritance which awaits them.

In this beneficent work sections and races should be forgotten, and partisanship should be unknown. Let our people find a new meaning in the divine oracle which declares that "A little child shall lead them;" for our own little children will soon control the destinies of the Republic.

My countrymen, we do not now differ in our judgment concerning the controversies of past generations, and fifty years hence our children will not be divided in their opinions concerning our controversies. They will surely bless their fathers and their fathers' God that the Union was preserved, that slavery was overthrown, and that both races were made equal before the law. We may hasten or we may retard, but we cannot prevent, the final reconciliation. Is it not possible for us now to make a truce with time by anticipating and accepting its inevitable verdict?

Enterprises of the highest importance to our

moral and material well-being invite us, and offer ample employment for our best powers. Let all our people, leaving behind them the battle-fields of dead issues, move forward, and, in the strength of liberty and the restored Union, win the grander victories of peace.

V.

The Gist of the "Southern Question."

REPLY MADE AT MENTOR TO A DELEGATION OF COLORED
CITIZENS FROM SOUTH CAROLINA AND
OTHER SOUTHERN STATES,
JAN. 14, 1881.

V.

THE GIST OF THE "SOUTHERN QUESTION."

GENERAL ELLIOTT AND GENTLEMEN,
—I thank you for your congratulations on the successful termination of the campaign recently closed, and especially for your kind allusion to me personally for the part I bore in that campaign. What I have done, what I have said concerning your race and the great problem that your presence on this continent has raised, I have said as a matter of profound conviction, and hold to with all the meaning of the words employed in expressing it.

What you have said in regard to the situation of your people, the troubles that they encounter, the evils from which they have suffered and still suffer, I have listened to with deep attention, and shall give it the full measure of reflection. This is not the time or the place for me to indicate any thing as to what I shall have to say and do by and by in an official way. But this I may say: I note as peculiarly significant one sentence in the remarks of General Elliott to the effect that a majority of citizens, as he alleges, in some portions of the South, are oppressed by the minority. If this be so, why is it so? It is because a trained man is two or three men in one, in comparison with an untrained man; and outside of politics, and outside of parties, the suggestion is full — brimful — of significance, that the way to make the majority always powerful over any minority is to make its members as trained and intelligent as is the minority itself. That brings the equality of citizenship; and no law can reasonably confer and maintain, in the long-run, equality that is not upheld by culture and intelligence. Legislation ought to do all it can.

I have made these suggestions, simply to indicate, that, in my judgment, the education of your race lies at the basis of the final solution of your great question, and that that cannot be altogether in the hands of the government. The government ought to do all it properly can; but the native hungering and thirsting for knowledge that the Creator has planted in every child must be cultivated by the parents of the child to the last possible degree of their ability, so that the hands of the people shall reach out and grasp in the darkness the hand of the government extending its help. By that union of effort, time will bring what mere legislation alone cannot immediately bring in any locality.

I rejoice that you have expressed so strongly and earnestly your views in regard to the necessity of your education. I have felt for years that that was the final solution, the final hope. Those efforts that are humble, and comparatively out of sight, are, in the long-run, the efforts that tell. I have sometimes thought that the men who sink the coffer-dam, and work for months in anchoring the great stones that make the solid abutments and piers, whose work is by and by entirely flooded by the water and out of sight, do not get their share of credit. The gaudy structure of the bridge that rests on these piers, and across which the trains thunder, is the thing that strikes the eye of the general public. The sunken piers, the hard work, the additional growth, the building-up of industry and economy, all that can help to be the foundation of real prosperity, is the work that in the long-run tells.

Some Scottish poet has said, or put it into the

mouth of some other prophet to say, that the time would come

> "When Bertram right and Bertram might
> Shall meet on Ellengowan's height."

And it is when the might and the right of the people meet, that majorities are never oppressed by minorities.

Gentlemen, that you may take part in this earnest work of building up your race from the foundation into the solidity of intelligence and industry and strength, and upon those bases at last see all your rights recognized and acknowledged, is my personal wish and hope for your people.

VI.

Relation of the National Government to Science.

SPEECH IN THE HOUSE OF REPRESENTATIVES,
FEB. 11, 1879.

VI.

RELATION OF THE NATIONAL GOVERNMENT TO SCIENCE.[1]

MR. CHAIRMAN,—I think it a misfortune that so important a measure as this is, is placed upon one of the annual appropriation bills. I have had occasion hitherto to characterize that method of legislation, and I think it is well illustrated in this case. If it could have been avoided in any way, it ought, it seems to me, to have been avoided here. The subject embraced in the sections which relate to the surveys of the public land should have been embodied in a separate bill, and subjected to the most careful scrutiny. But as the sections are here, and may be ruled in

[1] This speech was made in the Committee of the Whole upon the State of the Union, upon House Bill No. 640, making appropriations for the legislative, executive, and judicial expenses of the government for the fiscal year ending June 30, 1880, and for other purposes. The immediate subject was the sections of the bill consolidating the geological and other surveys.

order, I offer a few suggestions upon their merits.

I will say, however, that one subject provided for in these sections has had no other place in our laws except in appropriation bills, and probably cannot be ruled out on the point of order. I speak of those scientific surveys which for the last ten or twelve years have been supported by the government. I think I am right in saying that there is no independent statute touching them: all the legislation in regard to them is to be found in the appropriation bills. And what I shall say in the short time I propose to address the committee this morning, will relate chiefly to those surveys.

It is of the utmost importance that whatever the United States undertakes to do in reference to science shall be done upon some well-understood, well-reasoned, and well-defined system. And I venture to ask the attention of the Committee of the Whole for a few minutes to some general views on the relation of the National Government to this subject.

We are accustomed to hear it said that the great powers of government in this country are divided into two classes, — National powers and

NATIONAL GOVERNMENT AND SCIENCE. 261

State powers. That is an incomplete classification. Our fathers carefully divided all governmental powers into three classes: one they gave to the States; another, Nation; but the third great class, comprising the most precious of all powers, they refused to confer upon the States or the Nation, but reserved to themselves. This third class of powers has been almost uniformly overlooked by men who have discussed the American system.

My attention was called to this in a striking way not long since, in reading a speech of Bismarck's before the Reichstag of Germany. A proposition was pending to grant some political rights to the Jews in the German empire. Bismarck opposed it; and in doing so he took occasion to state what, in his view, was the primary object of the Prussian government; and I was startled at the statement: —

"All gentlemen around me will admit," said he, " that the primary object of the Prussian government is to maintain and defend the gospel of our Lord Jesus Christ. How, then, can one who disbelieves in Christ be properly admitted as a sharer of power in this kingdom?"

I was struck with the fact that the great statesman of Germany — probably the foremost man in

Europe to-day — stated as an unquestioned principle, that the support, defence, and propagation of the Christian gospel is the central object of the German government. Then I considered, in contrast with that, the peculiarity of our own government. Our fathers, though recognizing, in common with Germany and the other Christian nations of the earth, the supreme importance of religion among men, deliberately turned to the great nation they were to establish, and said, " You shall never make any law about religion ; " and to the States they virtually said, " You shall never make any law establishing any form of religion." In other words, here was an interest too precious to be trusted, either to the Nation or to the States. Our fathers said, " This highest of all human interests we will reserve to the people themselves. We will not delegate our power over it to any organized government, State or National. We will not even allow legislatures to make any law concerning it."

To my mind, it is the sublimest fact in our American system, that, in defining the boundaries of delegated powers, they chose to intrust the most precious of all the interests of human beings on this earth absolutely to the voluntary action of the individual people of the Republic, not to be voted upon by their representatives, but to be regulated, protected, and cherished by their own voluntary action, leaving themselves perfectly free to have no religion if they chose, or any religion that they pleased. Thus they exhibited their regard for liberty, their faith in the voluntary action of the people, and their belief that the most precious interests would be safest under the immediate guardianship of freemen. In my view, we have spent too much time in discussing State sovereignty and National supremacy, and have neglected to recognize and appreciate the vast importance of the reserved rights of the people.

It is a safe and wise rule to follow in all legislation, that whatever the people can do without legislation will be better done by them than by the intervention of the State or the Nation.

What I have said in reference to religion applies with almost equal force to science. In the main, the framers of our government trusted science to the same jurisdiction to which they intrusted religion. With the single exception of one clause in the Constitution authorizing Congress to promote science by granting copyrights and patents, the chief support and maintenance of science are left, and I think wisely left, to the voluntary action of our people; and this was done, not in the interest of liberty alone, but in the interest of science itself.

This leads me to inquire, What ought to be the relation of the National Government to science? What, if any thing, ought we to do in the way of promoting science? For example, if we have the power, would it be wise for Congress to appropriate money out of the treasury to employ naturalists to find out all that is to be known of our American birds? Ornithology is a delightful and useful study; but would it be wise for Congress to make an appropriation for the advancement of that science? In my judgment, manifestly not. We would thereby make one favored class of men the rivals of all the ornithologists who, in their private way, following the bent of their genius, may be working out the results of science in that field. I have no doubt that an appropriation out of our treasury for that purpose would be a positive injury to the advancement of science, just as an appropriation to establish a church would work injury to religion.

Generally the desire of our scientific men is to be let alone, to work in free competition with all the scientific men of the world; to develop their own results, and get the credit of them each for himself; not to have the government enter the lists as the rival of private enterprise.

As a general principle, therefore, the United States ought not to interfere in matters of science, but should leave its development to the free, voluntary action of our third great estate, — the people themselves.

In this non-interference theory of the government, I do not go to the extent of saying that we should do nothing for education, — for primary education. That comes under another consideration, — the necessity of the nation to protect itself, and the consideration that it is cheaper and wiser to give education than to build jails. But I am speaking now of the higher sciences.

To the general principle I have stated, there are a few obvious exceptions, which should be clearly understood when we legislate on the subject. In the first place, the government should aid all sorts of scientific inquiry that are necessary to the intelligent exercise of its own functions.

For example, as we are authorized by the Constitution, and compelled by necessity, to build and maintain light-houses on our coast, and establish fog-signals, we are bound to make all necessary scientific inquiries in reference to light and its laws, sound and its laws, — to do whatever in the way of science is necessary to achieve the best results in lighting our coasts and warning our mariners of danger. So, when we are building iron-clads for our navy, or casting guns for our army, we ought to know all that is scientifically possible to be known about the strength of materials and the laws of mechanics which apply to such structure. In short, wherever, in exercising any of the necessary functions of the government, scientific inquiry is needed, let us make it to the fullest extent, and at the public expense.

There is another exception to the general rule of leaving science to the voluntary action of the people. Wherever any great popular interest, affecting whole classes, possibly all classes of the community, imperatively needs scientific investigation, and private enterprise cannot accomplish it, we may wisely intervene and help where the Constitution gives us authority. For example, in discovering the origin of yellow-fever, and the methods of preventing its ravages, the Nation should do, for the good of all, what neither the States nor individuals can accomplish. I might perhaps include, in a third exception, those inquiries which, in consequence of their great magnitude and cost, cannot be successfully made by private individuals. Outside these three classes of inquiries, the government ought to keep its hands off, and leave scientific experiment and inquiry to the free competition of those bright, intelligent men whose genius leads them into the fields of research.

And I suspect, when we read the report of our Commissioner to the late Paris Exposition, which shows such astonishing results, so creditable to our country, so honorable to the genius of our people, it will be found in any final analysis of causes, that the superiority of Americans in that great exposition resulted mainly from their superior freedom, and the greater competition between mind and mind, untrammelled by government interference. I believe it will be found we are best serving the cause of religion and science, and all those great primary rights which we did not delegate to the Congress or the States, but left the people free to enjoy and maintain them.

Mr. Chairman, leaving these general reflections, I come to the special question of our geological surveys. Leaving out of the account all the government works proper, such as light-houses, such as the survey of our coast, such as the survey of our rivers and harbors, such as the surveys of the lakes, of military surveys proper, — leaving all these out, we have spent almost two million dollars in the last twelve years for purely scientific surveys. While the results have been very gratifying, while they have been exceedingly interesting to men of science, and also of commercial value to the country, I believe we have spent a large part of that money upon an unwise system, and in a way which has tended to discourage the private pursuit of science by our people.

We have made the government a formidable and crushing competitor of private students of science; and I think we have, in some cases, gone beyond the fair limit of what the government ought to do in the way of scientific investigation. We have had the War Department, with two or three separate expeditions, exploring our Western territory; we have had two separate organizations from the Interior Department, also exploring: and it has all been done on a system which has invited and fostered a personal seeking of favor from Congress. There have been good men, intelligent men, scientific men, who have sought for authority and aid to make scientific investigations in fields which private citizens were exploring; and in employing so many separate and independent parties, there have been many cases, if not of collision, at least of overlapping and duplication, in the same field of examination. It seems to me it is high time for us, first, to restrict our scientific work plainly and narrowly within the limits of the rules I have tried to lay down; and, second, to consolidate the scientific part of our work of survey under one responsible head, and, having done that, with all the economy which can be fairly used, let us make our outlay only in the direction of public necessity.

Now, lest some one should think I am attacking the geological surveys, I hasten to say that it is absolutely vital to an intelligent discharge of our duties as trustees, or rather as owners, of the great public domain yet unsurveyed and unsold, to give to our people all the light that science can shed upon the character and quality of those lands.

While I may doubt the propriety of making at once the whole change proposed in this bill, it is perfectly clear to my mind that we have reached a natural crisis in the management and disposition of our public domain. We have now reached the foot-hills of the great Rocky-Mountain chain; and the old plans, the old methods, both of survey and of settlement, are in the main no longer applicable. Of what possible use can it be to checkerboard the slopes and the tops of mountains that are full of ores with the old system of sections, half-sections, and quarter-sections?

To say that the old plan has worked well for a hundred years, is to praise our past properly; but to say that the same plan will work well for the next hundred years, is to say the match-locks, gun-flints, the spontoons, and other nameless and obsolete implements of war, that were in vogue a hundred years ago, will be good for a hundred years to come, and should not be abandoned. We must not revolutionize merely for the sake of change; but we must wisely and intelligently adapt our policy to the progress of events; and I believe it has been clearly shown, that, if the old rectangular system is continued, it will be substantially worthless in its application to most of our unsurveyed territory.

Mr. KEIFER. It never was applied to them.

Mr. GARFIELD. We do not want it to be.

NATIONAL GOVERNMENT AND SCIENCE. 271

Mr. KEIFER. And it never will be.

Mr. GARFIELD. But I am confining what I say to-day almost exclusively to that clause of the bill which relates to the scientific surveys. As regards the land-surveys, I confess I have not studied that subject so fully as some of the gentlemen around me.

Mr. PAGE. May I ask the gentleman a question?

Mr. GARFIELD. Yes, sir.

Mr. PAGE. I ask the gentleman from Ohio if he is not aware that the amendment of which he is now speaking is directly in violation of, or changes, existing law, and makes an appropriation for an additional officer not now known to the law? and whether he is in favor of new legislation on an appropriation bill?

Mr. GARFIELD. I said in the outset of my remarks, that I am opposed to that mode of legislation, and that I regret for that reason that this provision is here and not in a bill by itself. My record is too well known to leave any doubt on that subject.

I say this: Let us consolidate these scientific explorations and surveys, and unite them under one head, and not scatter them as we have done hitherto, and waste money, and duplicate work, and make the name of science ridiculous in the United States. As to the other parts of these sections, let us at least make an arrangement, if we do no more, by which we shall have a full and complete report upon the whole subject, so that we may make these changes soon if not now.

In this hurried way I have said nearly all I intended to say, except to call attention to one other point. Besides going too far in scientific explorations, we have greatly wronged the scientific publication societies of this country. I suppose some gentlemen may not know that there are twenty-seven voluntary scientific associations in this country that publish their proceedings, besides five or six journals specially devoted to publishing the discoveries of science.

These are a part of the means by which discoveries in science can find their way to the public through the press; and yet we are printing thousands of volumes in competition with the private associations of the country, and thereby injuring and crippling them. I believe we ought simply to confine ourselves to our own business, and not needlessly travel into their field. Without very much reflection, and in a manner quite unsatisfactory to myself, I have offered these suggestions. If I have stimulated any one to do the subject better justice, I shall not altogether have failed of my purpose.

VII.

College Education.

AN ADDRESS BEFORE THE LITERARY SOCIETIES OF THE
ECLECTIC INSTITUTE, HIRAM, O.,
JUNE 14, 1867.

VII.

COLLEGE EDUCATION.

GENTLEMEN OF THE LITERARY SOCIETIES, — I congratulate you on the significant fact, that the questions which most vitally concern your personal work, are at this time rapidly becoming, indeed have already become, questions of first importance to the whole nation. In ordinary times, we could scarcely find two subjects wider apart than the meditations of a schoolboy, when he asks what he shall do with himself, and how he shall do it, and the forecastings of a great nation, when it studies the laws of its own life, and endeavors to solve the problem of its destiny. But now there is more than a resemblance between the nation's work and yours. If the two are not identical, they at least bear the relation of the whole to a part.

The nation, having passed through the childhood of its history, and being about to enter upon a new life, based on a fuller recognition of the rights of manhood, has discovered that liberty can be safe only when the suffrage is illuminated by education. It is now perceived that the life and light of a nation are inseparable. Hence the Federal Government has established a National Department of Education, for the purpose of teaching young men and women how to be good citizens.

You, young gentlemen, having passed the limits of childhood, and being about to enter the larger world of manhood, with its manifold struggles and aspirations, are now confronted with the question, "What must I do to fit myself most completely, not for being a citizen merely, but for being 'all that doth become a man,' living in the full light of the Christian civilization of America?" Your disinthralled and victorious country asks you to be educated for her sake, and the noblest aspirations of your being still more imperatively ask it for your own sake.

In the hope that I may aid you in solving some of these questions, I have chosen for my theme on this occasion: —

"The Course of Study in American Colleges, and its Adaptation to the Wants of our Time."

Before examining any course of study, we

should clearly apprehend the objects to be obtained by a liberal education.

In general, it may be said that the purpose of all study is twofold, — to discipline our faculties, and to acquire knowledge for the duties of life. It is happily provided in the constitution of the human mind, that the labor by which knowledge is acquired is the only means of disciplining the powers. It may be stated as a general rule, that if we compel ourselves to learn what we ought to know, and use it when learned, our discipline will take care of itself.

Let us, then, inquire, What kinds of knowledge should be the objects of a liberal education? Without adopting in full the classification of Herbert Spencer, it will be sufficiently comprehensive for my present purpose to propose the following kinds of knowledge, stated in the order of their importance: —

First, That knowledge which is necessary for the full development of our bodies and the preservation of our health.

Second, The knowledge of those principles by which the useful arts and industries are carried on and improved.

Third, That knowledge which is necessary to

a full comprehension of our rights and duties as citizens.

Fourth, A knowledge of the intellectual, moral, religious, and æsthetic nature of man, and his relations to nature and civilization.

Fifth, That special and thorough knowledge which is requisite for the particular profession or pursuit which a man may choose as his life-work after he has completed his college studies.

In brief, *the student should study himself, his relations to society, to nature, and to art; and above all, in all, and through all these, he should study the relations of himself, society, nature, and art, to God, the Author of them all.* Of course it is not possible, nor is it desirable, to confine the course of development exclusively to this order; for Truth is so related and correlated, that no department of her realm is wholly isolated. We cannot learn much that pertains to the industry of society, without learning something of the material world, and the laws which govern it. We cannot study nature profoundly without bringing ourselves into communion with the spirit of art, which pervades and fills the universe. But what I suggest is, that we should make the course of study conform generally to the order here indicated; that the student shall first study what he most needs to know; that the order of his needs shall be the order of his work. Now, it will not be denied, that from the day that the child's foot first presses the green turf till the day when, an old man, he is ready to be laid under it, there is not an hour in which he does not need to know a thousand things in relation to his body, — "what he shall eat, what he shall drink, and wherewithal he shall be clothed." Unprovided with that instinct which enables the lower animals to reject the noxious, and select the nutritive, man must learn even the most primary truth that ministers to his self-preservation. If parents were themselves sufficiently educated, most of this knowledge might be acquired at the mother's knee; but, by the strangest perversion and misdirection of the educational forces, these most essential elements of knowledge are more neglected than any other.

School-committees would summarily dismiss the teacher who should have the good sense and courage to spend three days of each week with her pupils in the fields and woods, teaching them the names, peculiarities, and uses of rocks, trees, plants, and flowers, and the beautiful story of the animals, birds, and insects, which fill the world with life and beauty. They will applaud her for continuing to perpetrate that undefended and indefensible outrage upon the laws of physical and intellectual life, which keeps a little child sitting in silence, in a vain attempt to hold his mind to the words of a printed page, for six hours in a day. Herod was merciful, for he finished his slaughter of the innocents in a day; but this practice kills by the savagery of slow torture. And what is the child directed to study? Besides the mass of words and sentences which he is compelled to memorize, not one syllable of which he understands, at eight or ten years of age he is set to work on English grammar, — one of the most complex, intricate, and metaphysical of studies, requiring a mind of much muscle and discipline to master it. Thus are squandered — nay, far worse than squandered — those thrice precious years, when the child is all ear and eye, when its eager spirit, with insatiable curiosity, hungers and thirsts to know the what and the why of the world and its wonderful furniture. We silence its sweet clamor by cramming its hungry mind with words, words, — empty, meaningless words. It asks for bread, and we give it a stone. It is to me a perpetual wonder that any child's love of knowledge survives the outrages of the schoolhouse. It would be foreign from my present purpose to consider further the subject of primary education; but it is worthy your profoundest thought, for "out of it are the issues of life." That man will be a benefactor of his race who shall teach us how to manage rightly the first years of a child's education. I, for one, declare that no child of mine shall ever be *compelled* to study one hour, or to learn even the English alphabet, before he has deposited under his skin at least seven years of muscle and bone.

What are our seminaries and colleges accomplishing in the way of teaching the laws of life and physical well-being? I should scarcely wrong them, were I to answer, Nothing: absolutely nothing. The few recitations which some of the colleges require in anatomy and physiology, unfold but the alphabet of those subjects. The emphasis of college culture does not fall there. The graduate has learned the *Latin* of the old maxim, "*Mens sana in corpore sano;*" but how to strengthen the mind by the preservation of the body, he has never learned. He can read you in Xenophon's best Attic Greek, that Apollo flayed the unhappy Marsyas, and hanged up his skin as a trophy; but he has never examined the wonderful texture of his own skin, or the laws by which he may preserve it. He would blush, were he to mistake the place of a Greek accent, or put the ictus on the second syllable of Eolus; but the whole circle "*liberalium artium,*" so pompously referred to in his diploma of graduation, may not have taught him, as I can testify in an instance personally known to me, whether the *jejunum* is a bone, or the *humerus* an intestine. Every hour of study consumes a portion of his muscular and vital force. Every tissue of his body requires its appropriate nourishment, the elements of which are found in abundance in the various products of nature; but he has never inquired where he shall find the phosphates and carbonates of lime for his bones, albumen and fibrine for his blood, and phosphorus for his brain. His chemistry, mineralogy, botany, anatomy, and physiology, if thoroughly studied, would give all this knowledge; but he has been intent on things remote and foreign, and has given but little heed to those matters which so nearly concern the chief functions of life. But the student should not be blamed. The great men of history have set him the example. Copernicus discovered and announced the true theory of the solar system a hundred years before the circulation of the blood was known. Though from the heart to the surface, and from the surface back to the heart, of every man of the race, some twenty pounds of blood had made the circuit once every three minutes, yet men were looking so steadily away from themselves that they did not observe the wonderful fact. His habit of thought has developed itself in all the courses of college study.

In the next place, I inquire, What kinds of knowledge are necessary for carrying on and improving the useful arts and industries of civilized life? I am well aware of the current notion, that these muscular arts should stay in the fields and shops, and not invade the sanctuaries of learning. A finished education is supposed to consist mainly of literary culture. The story of the forges of the Cyclops, where the thunderbolts of Jove were fashioned, is supposed to adorn elegant scholarship more gracefully than those sturdy truths which are preaching to this generation in the wonders of the mine, in the fire of the furnace, in the clang of the iron-mills, and the other innumerable industries, which, more than all other human agencies, have made our civilization what it is, and are destined to achieve wonders yet undreamed of. This generation is beginning to understand that education should not be forever divorced from industry, — that the highest results can be reached only when science guides the hand of labor. With what eagerness and alacrity is industry seizing every truth of science, and putting it in harness! A few years ago Bessemer of England, studying the nice affinities between carbon and the metals, discovered that a slight change of combination would produce a metal possessing the ductility of iron and the compactness of steel, and which would cost but little more than common iron. One rail of this metal will outlast fifteen of the iron rails now in use. Millions of capital are already invested to utilize this thought of Bessemer's, which must soon revolutionize the iorn-manufacture of the world.

Another example: The late war raised the price of cotton, and paper made of cotton rags. It was found that good paper could be manufactured from the fibre of soft wood; but it was expensive and difficult to reduce to a pulp, without chopping the fibre in pieces. A Yankee mechanic, who had learned in the science of vegetable anatomy that a billet of wood was composed of millions of hollow cylinders, many of them so small that only the microscope could reveal them, and having learned also the penetrative and expansive power of steam, wedded these two truths in an experiment, which, if exhibited to Socrates, would have been declared a miracle from the gods. The experiment was very simple. Putting his block of wood in a strong box, he forced into it a volume of superheated steam which made its way into the minutest pore and cell of the wood. Then through a trap-door suddenly opened, the block was tossed out. The outside pressure being removed, the expanding steam instantly burst every one of the million tubes; every vegetable flue collapsed, and his block of wood lay before him a mass of fleecy fibre, more delicate than the hand of man could make it.

Machinery is the chief implement with which civilization does its work; but the science of mechanics is impossible without mathematics.

But for her mineral resources, England would be only the hunting-park of Europe, and it is believed that her day of greatness will terminate when her coal-fields are exhausted. Our mineral wealth is a thousand times greater than hers; and yet, without the knowledge of geology, mineralogy, metallurgy, and chemistry, our mines could be of but little value. Without a knowledge of astronomy, commerce on the sea is impossible; and now at last it is being discovered that the greatest of all our industries, the agricultural, in which three-fourths of all our population are engaged, must call science to its aid, if it would keep up with the demands of civilization. I need not enumerate the extent and variety of knowledge, scientific and practical, which a farmer needs in order to reach the full height and scope of his noble calling. And what has our American system of education done for this controlling majority of the people? I can best answer that question with a single fact. Notwithstanding there are in the United States one hundred and twenty thousand common schools and seven thousand academies and seminaries; notwithstanding there are two hundred and seventy-five colleges where young men may be graduated as bachelors and masters of the liberal arts, — yet in all these the people of the United States have found so little being done, or likely to be done, to educate men for the work of agriculture, that they have demanded, and at last have secured from their political servants in Congress, an appropriation sufficient to build and maintain, in each State of the Union, a college for the education of farmers. This great outlay would have been totally unnecessary, but for the stupid and criminal neglect of college, academic, and common-school boards of education to furnish that which the wants of the people require. The scholar and the worker must join hands, if both would be successful.

I next ask, What studies are necessary to teach our young men and women the history and spirit of our government, and their rights and duties as citizens? There is not now, and there never was on this earth, a people who have had so many and weighty reasons for loving their country, and thanking God for the blessings of civil and religious liberty, as our own. And yet, seven years ago, there was probably less strong, earnest, open love of country in the United States than in any other nation of Christendom. It is true, that the gulf of anarchy and ruin into which treason threatened to plunge us, startled the nation as by an electric shock, and galvanized into life its dormant and dying patriotism. But how came it dormant and dying? I do not hesitate to affirm, that one of the chief causes was our defective system of education. Seven years ago there was scarcely an American college in which more than four weeks out of the four-years' course were devoted to studying the government and history of the United States. For this defect of our educational system I have neither respect nor toleration. It is far inferior to that of Persia three thousand years ago. The uncultivated tribes of Greece, Rome, Libya, and Germany, surpassed us in this respect. Grecian children were taught to reverence and emulate the virtues of their ancestors. Our educational forces are so wielded as to teach our children to admire most that which is foreign and fabulous and dead. I have recently examined the catalogue of a leading New-England college, in which the geography and history of Greece and Rome are required to be studied five terms; but neither the history nor the geography of the United States is named in the college course, or required as a condition of admission. Our American children must know all the classic rivers, from the Scamander to the Yellow Tiber; must tell you the length of the Appian Way, and of the canal over which Horace and Virgil sailed on their journey to Brundusium: but he may be crowned with baccalaureate honors without having heard, since his first moment of Freshman life, one word concerning the one hundred and twenty-two thousand miles of coast and river navigation, the six thousand miles of canal, and the thirty-five thousand miles of railroad, which indicate both the prosperity and the possibilities of his own country.

It is well to know the history of those magnificent nations whose origin is lost in fable, and whose epitaphs were written a thousand years ago; but, if we cannot know both, it is far better to study the history of our own nation, whose origin we can trace to the freest and noblest aspirations of the human heart, — a nation that was formed from hardiest, purest, and most enduring elements of European civilization; a nation that, by its faith and courage, has dared and accomplished more for the human race in a single century than Europe accomplished in the first thousand years of the Christian era. The New-England township was the type after which our Federal Government was modelled; yet it would be rare to find a college student who can make a comprehensive and intelligent statement of the municipal organization of the township in which he was born, and tell you by what officers its legislative, judicial, and executive functions are administered. One-half of the time which is now almost wholly wasted in district schools on English grammar, attempted at too early an age, would be sufficient to teach our children to love the Republic, and to become its loyal and life-long supporters. After the bloody baptism from which the nation has arisen to a higher and nobler life, if this shameful defect in our system of education be not speedily remedied, we shall deserve the infinite contempt of future generations. I insist that it should be made an indispensable condition of graduation in every American college, that the student must understand the history of this continent since its discovery by Europeans; the origin and history of the United States, its constitution of government, the struggles through which it has passed, and the rights and duties of citizens who are to determine its destiny and share its glory.

Having thus gained the knowledge which is necessary to life, health, industry, and citizenship, the student is prepared to enter a wider and grander field of thought. If he desires that large and liberal culture which will call into activity all his powers, and make the most of the material God has given him, he must study deeply and earnestly the intellectual, the moral, the religious, and the æsthetic nature of man; his relations to nature, to civilization past and present; and, above all, his relations to God. These should occupy, nearly, if not fully, half the time of his college course. In connection with the philosophy of the mind, he should study logic, the pure mathematics, and the general laws of thought. In connection with moral philosophy, he should study political and social ethics, a science so little known either in colleges or congresses. Prominent among all the rest, should be his study of the wonderful history of the human race, in its slow and toilsome march across the centuries, — now buried in ignorance, superstition, and crime; now rising to the sublimity of heroism, and catching a glimpse of a better destiny; now turning remorselessly away from, and leaving to perish, empires and civilizations in which it had invested its faith and courage and boundless energy for a thousand years, and plunging into the forests of Germany, Gaul, and Britain, to build for itself new empires, better fitted for its new aspirations; and at last crossing three thousand miles of unknown sea, and building in the wilderness of a new hemisphere its latest and proudest monuments. To know this as it ought to be known, requires not only a knowledge of general history, but a thorough understanding of such works as Guizot's "History of Civilization" and Draper's "Intellectual Development of Europe," and also the rich literature of ancient and modern nations.

Of course, our colleges cannot be expected to lead the student through all the paths of this great field of learning; but they should at least point out its boundaries, and let him taste a few clusters from its richest vines.

Finally, in rounding up the measure of his work, the student should crown his education with that æsthetic culture which will unfold to him the delights of nature and art, and make his mind and heart a fit temple where the immortal spirit of Beauty may dwell forever.

While acquiring this kind of knowledge, the student is on a perpetual voyage of discovery,— searching what he is, and what he may become; how he is related to the universe, and how the harmonies of the outer world respond to the voice within him. It is in this range of study that he learns most fully his own tastes and aptitudes — and generally determines what his work in life shall be.

The last item in the classification I have suggested, that special knowledge which is necessary to fit a man for the particular profession or calling he may adopt, I cannot discuss here, as it lies outside the field of general education; but I will make one suggestion to any of the young gentlemen before me who may intend to choose, as his life-work, some one of the learned professions. You will make a fatal mistake if you make only the same preparations which your predecessors made fifty or even ten years ago. Each generation must have a higher cultivation than the preceding one, in order to be equally successful; and each must be educated for his own times. If you become a lawyer, you must remember that the science of law is not fixed like geometry, but is a growth which keeps pace with the progress of society. The developments of the late war will make it necessary to re-write many of the leading chapters of international and maritime law. The destruction of slavery and the enfranchisement of four millions of colored men will almost revolutionize American jurisprudence. If Webster were now at the bar, in the full glory of his strength, he would be compelled to reconstruct the whole fabric of his legal learning. Similar changes are occurring, both in the medical and military professions. Ten years hence the young surgeon will hardly venture to open an office till he has studied thoroughly the medical and surgical history of the late war. Since the experience at Sumter and Wagner, no nation will again build fortifications of costly masonry; for they have learned that earth-works are not only cheaper, but a better defence against artillery. The text-books on military engineering must be re-written. Our Spencer rifle and Prussian needle-gun have revolutionized, both the manufacture and the manual of arms; and no great battle will ever again be fought with muzzle-loading muskets. Napoleon, at the head of his Old Guard, could to-day win no Austerlitz till he had read the military history of the last six years.

It may perhaps be thought that the suggestion I have made concerning the professions will not apply to the work of the Christian minister, whose principal text-book is a divine and perfect revelation; but, in my judgment, the remark applies to the clerical profession with even more force than to any other. There is no department of his duties in which he does not need the fullest and the latest knowledge. He is pledged to the defence of revelation and religion; but it will not avail him to be able to answer the objections of Hume and Voltaire. The arguments of Paley were not written to answer the scepticisms of to-day. His "Natural Theology" is now less valuable than Hugh Miller's "Footprints of the Creator," or Guyot's lectures on "Earth and Man." The men and women of to-day know but little, and care less, about the thousand abstract questions of polemic theology which puzzled the heads and wearied the hearts of our Puritan fathers and mothers. That minister will make, and deserves to make, a miserable failure, who attempts to feed hungry hearts on the dead dogmas of the past. More than that of any other man it is his duty to march abreast with the advanced thinkers of his time, and be not only a learner, but a teacher, of its science, its literature, and its criticism.

But I return to the main question before me. Having endeavored to state what kinds of knowledge should be the objects of a liberal education, I shall next inquire how well the course of study in American colleges is adapted to the attainment of these objects. In discussing this question, I do not forget that he is deemed a rash and imprudent man who invades with suggestions of change these venerable sanctuaries of learning. Let him venture to suggest that much of the wisdom there taught is foolishness, and he may hear from the college chapels of the land, in good Virgilian hexameter, the warning cry, "*Procul O! procul este profani!*" Happy for him if the whole body of alumni do not with equal pedantry respond in Horatian verse, "*Fenum habet in cornu; longe fuge.*" But I protest that a friend of American education may suggest changes in our college studies without committing profanation, or carrying hay on his horns. Our colleges have done, and are doing, a noble work, for which they deserve the thanks of the nation; but he is not their enemy who suggests that they ought to do much better. As an alumnus of one which I shall always reverence, and as a friend of all, I will venture to discuss the work they are doing. I have examined some twenty catalogues of Eastern, Western, and Southern colleges, and find the subjects taught, and the relative time given to each, about the same in all. The chief difference is in the quantity of work required. I will take Harvard as a representative; it being the oldest of our colleges, and certainly requiring as much study as any other. Remembering that the standard by which we measure a student's work for one day is three recitations of one hour each, and that his year usually consists of three terms of thirteen or fourteen weeks each, for convenience' sake I will divide the work required to admit him to college, and after four years to graduate him, into two classes: —

1st, That which belongs to the study of Latin and Greek; and, 2d, That which does not.

Now, from the annual catalogue of Harvard for 1866-67 (p. 26), I find that the candidate for admission to the Freshman class must be examined in what will require the study of eight terms in Latin, six in Greek, one in ancient geography, one in Grecian history, and one in Roman history, which make seventeen terms in the studies of class first. Under the head of class second the candidate is required to be examined in reading, in common-school arithmetic and geography, in one term's study of algebra, and one term of geometry. English grammar is not mentioned.

Thus, after studying the elementary branches which are taught in all our common schools, it requires about two years and a half of study to enter a college; and of that study seventeen parts are devoted to the language, history, and geography of Greece and Rome, and two parts to all other subjects!

Reducing the Harvard year to the usual division of three terms, the analysis of the work will be found as follows: not less than nine terms of Latin (there may be twelve if the student chooses it); not less than six terms of Greek (but twelve if he chooses it); and he may elect, in addition, three terms in Roman history. With the average of three recitations per day, and three terms per year, we may say that the whole work of college study consists of thirty-six parts. Not less than fifteen of these *must* be devoted to Latin and Greek, and not more than twenty-one to all other subjects. If the student chooses, he *may* devote twenty-four parts to Latin and Greek, and twelve to all other subjects. Taking the whole six and a half years of preparatory and college study, we find, that, to earn a bachelor's diploma at Harvard, a young man, after leaving the district school, must devote four-sevenths of all his labor to Greece and Rome.

Now, what do we find in our second, or *unclassical*, list? It is chiefly remarkable for what it does not contain. In the whole programme of study, lectures included, no mention whatever is made of physical geography, of anatomy, physiology, or the general history of the United States.

A few weeks of the Senior year given to Guizot and the history of the Federal Constitution, and a lecture on general history once a week during half that year, furnish all that the graduate of Harvard is required to know of his own country and the living nations of the earth.

He must apply years of arduous labor to the history, oratory, and poetry of Greece and Rome; but he is not required to cull a single flower from the rich fields of our own literature. English literature is not named in the curriculum, except that the student may, if he chooses, attend a few general lectures on modern literature.

Such are some of the facts in reference to the educational work of our most venerable college, where there is probably concentrated more general and special culture than at any other in America.

I think it probable, that in some of the colleges the proportion of Latin and Greek to other studies may be less; but I believe that in none of them the preparatory and college work devoted to these two languages is less than half of all the work required.

Now, the bare statement of this fact should challenge, and must challenge, the attention of every thoughtful man in the nation. No wonder that men are demanding, with an earnestness that will not be repressed, to know how it happens, and why it happens, that, placing in one end of the balance all the mathematical studies; all the physical sciences, in their recent rapid developments; all the study of the human mind and the laws of thought; all the principles of political economy and social science, which underlie the commerce and industry, and shape the legislation, of nations; the history of our own nation, — its constitution of government and its great industrial interests; all the literature and history of modern civilization, — placing all this, I say, in one end of the balance, they kick the beam when Greece and Rome are placed in the other. I hasten to say that I make no attack upon the study of these noble languages as an important and necessary part of a liberal education. I have no sympathy with that sentiment which would drive them from academy and college as a part of the dead past that should bury its dead. It is the *proportion* of the work given to them of which I complain.

These studies hold their relative rank in obedience to the tyranny of custom. Each new college is modelled after the older ones, and all in

America have been patterned on an humble scale after the universities of Europe. The prominence given to Latin and Greek at the founding of these universities was a matter of inexorable necessity. The continuance of the same, or anywhere near the same, relative prominence to-day, is both unnecessary and indefensible. I appeal to history for the proof of these assertions.

Near the close of the fifth century we date the beginning of those dark ages which enveloped the whole world for a thousand years. The human race seemed stricken with intellectual paralysis. The noble language of the Cæsars, corrupted by a hundred barbarous dialects, ceased to be a living tongue long before the modern languages of Europe had been reduced to writing.

In Italy the Latin died in the tenth century; but the oldest document known to exist in Italian was not written till the year 1200. Italian did not really take its place in the family of written languages till a century later, when it was crystallized into form and made immortal by the genius of Dante and Petrarch.

The Spanish was not a written language till the year 1200, and was scarcely known to Europe till Cervantes convulsed the world with laughter in 1605.

The Latin ceased to be spoken by the people of France in the tenth century, and French was not a written language till the beginning of the fourteenth century. Pascal, who died in 1662, is called the father of modern French prose.

The German, as a literary language, dates from Luther, who died in 1546. It was one of his mortal sins against Rome, that he translated the Bible into the uncouth and vulgar tongue of Germany.

Our own language is also of recent origin. Richard I. of England, who died in 1199, never spoke a word of English in his life. Our mother-tongue was never heard in an English court of justice till 1362. The statutes of England were not written in English till three years before Columbus landed in the New World. No philologist dates modern English farther back than 1500. Sir Thomas More, the author of "Utopia," who died in 1535, was the father of English prose.

The dark ages were the sleep of the world, while the languages of the modern world were being born out of chaos.

The first glimmer of dawn was in the twelfth century, when in Paris, Oxford, and other parts of Europe, universities were established. The fifteenth century was spent in saving the remnants of classic learning which had been locked up in the cells of monks, — the Greek at Constantinople, and the Latin in the cloisters of Western Europe.

During the first three hundred years of the life of the older universities, it is almost literally true, that no modern tongue had become a written language. The learning of Europe was in Latin and Greek. In order to study either science or literature, these languages must first be learned. European writers continued to use Latin long after the modern languages were fully established. Even Milton's great "Defence of the People of England" was written in Latin, — as were also the "Principia," and other scientific works of Newton, who died in 1727.

The pride of learned corporations, the spirit of exclusiveness among learned men, and their want of sympathy with the mass of the people, united to maintain Latin as the language of learning long after its use was defensible.

Now, mark the contrast between the objects and demands of education when the European universities were founded, — or even when Harvard was founded, — and its demands at the present time. We have a family of modern languages almost equal in force and perfection to the classic tongues, and a modern literature, which, if less perfect in æsthetic form than the ancient, is immeasurably richer in truth, and is filled with the noblest and bravest thoughts of the world. When the universities were founded, modern science was not born. Scarcely a generation has passed since then, without adding some new science to the circle of knowledge. As late as 1809 "The Edinburgh Review" declared that "lectures upon political economy would be discouraged in Oxford, probably despised, probably not permitted." At a much later date, there was no text-book in the United States on that subject. The claims of Latin and Greek to the chief place in the *curriculum* have been gradually growing less, and the importance of other knowledge has been constantly increasing; but the colleges have generally opposed all innovations, and still cling to the old ways with stubborn conservatism. Some concessions, however, have been made to the necessities of the times, both in Europe and America. Harvard would hardly venture to enforce its law (which prevailed long after Cotton Mather's day), forbidding its students to speak English within the college limits, under any pretext whatever; and British Cantabs have had their task of composing hexameters in bad Latin reduced by a few thousand verses during the last century.

It costs me a struggle to say any thing on this subject which may be regarded with favor by those who would reject the classics altogether, for I have read them and taught them with a pleasure and relish which few other pursuits have ever afforded me; but I am persuaded that their supporters must soon submit to a re-adjustment of their relations to college study, or they may be driven from the course altogether. There are most weighty reasons why Latin and Greek should be retained as part of a liberal education. He who would study our own language profoundly must not forget that nearly thirty per cent of its words are of Latin origin, — that the study of Latin is the study of universal grammar, and renders the acquisition of any modern language an easy task, and is indispensable to the teacher of language and literature, and to other professional men.

Greek is perhaps the most perfect instrument of thought ever invented by man, and its literature has never been equalled in purity of style, and boldness of expression. As a means of intellectual discipline, its value can hardly be overestimated. To take a long and complicated sentence in Greek, to study each word in its meanings, inflections, and relations, and to build up in the mind, out of these polished materials, a sentence perfect as a temple, and filled with Greek thought which has dwelt there two thousand years, is almost an act of creation: it calls into activity all the faculties of the mind.

That the Christian Oracles have come down to us in Greek, will make Greek scholars forever a necessity.

These studies, then, should not be neglected: they should neither devour nor be devoured. I insist they can be made more valuable, and at the same time less prominent, than they now are. A large part of the labor now bestowed upon them is devoted, not to learning the genius and spirit of the language, but is more than wasted on pedantic trifles. More than half a century ago, in his essay entitled "Professional Education," Sydney Smith lashed this trifling as it deserves. Speaking of classical Englishmen, he says, —

"Their minds have been so completely possessed of exaggerated notions of classical learning, that they have not been able, in the great school of the world, to form any other notion of real greatness. Attend, too, to the public feelings; look to all the terms of applause. A learned man! a scholar! a man of erudition! Upon whom are these epithets of approbation bestowed? Are they given to men acquainted with the science of government, thoroughly masters of the geographical and commercial relations of Europe? to men who know the properties of bodies and their action upon each other? No: this is not learning; it is chemistry or political economy, not learning. The distinguishing abstract term, the epithet of scholar, is reserved for him who writes on the Æolic reduplication, and is familiar with the Sylburgian method of arranging defectives in ω and μ. . . . The object of the young Englishman is not to reason, to imagine, or to invent, but to conjugate, decline, and derive. The situations of imaginary glory which he draws for himself are the detection of an anapest in the wrong place, or the restoration of a dative case which Cranzius has passed over and the never-dying Ernesti failed to observe. If a young classic of this kind were to meet the greatest chemist, or the greatest mechanician, or the most profound political economist of his time, in company with the greatest Greek scholar, would the slightest comparison between them ever come across his mind? Would he ever dream that such men as Adam Smith and Lavoisier were equal in dignity of understanding to, or of the same utility as, Bentley or Heyné? We are inclined to think that the feeling excited would be a good deal like that which was expressed by Dr. George about the praises of the great King of Prussia, who entertained considerable doubts whether the king, with all his victories, knew how to conjugate a Greek verb in μι."

He concludes another essay, written in 1826, with these words: —

"If there is any thing which fills reflecting men with melancholy and regret, it is the waste of mortal time, parental money, and puerile happiness, in the present method of pursuing Latin and Greek."

To write verse in these languages; to study elaborate theories of the Greek accent and the ancient pronunciation of both Greek and Latin, which no one can ever know he has discovered, and which would be utterly valueless if he did discover it; to toil over the innumerable exceptions to the arbitrary rules of poetic quantity, which few succeed in learning, and none remember,— these, and a thousand other similar things which crowd the pages of Zumpt and Kühner, no more constitute a knowledge of the spirit and genius of the Greek and Latin languages than counting the number of threads to the square inch in a man's coat and the number of pegs in his boots makes us acquainted with his moral and intellectual character. The greatest literary monuments of Greece existed hundreds of years before the science of grammar was born. Plato and Thucydides had a tolerable acquaintance with the Greek language; but Crosby goes far beyond their depth.

Our colleges should require a student to understand thoroughly the structure, idioms, and spirit of these languages, and to be able, by the aid of a lexicon, to analyze and translate them with readiness and elegance. They should give him the key to the storehouse of ancient literature, that he may explore its treasures for himself in after-life. This can be done in two years less than the usual time, and nearly as well as it is now done.

I am glad to inform you, young gentlemen, that the trustees of the institution in this place have this day resolved that in the course of study to be pursued here, Latin and Greek shall not be *required* after the Freshman year. They must be studied the usual time as a requisite to admission, and they may be carried farther than Freshman year as elective studies; but in the regular course their places will be supplied by some of the studies I have already mentioned. Three or four terms in general literature will teach you that the republic of letters is larger than Greece or Rome.

The board of trustees have been strengthened in the position they have taken, by the fact that a similar course for the future has recently been announced by the authorities of Harvard University. Within the last six days, I have received a circular from the secretary of that venerable college, which announces that two-thirds of the Latin and Greek are hereafter to be stricken from the list of required studies of the college course.

I rejoice that the movement has begun. Other colleges must follow the example; and the day will not be far distant when it shall be the pride of a scholar that he is also a worker, and when the worker shall not refuse to become a scholar because he despises a trifler.

I congratulate you that this change does not reduce the amount of labor required of you. If it did, I should deplore it. I beseech you to remember that the genius of success is still the genius of labor. If hard work is not another name for talent, it is the best possible substitute for it. In the long-run, the chief difference in men will be found in the amount of work they do. Do not trust to what lazy men call the spur of the occasion. If you wish to wear spurs in the tournament of life, you must buckle them to your own heels before you enter the lists.

Men look with admiring wonder upon a great intellectual effort, like Webster's reply to Hayne, and seem to think that it leaped into life by the inspiration of the moment. But if by some intellectual chemistry we could resolve that masterly speech into its several elements of power, and trace each to its source, we should find that every constituent force had been elaborated twenty years before, — it may be, in some hour of earnest intellectual labor. Occasion may be the bugle-call that summons an army to battle; but the blast of a bugle cannot ever make soldiers, or win victories.

And finally, young gentlemen, learn to cultivate a wise reliance, based not on what you hope, but on what you perform. It has long been the habit of this institution, if I may so speak, to throw young men overboard, and let them sink or swim. None have yet drowned who were worth the saving. I hope the practice will be continued, and that you will not rely upon outside help for growth or success. Give crutches to cripples; but go you forth with brave true hearts, knowing that fortune dwells in your brain and muscle, and that labor is the only human symbol of Omnipotence.

VIII.

Elements of Success.

ADDRESS BEFORE THE STUDENTS OF THE SPENCERIAN
BUSINESS COLLEGE, WASHINGTON, D.C.,
JUNE 29, 1869.

VIII.

ELEMENTS OF SUCCESS.

LADIES AND GENTLEMEN, — I have consented to address you this evening, chiefly for two reasons, — one of them personal to myself, the other public. The personal reason is, that I have a·deep and peculiar sympathy with young people who are engaged in any department of education. Their pursuits are to me, not only matters of deep interest, but of profound mystery. It will not, perhaps, flatter you older people when I say that I have far less interest in you than in these young people. With us, the great questions of life are measurably settled. Our days go on, their shadows lengthening as we approach nearer to the evening which will soon deepen into the night of life ; but before these young people are the dawn, the sunrise, the coming noon, all the wonders and mysteries of life. For ourselves, much of all that belongs to the possibilities of life is ended; and the very angels look down upon us with less curiosity than upon these whose lives are just opening. Pardon me, then, if I feel more interest in them than in you.

I feel a profounder reverence for a boy than for a man. I never meet a ragged boy of the street without feeling that I may owe him a salute, for I know not what possibilities may be buttoned up under his shabby coat. When I meet you in the full flush of mature life, I see nearly all there is of you; but among these boys are the great men of the future, — the heroes of the next generation, the philosophers, the statesmen, the philanthropists, the great reformers and moulders of the next age. Therefore, I say, there is a peculiar charm to me in the exhibitions of young people engaged in the business of education.

But there was a reason of public policy which brought me here to-night; and it was to testify to the importance of these business colleges, and to give two or three reasons why they have been established in the United States. I wish every college president in the United States could hear the first reason I propose to give. Business colleges, my fellow-citizens, originated in this country as a protest against the insufficiency of our system of education, — as a protest against the failure, the absolute failure, of our American schools and colleges to fit young men and women for the business of life. Take the great classes graduated from the leading colleges of the country during this and the next month, and how many, or, rather, how few, of their members are fitted to go into the practical business of life, and transact it like sensible men! These business colleges furnish their graduates with a better education for practical purposes than Princeton, Harvard, or Yale.

The people are making a grave charge against our system of higher education when they complain that it is disconnected from the active business of life. It is a charge to which our colleges cannot plead guilty, and live. They must rectify the fault, or miserably fail of their great purpose. There is scarcely a more pitiable sight than to see here and there learned men, so called, who have graduated in our own and the universities of Europe with high honors, — men who know the whole gamut of classical learning, who have sounded the depths of mathematical and speculative philosophy, — and yet who could not harness a horse, or make out a bill of sale, if the world depended upon it.

The fact is, that our curriculum of college

studies was not based on modern ideas, and has not grown up to our modern necessities. The prevailing system was established at a time when the learning of the world was in Latin and Greek, — when, if a man would learn arithmetic, he must first learn Latin; and, if he would learn the history and geography of his own country, he would acquire that knowledge only through the Latin language. Of course, in those days, it was necessary to lay the foundation of learning in a knowledge of the learned languages.

The universities of Europe, from which our colleges were copied, were founded before the modern languages were born. The leading languages of Europe are scarcely six hundred years old. The reasons for a course of study then are not good now. The old necessities have passed away. We now have strong and noble living languages, rich in literature, replete with high and earnest thought, the language of science, religion, and liberty; and yet we bid our children feed their spirits on the life of dead ages, instead of the inspiring life and vigor of our own times. I do not object to classical learning, — far from it; but I would not have it exclude the living present. Therefore I welcome the business college in the form it has taken in the United States, because it meets an acknowledged want, by affording to young people of only common scholastic attainments, and even to the classes that graduate from Harvard and Yale, an opportunity to learn important and indispensable lessons before they go out into the business of life.

The present Chancellor of the British Exchequer, the Right Honorable Robert Lowe, one of the brightest minds in that kingdom, said in a recent address before the venerable University of Edinburgh, "I was a few months ago in Paris, and two graduates of Oxford went with me to get our dinner at a restaurant; and, if the white-aproned waiter had not been better educated than all three of us, we might have starved to death. We could not ask for our dinner in his language, but fortunately he could ask us in our own language what we wanted." There was one test of the insufficiency of modern education.

There is another reason why I am glad that these business colleges have been established in this country, and particularly in the city of Washington. If there be any city on this continent where such institutions are needed more than in any other, it is here in this city, for the benefit of the employees of the United States.

Allow me, young ladies and gentlemen, to turn aside for one moment to speak of what relates to your business life. If I could speak one sentence which could be echoed through every department of the government, addressing myself not to those in middle life, whose plans for the future are fixed, but to those who are beginning life, I would say to every young man and woman in the civil service of the government, "Hasten by the most rapid steps to get out of these departments into active, independent business life." Do not misunderstand me. Your work is honorable, — honorable to yourselves, and necessary to the government. I make no charge on that score; but to a young man, who has in himself the magnificent possibilities of life, it is not fitting that he should be permanently commanded: he should be a commander. You must not continue to be *the employed:* you must be an *employer.* You must be promoted from the ranks to the command. There is something, young men, which you can command: go and find it, and command it. You can at least command a horse and dray, can be generalissimo of them, and may carve out a fortune with them. And I did not fall on that illustration by accident, young gentlemen. Do you know the fact? If you do not, let me tell it you, — that more fortunes have been won, and fewer failures known, in the dray business than in wholesale merchandising.

Do not, I beseech you, be content to enter upon any business which does not require and compel constant intellectual growth. Do not enter into any business which will leave you no farther advanced mentally than it found you, — which will require no more ability and culture at the end than it did at the beginning of twenty-five years. I ask you whether your work in the departments is not mainly of that kind, and whether it must not continue to be of that kind. If you take advantage of our magnificent libraries here; of the law colleges or the medical colleges; if, whatever your plans may be, you complete and utilize your education by taking a course in the business college; if you hold office in the departments for a few years to enable you to live while you obtain a legal, medical, or business education, — you are doing a worthy work. It always pleases me to see young men obtain such places for such a purpose. But, while I will cheerfully help a young man to secure such a place for such a reason, I would warn him not to continue in it, but to get out of it as soon as possible, and take a place of active personal responsibility in the great industrial family of the nation.

There is another reason, — the last I shall give in illustrating the importance of business colleges, — and that is the consideration which was so beautifully and cogently urged a few moments since, by the young lady who delivered the valedictory of her class, that it is almost surplusage to add a word to her discussion. The career opened in business colleges, especially in this one, for young women, is a most important and noteworthy feature of these institutions.

Laugh at it as we may, put it aside as a jest if we will, keep it out of Congress or political campaigns, still the woman question is rising in our horizon larger than the size of a man's hand; and some solution ere long that question must find. I have not yet committed my mind to any formula that embraces the whole question. I halt on the threshold of so great a problem. But there is one point on which I have reached a conclusion; and that is, that this nation must open up new avenues of work and usefulness to the women of the country, so that everywhere they may have something to do. This is, just now, infinitely more valuable to them than the platform or the ballot-box. Whatever conclusion shall be reached on that subject by and by, at present the most valuable gift which can be bestowed on women is something to do, which they can do well and worthily, and thereby maintain themselves. Therefore I say that every thoughtful statesman will look with satisfaction upon such business colleges as are opening a career for our young women. On that score we have special reasons to be thankful for the establishment of these institutions.

Now, young gentlemen, let me for a moment address you touching your success in life; and I hope the very brevity of my remarks will increase the chance of their making a lodgement in your minds. Let me beg you, in the outset of your career, to dismiss from your minds all ideas of succeeding by luck. There is no more common thought among young people than that foolish one, that by and by something will turn up by which they will suddenly achieve fame or fortune. No, young gentlemen, things don't turn up in this world unless somebody turns them up. Inertia is one of the indispensable laws of matter; and things lie flat where they are until by some intelligent spirit (for nothing but spirit makes motion in this world) they are endowed with activity and life. Do not dream that some good luck is going to happen to you, and give you a fortune. Luck is an *ignis fatuus*: you may follow it to ruin, but not to success. The great Napoleon, who believed in his destiny, followed it until he saw his star go down in blackest night, when the Old Guard perished around him, and Waterloo was lost. A pound of pluck is worth a ton of luck.

Young men talk of trusting to the spur of the occasion. That trust is vain. Occasions cannot make spurs, young gentlemen. If you expect to wear spurs, you must win them. If you wish to use them, you must buckle them to your own heels before you go into the fight. Any success you may achieve is not worth the having unless you fight for it. Whatever you win in life you must conquer by your own efforts; and then it is yours, — a part of yourself.

Again: in order to have any success in life, or any worthy success, you must resolve to carry into your work a fulness of knowledge, — not merely a sufficiency, but more than a sufficiency. In this respect, follow the rule of the machinists. If they want a machine to do the work of six horses, they give it nine-horse power, so that they may have a reserve of three. To carry on the business of life, you must have surplus power. Be fit for more than the thing you are now doing. Let every one know that you have a reserve in yourself, — that you have more power than you are now using. If you are not too large for the place you occupy, you are too small for it. How full our country is of bright examples, not only of those who occupy some proud eminence in public life, but in every place you may find men going on with steady nerve, attracting the attention of their fellow-citizens, and carving out for themselves names and fortunes from small and humble beginnings and in the face of formidable obstacles. Let me cite an example of a man I recently saw in the little village of Norwich, New York. If you wish to know his name, go into any hardware-store, and ask for the best hammer in the world; and, if the salesman be an intelligent man, he will bring you a hammer bearing the name of D. Maydole. Young gentlemen, take that hammer in your hand, drive nails with it, and draw inspiration from it.

Thirty years ago a boy was struggling through the snows of Chenango Valley, trying to hire himself to a blacksmith. He succeeded, and learned his trade; but he did more. He took it into his head that he could make a better hammer than any other man had made. He devoted himself to the task for more than a quarter of a century. He studied the chemistry of metals, the strength of materials, the philosophy of form. He studied failures. Each broken hammer taught him a lesson. There was no part of the process that he did not master. He taxed his wit to invent machines to perfect and cheapen his processes. No improvement in working steel or iron escaped his notice. What may not twenty-five years of effort accomplish when concentrated on a single object? He earned success; and now, when his name is stamped on a steel hammer, it is his note, his bond, his integrity embodied in steel. The spirit of the man is in each hammer; and the work, like the workman, is unrivalled. Mr. Maydole is now acknowledged to have made the best hammer in the world. Even the sons of Thor, across the sea, admit it.

While I was there, looking through his shop, with all its admirable arrangement of tools and machinery, there came to him a large order from China. The merchants of the Celestial Kingdom had sent down to the little town, where the persistent blacksmith now lives in affluence, to get the best that Anglo-Saxon skill had accomplished in the hammer business. It is no small achievement to do one thing better than any other man in the world has done it.

Let me call your attention to something nearer your own work in this college. About forty years ago a young lad who had come from the Catskill Mountains, where he had learned the rudiments of penmanship by scribbling on the sole-leather of a good old Quaker shoemaker (for he was too poor to buy paper) till he could write better than his neighbors, commenced to teach in that part of Ohio which has been called "benighted Ashtabula" (I suggest "beknighted" as the proper spelling of the word). He set up a little writing-school in a rude log cabin, and threw into the work the fervor of a poetic soul and a strength of heart and spirit that few men possess. He caught his ideals of beauty from the waves of the lake and the curves they make upon the white sand beach, and from the tracery of the spider's web. Studying the lines of beauty as drawn by the hand of Nature, he wrought out that system of penmanship which is now the pride of our country, and the model of our schools. It is the system you have been learning in this college, and which is so worthily represented by the son of its author, my friend Professor Spencer, your able instructor. This is an example of what a man may do by putting his whole heart into the work he undertakes.

Only yesterday, on my way here, I learned a fact which I will give you to show how, by attending to things, and putting your mind to the work, you may reach success. A few days ago, in the city of Boston, there was held an exhibition of photography; and to the great surprise of New England it turned out that Mr. Ryder, a photographer from Cleveland, O., took the prize for the best photography in America. But how did this thing happen? I will tell you. This Cleveland photographer happened to read in a German paper of a process practised by the artists of Bohemia, — a process of touching up the negative with the finest instruments, thus removing all chemical imperfections from the negative itself. Reading this, he sent for one of these artists, and at length succeeded in bringing the art of Bohemia into the service of his own profession.

The patient Bohemian sat down with his lenses,

and bringing a strong, clear light upon these negatives, working with the finest instruments, rounding and strengthening the outlines, was able at last to print from the negative a photograph more perfect than any I have seen made with the help of an India-ink finish. And so Mr. Ryder took the prize. Why not? It was no mystery: it was simply taking time by the forelock, securing the best aid in his business, and bringing to bear the force of an energetic mind to attain the best possible results. That is the only way, young ladies and gentlemen, in which success is gained. These men succeed because they deserve success. Their results are wrought out: they do not come to hand already made. Poets may be born, but success is made.

Young gentlemen, let not poverty stand as an obstacle in your way. Poverty is uncomfortable, as I can testify; but nine times out of ten the best thing that can happen to a young man is to be tossed overboard, and compelled to sink or swim for himself. In all my acquaintance, I have never known one to be drowned who was worth the saving. This would not be wholly true in any country but one of political equality like ours. The editor of one of the leading magazines of

England told me, not many months ago, a fact startling enough in itself, but of great significance to a poor man. He told me that he had never yet known, in all his experience, a single boy of the class of farm-laborers (not those who own farms, but mere farm-laborers) who had ever risen above his class. Boys from the manufacturing and commercial classes had risen frequently, but from the farm-labor class he had never known one.

The reason is this: In the aristocracies of the Old World, wealth and society are built up like the strata of rock which compose the crust of the earth. If a boy be born in the lowest stratum of life, it is almost impossible for him to rise through this hard crust into the higher ranks; but in this country it is not so. The strata of our society resemble rather the ocean, where every drop, even the lowest, is free to mingle with all others, and may shine at last on the crest of the highest wave. This is the glory of our country, young gentlemen; and you need not fear that there are any obstacles which will prove too great for any brave heart. You will recollect what Burns, who knew all meanings of poverty and struggle, has said in homely verse: —

ELEMENTS OF SUCCESS. 333

> "Though losses and crosses
> Be lessons right severe,
> There's wit there, you'll get there,
> You'll find no other where."

One thought more, and I will close. This is almost a sermon, but I cannot help it; for the occasion itself has given rise to the thoughts I am offering you. Let me suggest, that, in giving you being, God locked up in your nature certain forces and capabilities. What will you do with them? Look at the mechanism of a clock. Take off the pendulum and ratchet, and the wheels go rattling down, and all its force is expended in a moment; but properly balanced and regulated it will go on, letting out its force tick by tick, measuring hours and days, and doing faithfully the service for which it was designed. I implore you to cherish and guard and use well the forces that God has given to you. You may let them run down in a year, if you will. Take off the strong curb of discipline and morality, and you will be an old man before your twenties are passed. Preserve these forces. Do not burn them out with brandy, or waste them in idleness and crime. Do not destroy them. Do not use them unworthily. Save and protect them, that they may save for you fortune and fame. Honestly resolve to do this, and you will be an honor to yourself and to your country. I thank you, young friends, for your kind attention.

IX.

Some Tendencies of American Education.

SPEECH BEFORE THE DEPARTMENT OF SUPERINTENDENCE
OF THE NATIONAL EDUCATION ASSOCIATION,
WASHINGTON, D.C., FEB. 5, 1879.

IX.

SOME TENDENCIES OF AMERICAN EDUCATION.

GENTLEMEN, I am really not in a situation to say any thing to this convention, for I do not know where you are in the course of your deliberations; but Dr. Loring has said some things that have awakened in me a very lively interest, and I will "rake after his cradling," as the harvesters would say. It is a matter of great gratification to me to meet gentlemen who are engaged in the work of education. I feel at home among teachers; and, I may say, I look back with more satisfaction upon my work as a teacher than upon any other work I have done. It gives me a pleasant home feeling to sit among you, and revive old memories.

There is one thing to which I will venture to call your attention; and that is the great case, if I may speak as a lawyer, which is soon to be tried before the American people, — the case of *Brains* vs. *Brick and Mortar*. That, in my judgment, is to be a notable trial; and until the cause is fully argued and rightly decided, we shall have no end of trouble in our educational work. To insure its final and rightful settlement, the friends of our schools should unite to force the question to a hearing, and should go to the very bottom of the controversy. It has long been my opinion, that we are all educated, whether children, men, or women, far more by personal influence than by books and the apparatus of schools. If I could be taken back into boyhood to-day, and had all the libraries and apparatus of a university, with ordinary routine professors, offered me on the one hand, and on the other a great, luminous, rich-souled man, such as Dr. Hopkins was twenty years ago, in a tent in the woods alone, I should say, "Give me Dr. Hopkins for my college course, rather than any university with only routine professors." The privilege of sitting down before a great clear-headed, large-hearted man, and breathing the atmosphere of his life, and being drawn up to him and lifted up by him, and learning his methods of thinking and living, is in itself an enormous educating power. But America, I say, is running to brick and mortar. Colleges and universities are constantly receiving munificent gifts which the donors require to be built into walls inscribed with their names; but the real college sits starving under the stately shadows. Our Smithsonian Institution over here was, for a long time, engaged in this struggle between brick and brains. One of the first things done by Congress was to saddle it with a huge brick building. Another impediment we fortunately got rid of, — the great library of the Institution, which devoured five thousand dollars a year of the income; and we are now struggling to get off our hands the great museum, which costs still more. Museums and libraries are necessary and valuable; but the central purpose of Smithson, to encourage original discovery, was in great measure thwarted by the mere accumulation of materials. I hope the day is not distant when the income of that beneficent institution will be so liberated that every American who has the requisite genius and force can find there the help required for original investigation.

And so, in our schools, let us put less money in great schoolhouses, and more in the salaries of teachers. Smaller schools and more teachers, less machinery and more personal influence, will bring forth fruits higher and better than any we have yet seen.

In this connection I will refer to the tendency in our primary schools to overcrowd the children by giving them too many studies, and thus rendering them superficial in all. The professors at West Point tell us that for more than forty years their course of examinations of cadets for admission has been substantially the same, and that the questions now asked in the several branches are the same as those propounded in the same branches forty years ago. Now, these professors say that the percentage of failures to pass that preliminary examination has been increasing, especially of late, with alarming rapidity, and is very much greater than it was forty years ago. I understand that Professor Church says this fact does not arise from worse appointments, nor from lack of general information. Indeed, the young men who go there now have much more general culture than their earlier predecessors. Many of them, who have studied Latin, algebra, and physics, and other higher branches, utterly break down in spelling, penmanship, arithmetic, and grammar. In short, they know a little of many branches, but are thorough in none.

There is a limit of effort in a child; and if his culture is spread over too large a surface, it will be thin everywhere. The ambition of our schools to do too much results in doing nothing well. *Non multa sed multum* is the old and safe rule. I believe, therefore, that the two great points which the educators of this country should aim at if they would succeed are, first, smaller schools and more teachers, — remembering always that a teacher who is at all fit for his work is one who has the power of inspiring, who can pour his spirit into the darkness of the pupil's mind, and fill it with "sweetness and light;" secondly, they should cut off a large number of new studies which have been forced into the earlier course, and concentrate their efforts upon the old primary branches until these are thoroughly mastered.

Now, gentlemen, you who are conducting the educational affairs of this country cannot afford to rest under this charge of failure at West Point. You must answer by disproving the charge, or removing the evil. Every conference among educators should be directed to these questions; and when they are settled, you will have rendered one of the highest services that can be rendered to this country.

If I may refer to the national aspect of your profession, I will say we can never escape Macaulay's prophecy of the downfall of the Republic, unless we do it by the aid of the schoolmaster. Macaulay said that a government like ours must inevitably lead to anarchy; and I believe there is no answer to his prophecy unless the schoolmaster can give it. If we can fill the minds of all our children who are to be voters with intelligence which will fit them wisely to vote, and fill them with the spirit of liberty, then will we have averted the fatal prophecy. But if, on the other hand, we allow our youth to grow up in ignorance, this Republic will end in disastrous failure. All the encouragement that the National Government can give, every thing that States can do, all that good citizens every where can do, and most of all what the teacher himself can do, ought to be hailed as the deliverance of our country from the saddest distress.

X.
IN MEMORIAM.

S. F. B. Morse.

AN ADDRESS AT THE MORSE MEMORIAL MEETING, HELD IN THE HALL OF THE HOUSE OF REPRESENTATIVES, APRIL 16, 1872.

X.

S. F. B. MORSE.

THE grave has just closed over the mortal remains of one whose name will be forever associated with a series of achievements in the domain of discovery and invention the most wonderful our race has ever known, — wonderful in the results accomplished, more wonderful still in the agencies employed, most wonderful in the scientific revelations which preceded and accompanied its development.

The electro-magnetic telegraph is the embodiment — I might say the incarnation — of many centuries of thought, of many generations of effort to elicit from Nature one of her deepest mysteries.

No one man, no one century, could have achieved it. It is the child of the human race, — "the heir of all the ages." How wonderful were the steps which led to its creation! The very name of this telegraphic instrument bears record of its history, — "electric, magnetic!" The first named from the bit of yellow amber, whose qualities of attraction and repulsion were discovered by a Grecian philosopher twenty-four centuries ago; and the second from Magnesia, the village of Asia Minor, where first was found the loadstone whose touch turned the needle forever to the north. These were the earliest forms in which that subtle, all-pervading force revealed itself to men. In the childhood of the race, men stood dumb in the presence of its more terrible manifestations. When it gleamed in the purple aurora, or shot dusky-red from the clouds, it was the eye-flash of an angry God, before whom mortals quailed in helpless fear.

When the electric light burned blue on the spear-points of the Roman legions, it was to them and their leaders a portent from the gods, beckoning to victory. When the phosphorescent light, which the sailors still call St. Elmo's fire, hovered on the masts and spars of the Roman ship, it was Castor and Pollux, twin gods of the sea, guiding the mariner to port, or the beacon of an avenging god luring him to death.

When we consider the startling forms in which this element presents itself, it is not surprising that so many centuries elapsed before man dared to confront and question its awful mystery. And it was fitting that here, in this new, free world, the first answer came, revealing to our Franklin the great truth, that the lightning of the sky, and the electricity of the laboratory, were one; that in the simple electric toy were embodied all the mysteries of the thunderbolt. Until near the beginning of the present century, the only known method of producing electricity was by friction. But the discoveries of Galvani in 1790, and of Volta in 1810, resulted in the production of electricity by the chemical action of acids upon metals, and gave to the world the galvanic battery and the voltaic pile and the electric current. This was the first step in that path of modern discovery which led to the telegraph. But further discoveries were necessary to make the telegraph possible.

The next great step was taken by Oërsted, the Swedish professor, who, in 1819-20, made the discovery that the needle, when placed near the galvanic battery, was deflected at right angles with the electric current. In the four modest pages in which Oërsted announced this discovery to the world, the science of electro-magnetism was founded.

As Franklin had exhibited the relation between lightning and the electric fluid, so Oërsted exhibited the relation between magnetism and electricity. From 1820 to 1825 his discovery was further developed by Davy and Sturgeon of England, and Arago and Ampère of France. They found, that, by sending a current of electricity through a wire coiled around a piece of soft iron, the iron became a magnet while the current was passing, and ceased to be a magnet when the current was broken. This gave an intermittent power, — a power to grapple and to let go, at the will of the electrician. Ampère suggested that a telegraph was possible by applying this power to a needle.

In 1825 Barlow of England made experiments to verify this suggestion of the telegraph, and pronounced it impracticable on the ground that the batteries then used would not send the fluid through even two hundred feet of wire without a sensible diminution of its force.

In 1831 Joseph Henry, now secretary of the Smithsonian Institution, then a professor at Albany, N.Y., as the result of numerous experiments discovered a method by which he produced a battery of such intensity as to overcome the difficulty spoken of by Barlow in 1825.

By means of this his discovery, he magnetized soft iron at a great distance from the battery, pointed out the fact that a telegraph was possible, and actually rang a bell by means of the electromagnet acting on a long wire.

This was the last step in the series of great discoveries which preceded the invention of the telegraph.

When these discoveries ended, the work of the inventor began. It was in 1832, the year that succeeded the last of these great discoveries, when Professor Morse first turned his thoughts to that work whose triumph is the triumph of his race. He had devoted twenty-two years of his manhood to the study and practice of art. He had sat at the feet of the great masters of Europe, and had already, by his own works of art, achieved a noble name from the work of interpreting; and he now turned to the grander work of interpreting to the world that subtle and mysterious element with which the thinkers of the human race had so long been occupied.

I cannot here recount the story of that long struggle through which he passed to the accomplishment of his great result; how he struggled with poverty, with the vast difficulties of the subject itself, with the unfaith, the indifference, and the contempt which almost everywhere confronted him; how, at the very moment of his triumph, he was on the verge of despair, when in this very Capitol his project met the jeers of almost a majority of the National Legislature. But when has despair yielded to such a triumph? When has such a morning risen on such a night? To all cavillers and doubters, this instrument and its language are a triumphant answer. That chainless spirit which fills the immensity of space with its invisible presence; which dwells in the blaze of the sun, and follows the path of the farthest star, and courses the depths of earth and sea, — that mighty spirit has at last yielded to the human will. It has entered a body prepared for its dwelling. It has found a voice through which it speaks to the human ear. It has taken its place as the humble servant of man; and through all coming time its work will be associated with the name and fame of Samuel F. B. Morse.

Were there no other proof of the present value of his work, this alone would suffice, — that throughout the world, whatever the language or the dialect of those who use it, the telegraph speaks a language whose first element is the alphabet of Morse; and in 1869, of the sixteen thousand telegraphic instruments used on the lines of Europe, thirteen thousand were of the pattern invented by Morse. The future of this great achievement can be measured by no known standards. Morse gave us the instrument and the alphabet. The world is only beginning to spell out the lesson, whose meaning the future will read.

XI.

IN MEMORIAM.

Joseph Henry.

ADDRESS AT THE MEMORIAL MEETING HELD IN THE
HALL OF THE HOUSE OF REPRESENTATIVES,
TUESDAY EVENING, JAN. 16, 1879.

XI.

JOSEPH HENRY.

*" And who hath trod Olympus, from his eye
Fades not the broader outlook of the gods."*

MR. PRESIDENT,—In the presence of these fathers of science, who have honored this occasion with their wisdom and eloquence, I can do but little more than express my gratitude for the noble contribution they have made to this national expression of love and reverence. So completely have they covered the ground, so fully have they sketched the great life which we celebrate, that nothing is left but to linger a moment over the tributes they have offered, and select here and there a special excellence to carry away as a lasting memorial.

No page of human history is so instructive and significant as the record of those early influences which develop the character and direct the lives of eminent men. To every man of great original power, there comes in early youth a moment of sudden discovery, of self-recognition, when his own nature is revealed to himself, when he catches, for the first time, a strain of that immortal song to which his own spirit answers, and which becomes thenceforth and forever the inspiration of his life, —

"Like noble music unto noble words."

More than a hundred years ago, in Strasbourg on the Rhine, in obedience to the commands of his father, a German lad was reluctantly studying the mysteries of the civil law, but feeding his spirit as best he could upon the formal and artificial poetry of his native land, when a page of William Shakespeare met his eye, and changed the whole current of his life. Abandoning the law, he created and crowned with an immortal name the grandest epoch of German literature.

Recording his own experience, he says, —

"At the first touch of Shakespeare's genius I made the glad confession that something inspiring hovered above me. . . . The first page of his that I read made me his for life; and when I had finished a single play, I stood like one born blind on whom a miraculous hand bestows sight in a moment. I saw, I felt, in the most vivid manner, that my existence was infinitely expanded."

This old-world experience of Goethe's was strikingly reproduced, though under different conditions, and with different results, in the early life of Joseph Henry. You have just heard the incident worthily recounted; but let us linger over it a moment. An orphan boy of sixteen, of tough Scotch fibre, laboring for his own support at the handicraft of the jeweller, unconscious of his great power, delighted with romance and the drama, dreaming of a possible career on the stage, his attention was suddenly arrested by a single page of an humble book of science which chanced to fall into his hands. It was not the flash of poetic vision which aroused him: it was the voice of great Nature calling her child. With quick recognition and glad reverence his spirit responded; and from that moment to the end of his long and honored life, Joseph Henry was the devoted student of science, the faithful interpreter of nature.

To those who knew his gentle spirit, it is not surprising that ever afterward he kept the little volume near him, and cherished it as the source of his first inspiration. In the maturity of his fame, he recorded on its fly-leaf his gratitude. Note his words: —

"This book under Providence has exerted a remarkable influence on my life. . . . It opened to me a new world of thought and enjoyment, invested things before almost unnoticed with the highest interest, fixed my mind on the study of nature, and caused me to resolve at the time of reading it that I would devote my life to the acquisition of knowledge."

We have heard from his venerable associates with what resolute perseverance he trained his mind and marshalled his powers for the higher realms of science. He was the first American after Franklin who made a series of successful original experiments in electricity and magnetism. He entered the mighty line of Volta, Galvani, Oërsted, Davy, and Ampère, the great exploring philosophers of the world, and added to their work a final great discovery which made the electro-magnetic telegraph possible.

It remained only for the inventor to construct an instrument and an alphabet. Professor Henry refused to reap any pecuniary rewards from his great discovery, but gave freely to mankind what nature and science had given to him.

I observe that these venerable gentlemen who have spoken express some regret that Professor Henry left their higher circle to come down to us;

and to some extent I share their regret. Doubtless it was a great loss to science. I remember that Agassiz once said he had made it the rule of his life to abandon any scientific investigation so soon as it became useful. I fancied I saw him and his brethren going beyond the region of perpetual frost, up among the wild elements of nature and the hidden mysteries of science, and when they had made a discovery, and brought it down to the line of commercial value, leaving it there, knowing that the world would make it useful and profitable, while they went back to resume their original search. I do not wonder that these men regretted the loss of such a comrade as Joseph Henry.

But something is due to the millions of Americans outside the circle of science; and the Republic has the right to call on all her children for service. It was needful that the government should have, here at its capital, a great, luminous-minded, pure-hearted man, to serve as its counsellor and friend in matters of science. Such an adviser was never more needed than at the date of Professor Henry's arrival at the capital.

The venerable gentleman of almost eighty years, who has just addressed us so eloquently, has portrayed the difficulties which beset the government in its attempt to determine how it should wisely and worthily execute the trust of Smithson. It was a perilous moment for the credit of America when that bequest was made. In his large catholicity of mind, Smithson did not trammel the bequest with conditions. In nine words he set forth its object: "For the increase and diffusion of knowledge among men." He asked and believed that America would interpret his wish aright, and with the liberal wisdom of science.

A town-meeting is not a good place to determine scientific truths. And the yeas and nays that are called from this desk from day to day are not the supreme test of science, as the country finds when we attempt to settle any scientific question, whether it relates to the polariscope or to finance.

For ten years Congress wrestled with those nine words of Smithson, and could not handle them. Some political philosophers of that period held that we had no constitutional authority to accept the gift at all, and proposed to send it back to England. Every conceivable proposition was made. The colleges clutched at it; the libraries wanted it; the publication societies desired to scatter it. The fortunate settlement of the question was this: that, after ten years of wrangling, Congress was wise enough to acknowledge its own ignorance, and authorized a body of men to find some one who knew how to settle it. And these men were wise enough to choose your great comrade to undertake the task. Sacrificing his brilliant prospects as a discoverer, he undertook the difficult work. He draughted a paper, in which he offered an interpretation of the will of Smithson, mapped out a plan which would meet the demands of science, and submitted it to the suffrage of the republic of scientific scholars. After due deliberation it received the almost unanimous approval of the scientific world. With faith and sturdy perseverance, he adhered to the plan, and steadily resisted all attempts to overthrow it.

In the thirty-two years during which he administered the great trust, he never swerved from his first purpose; and he succeeded at last in realizing the ideas with which he started. But it has taken all that time to get rid of the incumbrance with which Congress had overloaded the Institution. In this work Professor Henry taught the valuable lesson to all founders and supporters of colleges, that they should pay less for brick and mortar, and more for brains. Under the first orders imposed upon him by Congress, he was required to expend twenty-five thousand dollars a year in purchasing books. By wise resistance he managed to lengthen out the period for that expenditure ten years; and a few years ago he had the satisfaction of seeing Congress remove from the Institution the heavy load, by transferring the Smithsonian Library to the Library of Congress. The fifty-eight thousand volumes and forty thousand pamphlets, of rare scientific value, which are now upon our shelves, have added greatly to the value of the national library; but their care and preservation would soon have absorbed the resources of the Smithsonian. When Congress shall have taken the other incumbrance, the National Museum, off the hands of the Institution, by making fit provision for the care of the great collection, they will have done still more to realize the ideas of Professor Henry.

He has stood by our side in all these years, meeting every great question of science with that calm spirit which knew no haste and no rest. At the call of his government he discovered new truths, and mustered them into its service. The twelve hundred light-houses that shine on our shores, the three thousand buoys along our rivers and coasts, testify to his faithfulness and efficiency.

When it became evident that we could no longer depend upon the whale-fisheries to supply our beacon-lights, he began to search for a substitute for sperm-oil; and after a thousand patient experiments he made the discovery that of all the oils of the world, when heated to 250° Fahrenheit, the common, cheap lard-oil of America became the best illuminant. That discovery gave us at once an unfailing supply, and for many years saved the treasury a hundred thousand dollars a year.

He had no such pride of authorship as to cling to his own methods when a better could be found. He has recently tested the qualities of petroleum as an illuminant, and recommended its use for the smaller lights. In instances far too numerous to be recounted, we have long had this man as our counsellor, our guide, and our friend.

During all the years of his sojourn among us, there has been one spot in this city across which the shadow of partisan politics has never fallen; and that was the ground of the Smithsonian Institution. We have seen in this city, at least one great, high trust so faithfully discharged for a third of a century that no breath of suspicion has ever dimmed its record. The Board of Regents have seen Professor Henry's accounts all closed; and, after the most rigid examination, the unanimous declaration is made, that, to the last cent, during the whole of that period, his financial administration was as faultless and complete as his discoveries in science. The blessing of such an example in this city ought at least to do something to reconcile these men of science to the loss they suffered when their friend was called to serve the government at its capital.

Remembering his great career as a man of science, as a man who served his government with singular ability and faithfulness, who was loved and venerated by every circle, who blessed with the light of his friendship the worthiest and the best, whose life added new lustre to the glory of the human race, we shall be most fortunate if ever in the future we see his like again.

XII.

IN MEMORIAM.

Life and Character of Almeda A. Booth.

AN ADDRESS DELIVERED AT HIRAM COLLEGE, O.,
JUNE 22, 1876.

TO THE THOUSANDS OF NOBLE MEN AND WOMEN WHOSE GENEROUS
AMBITION WAS AWAKENED, WHOSE EARLY CULTURE WAS GUIDED,
AND WHOSE LIVES HAVE BEEN MADE NOBLER, BY THE THOR-
OUGHNESS OF HER INSTRUCTION, BY THE WISDOM OF
HER COUNSEL, BY THE FAITHFULNESS OF HER
FRIENDSHIP, AND THE PURITY OF HER
LIFE, THIS TRIBUTE TO THE
MEMORY OF

ALMEDA A. BOOTH

IS AFFECTIONATELY DEDICATED.

XII.

ALMEDA A. BOOTH.

"The crown and head,
The stately flower of female fortitude."

MR. PRESIDENT,—You have called me to a duty at once most sad and most sacred. At every step of my preparation for its performance, I have encountered troops of thronging memories that swept across the field of the last twenty-five years of my life, and so filled my heart with the lights and shadows of their joy and sorrow that I have hardly been able to marshal them into order, or give them coherent voice. I have lived over again the life of this place. I have seen again the groups of young and joyous students ascending these green slopes, dwelling for a time on this peaceful height in happy and workful companionship, and then, with firmer step and with more serious and thoughtful faces, marching away to their posts in the battle of life.

And still nearer and clearer have come back

the memories of that smaller band of friends, the leaders and guides of those who encamped on this training-ground. On my journey to this assembly it has seemed that they, too, were coming, and that here I should once more meet and greet them. And I have not yet been able to realize that Almeda Booth will not be with us. After our great loss, how shall we gather up the fragments of the life we lived in this place? We are mariners, treading the lonely shore in search of our surviving comrades, and the fragments of our good ship wrecked by the tempest. To her, indeed, it is no wreck. She has landed in safety, and ascended the immortal heights beyond our vision.

What manner of woman she was, by what steps and through what struggles her character was developed, to what ends her life was directed, what she accomplished for herself and for us, and what rich fruitage may be gathered from the trees of her planting, I shall attempt to portray as best I can.

We can study no life intelligently except in its relations to causes and results. Character is the chief element, for it is both a result and a cause,— the result of all the elements and forces that combined to form it, and the chief cause of all that is accomplished by its possessor.

Who, then, was Almeda Ann Booth? and what were the elements and forces that formed her character and guided her life?

Every character is the joint product of nature and nurture. By the first, we mean those inborn qualities of body and mind inherited from parents, or, rather, from a long line of ancestors. Who shall estimate the effect of those latent forces infolded in the spirit of a new-born child, which may date back centuries, and find their origin in the unwritten history of remote ancestors; forces, the germs of which, enveloped in the solemn mystery of life, have been transmitted silently from generation to generation, and never perish? All-cherishing nature, provident and unforgetting, gathers up all these fragments, that nothing may be lost, but that all may re-appear in new combinations. Each new life is thus the "heir of all the ages," the possessor of qualities which only the events of life can unfold.

By the second element, — nurture, or culture, — we designate all those influences which act upon this initial force of character to retard or strengthen its development. There has been much discussion to determine which of these elements plays the more important part in the formation of character. The truth doubtless is, that sometimes the one and sometimes the other is the greater force; but, so far as life and character are dependent upon voluntary action, the second is no doubt the element of chief importance.

Not enough attention has been paid to the marked difference between the situation and possibilities of a life developed here in the West during the first half of the present century, and those of a life nurtured and cultivated in an old and settled community like that of New England.

Consider, for example, the measureless difference between the early surroundings of John Quincy Adams and Abraham Lincoln. Both were possessed of great natural endowments. Adams was blessed with parents whose native force of character and whose vigorous and thorough culture have never been surpassed by any married pair in America. Young Adams was thoroughly taught by his mother until he had completed his tenth year; and then, accompanying his father to France, he spent two years in a training-school at Paris and three years in the university at Leyden. After two years of diplomatic service under the skilful guidance of his father's hand, he returned to America, and devoted three years to study at Harvard, where he was graduated at the age of twenty-one; and three years later was graduated in the law under the foremost jurist of his time. With such parentage and such opportunities, who can wonder, that, by the time he reached the meridian of his life, he was a man of immense erudition, and had honored every great office in the gift of his country?

How startling the contrast, in every particular, between his early life and that of Abraham Lincoln! The facts concerning the latter are too well known to require a statement. Born to an inheritance of the extremest poverty, wholly unaided by his parents, surrounded by the rude forces of the wilderness, only one year in any school, never for a day master of his own time until he reached his majority, forcing his way to the profession of the law by the hardest and roughest road, and beginning its practice at twenty-eight years of age, yet by the force of unconquerable will and persistent hard work he attained a foremost place in his profession,

> "And, moving up from high to higher,
> Became, on fortune's crowning slope,
> The pillar of a people's hope, —
> The centre of a world's desire."

Who can tell what the results might have been if the situations of these two men had been reversed?

It is often remarked, as ground of encouragement to young men, that just such struggles as these in which Lincoln engaged are necessary to bring out the native force of character, and produce great results; and no doubt this is partly true. But, where one succeeds under such circumstances, how many thousands fail?

Our people frequently refer, with pride, to the exceptionally prominent place which Ohio has taken in all the walks of public and professional life during the last twenty years. That prominence is probably due to the fact, that those citizens of Ohio who have been leaders of their generation during the last twenty years are the first-born of the pioneer founders of our State. The inspirations of the Revolution were still acting in full vigor upon the people of the original thirteen States when the settlement of Ohio began. By the law of natural selection, those only became pioneers who were best fitted, by natural energy and force of character, to conquer the difficulties attending such a career; and their children have not only inherited a part of that energy, but have enjoyed means of culture which were far beyond the reach of the pioneers themselves. In old and settled communities, we find more culture; in pioneer life, more force. And it will doubtless prove true, that, in succeeding generations, Ohio will produce a higher type of scholars, — men of arts and letters; but it is also probable, that they will lose in rugged force a part, at least, of what they gain in culture.

Striking as was the difference between the two examples referred to, the contrast of such conditions is still greater when applied to the possibilities of the culture and development of woman. Man is better fitted for a rough struggle with rude elements. His is a coarser fibre, his "the wrestling thews that throw the world."

"Iron-jointed, supple-sinewed, he shall dive, and he shall run,
Catch the wild goat by the hair, and hurl his lances in the sun."

But woman's nature is of a finer fibre: her spirit is attuned to higher harmonies. "All dipped in angel-instincts," she craves more keenly than man the celestial food, — the highest culture which earth and heaven can give; and her loss is far greater than his, when she is deprived of those means of culture so rarely found in pioneer life. Success in intellectual pursuits, under such conditions, is the strongest possible test of her character.

With these general reflections as guides to the study of the life we have met to commemorate, let us inquire what were the elements and conditions out of which that life grew.

Almeda Ann Booth[1] was a child of the pioneers, and of hardy New-England stock. Her father, Ezra Booth, was born near the Housatonic River, in Newton, Fairfield County, Conn., Feb. 14, 1792; and her mother, Dorcas Taylor, was born in Great Barrington, Mass., June 30, 1800. Both were swept westward, in early childhood, by that tide of emigration which, in the beginning of the present century, began to people the wilderness of North-eastern Ohio. The precise date at which Ezra Booth came to the West, I have not ascertained. The parents of Dorcas Taylor came in 1813, and found a home in the woods of Nelson.

As we know the Western Reserve to-day, with

[1] In the Booth family-Bible it is recorded Almedah; and she followed that spelling until she was twenty years of age.

its 350,000 people, its growing cities, its vast industries, and its thousands of comfortable and elegant homes, we can hardly realize what it was when the parents of Miss Booth first saw it.

At the beginning of the century it was an unbroken wilderness, with but 1,302 white inhabitants. Indeed, in 1810 the whole number of white inhabitants within the present limits of Portage County was considerably less than the population of Hiram to-day. Between 1810 and 1830, 17,000 pioneers had settled in this county, and 70,000 had found homes in the Western Reserve. They brought with them little wealth, and few of the comforts of life. Patient and courageous toil was the first necessity of the men and women who wrought the transformation of that wilderness into the beautiful and happy homes inherited by their children. But the pioneers did not forget the faith and traditions of their fathers. While building their homes, they planted also the school and the church, and thus laid deep and strong the foundations of prosperity.

In the midst of such stirring scenes, Ezra Booth began his career. He was a man of more than ordinary powers of mind, — gentle, affectionate, impressible, and deeply religious. His early intellectual training did not go beyond the rudiments taught in the common schools of Connecticut. But he was an inveterate reader of books; and the armful of choice volumes that lay on the shelves of his little library was probably a greater number than could have been found in one house out of every thousand on the Reserve. Possessed of slender means, he adopted a profession which rendered the acquirement of wealth well-nigh impossible. He early entered the ministry of the Methodist Episcopal Church, and was assigned to a circuit of nearly a thousand miles, embracing in its range the township of Nelson; and there, in 1819, he married Dorcas Taylor, and fixed his home.

Soon after entering the ministry, he sent eleven silver dollars to England to purchase a Greek lexicon; and he so far mastered the language as to read the Greek Testament with ease. He used to say, that, in the early days of his ministry, he and a Mr. Charles Elliott were the only Methodist preachers west of the Alleghanies who were able to read Greek.

In a small frame house about three and a half miles eastward from this place, on the farm now owned by Mrs. Ferris Couch, Almeda, the only child of Ezra and Dorcas Booth, was born on the fifteenth day of August, 1823. She inherited a hardy and vigorous constitution, a clear and powerful intellect, and a spirit of remarkable sweetness and gentleness. These qualities of mind and heart shone with clear and steady light, from early childhood until her last hour.

Her life appears to fall into three very distinct periods, separated from each other by marked events. Indeed, she may be said to have lived three separate lives. These will appear as we review her history.

Her first twelve years were passed in Nelson. All the traditions that have come to us from that period are redolent of the fragrance of a sweet and loving childhood. In her fourth year she attended the district school at Nelson Centre, a mile and a half distant from her home. The school was taught at that time by Miss Jane Hopkins, afterwards Mrs. Nathan Wadsworth. How long she continued with this teacher, I have not learned; but, at the close of Miss Hopkins's school, Almeda received a locket, as the prize for making the greatest progress in spelling. Miss Clarissa Colton was also her teacher in

Nelson for several terms, and was remembered with great affection in after-years. I have not been able to learn the names of her other teachers in that place. The honored President of the Board of Trustees of this college, who saw her frequently when she was a little child, tells us this pleasing and characteristic incident: —

When Almeda was about twelve years of age, she used to puzzle her teachers with questions, and distress them by correcting their mistakes; and one of them (a male teacher, of course), who was too proud to acknowledge the corrections of a child, called upon Mr. Udall[1] for help and advice in regard to a point of dispute between them. Mr. Udall told him he was evidently in error, and must acknowledge his mistake. The teacher was manly enough to follow this wise advice, and thereafter made the little girl his friend and helper in the scholastic difficulties which he encountered. It was like her to help him quietly, and without boasting. During her whole life, what one of her friends ever heard an intimation from her that she had ever achieved an intellectual triumph over anybody in the world?

In 1835 her family removed to Mantua, about

[1] The President aforesaid.

four miles to the north-west of this place, where they resided for more than thirty years. Her progress had been so great under the instruction of her favorite teacher, Miss Colton, that her parents induced that young lady also to remove to Mantua. Almeda's progress as a scholar was continuous and rapid. Dr. Squire, who knew her well from the time she first attended the district school at Mantua, in the winter of 1835-36, tells us that "she was known as a thorough scholar, the best speller in the district, and, though dressed in the plainest style possible, was the pride of the neighborhood for her youthful attainments and gentleness."

Hon. A. G. Riddle, who knew her as a child in Mantua, has drawn this charming picture: —

"You ask me for my recollections of Almeda Booth. What I can recall of her associates her with a single spring and summer, — idyllic, as one long day of green foliage, apple-blossoms, humming bees, and sunshine, coming from nothing which preceded, and connected with nothing which followed.

"There was a beautiful, secluded neighborhood in northeast Mantua, where two little-travelled highways crossed. In the north-west angle thus formed stood the farmhouse, the homestead of Deacon Seth Harmon, my home at that time. The east-and-west road in its front was filled with cherry-trees. South of this highway stood a grand old and quite extensive apple-orchard, over the tops of which, and two or three hundred yards away, embowered in fruit and forest-trees, could be seen the roof of Almeda's home. A winding foot-path led down from it to the road in front of the Harmon homestead.

"I knew Almeda as an only child, — a maiden of twelve or thirteen years, well-grown, ruddy-cheeked, and buxom. Martha Harmon, dark and slight, was of about the same age. They were quite constant companions.

"About the Harmon house and grounds, in the highway, along that foot-path, through the orchard, amid falling apple-blossoms and humming bees, I can see and hear these two laughing, light-hearted girls; and that is all. I can connect them with no incident, or any certain time.

"I have a sort of an impression, and only that, of attending a winter school with Almeda.

"She must have had the power of fixing herself well in one's memory. I did not see her again for ten years, and knew her at once; and I recall the lively satisfaction I felt at being remembered by her. Through all the years since, I have been familiar with her name, though meeting her but seldom."

There must necessarily be much loneliness in the life of an only child. That Almeda felt this, is evident from one of her early essays which has been preserved, and in which she says, — "I am one of those unfortunate beings whom

Mrs. Sigourney so much pities, — a person destitute of brothers and sisters." And yet, for a thoughtful child, such a life had its compensations. She found early and sweet companionship with her father in his studies, and, like him, became an ardent lover of books. At that period few juvenile books were published; and the stirring works of legend and romance rarely found their way to the shelves of a preacher's library. The extent and character of her early reading I have not learned; but she once told me that she read Rollin's "Ancient History" and Gibbon's "Decline and Fall of the Roman Empire" when she was twelve years of age. I doubt if, at so early an age, any person in this assembly had done as much.

At the age of fourteen she had pretty thoroughly mastered the studies then taught in the district school; and, for a short time, she attended a select school in Painesville, boarding at the house of a Rev. Mr. Winans. When she was seventeen, she taught her first school, in a log schoolhouse, near her home in Mantua. She next engaged to teach, for five months, the school near what was known as the "Brick Tavern," south of Mantua Centre. There, as in her first school, she was very popular; but she became homesick, and by the aid of friends secured a change in the contract, by which the term was shortened to three months. She greatly disliked the custom of that time, which required her to "board around the district;" because it resulted in such a waste of her time, and cut her off from the opportunity of reading which she so highly prized. But she conquered all the discomforts of the work, and continued to teach, using for the advancement of her own culture the pittance then paid to a woman teacher, which sometimes did not exceed four dollars per month.[1]

---

[1] Dr. Squire has furnished me with the following interesting facts concerning Miss Booth's teaching in Mantua. He says, "I learn from the records of the Booth school-district, that Almeda taught there during the winter 1844-45. The studies taught were reading, writing, arithmetic, grammar, and geography. The term ended Feb. 14, 1845; wages, eight dollars per month. The report is signed 'Almeda A. Booth.' Similar report for the same district for the term ending March 6, 1846: wages seven dollars per month. For same district, term ending Aug. 28, 1846: average daily attendance, sixteen. Philosophy, history, and botany taught, in addition to common branches: wages four dollars per month. Report for term ending March 5, 1847: algebra and common branches; wages nine dollars per month. The month, at that time, probably meant twenty-six days of school." It will be seen that wages for summer were much lower than for winter.

In 1842 and 1843 she attended during several terms the Asbury Seminary, at Chagrin Falls, which at that time was under the charge of L. D. Williams, who was afterwards a distinguished professor in Meadville College. In later years she frequently spoke of him in terms of the highest respect and reverence. I have not been able to learn the range of her studies at Chagrin Falls; but she has left a small package of essays, written as school exercises while there, which exhibit that clearness and masterful force of expression so characteristic of her style in later years. The penmanship bears a few traces of the .formal school-girl hand, especially in the construction of the capital letters; but it also shows the outline of that elegant and graceful chirography with which we are now so familiar. The brief marginal notes and criticisms of her instructors indicate the pride and satisfaction they felt in her development. One of these notes is signed "Mattison;" another, "H. H. Moore;" and another is in these words: "Very good. The errors are few, and none of them bad ones. L. D. W." (evidently L. D. Williams).

I have read these short essays with a deep and mournful interest. Though written as formal school exercises, they are charming pictures of the progress of her mind and the genuine earnestness of her convictions. To quote them here, however, would be unjust to her maturer fame. Among them is a dialogue, in her handwriting, between herself and Miss Elizabeth Hayden, daughter of the late Rev. William Hayden. Even at that early age, Miss Booth exhibited unusual aptitude for that species of dramatic composition in which she subsequently developed so much power.

Until she reached the age of twenty-four, her life had been devoted to home duties, to study, and teaching. In the family of her nearest neighbor, she had formed the intimate acquaintance of Martyn Harmon, a young man of rare and brilliant promise. Like herself, he was an enthusiastic student. Ambitious of culture, he had pushed his way through the studies of Meadville College, and was graduated with honor. He had given Almeda his love, and received in return the rich gift of her great heart. The day of their wedding had been fixed. He was away in Kentucky, teaching; while she was in Mantua, preparing to adorn and bless the home of their love. On the 6th of March, 1848, he died of some sudden illness, and was buried near Frankfort, Ky. Funeral services were held in Mantua, at which Almeda took her place as chief mourner. Her plans of life and the hopes of her earthly future seemed buried in his grave.

This event closes the first period of her history. It seemed for a time to end her ambition and her hopes. Her heart was wedded by ties as sacred as any which marriage can consecrate. From that time forward she walked alone in the solitude of virgin widowhood.

In her subsequent life she rarely spoke of the suffering of that period; but she never ceased to cherish the memory of Martyn Harmon as that of an immortal husband who awaited her coming in the life beyond. Her faithfulness to him excluded the thought of marriage with any other.

After such a loss, what was left to a soul like hers? To her heart, the consolations of the Christian faith; and, to her life, the power of serving and blessing others. It is one of the precious mysteries of sorrow, that it finds solace in unselfish work. Patient and uncomplaining, with a spirit chastened and sweetened by her great sorrow, Almeda gathered up the fragments of her broken life, and devoted her powers to the work of teaching.

Making her father's home the centre of her activities, she commenced teaching in the most difficult and unpromising districts in her neighborhood. Her success was such as few teachers in a similar field have ever achieved. She found happiness in her work, and was rewarded with the admiration and love of those whose minds were moulded and guided by her influence.

Besides this, she found solace and strength in her old habit of reading. Her spirit, ranging beyond the narrow circle of her every-day life, found in books a noble companionship with the good and great of other days.

I find among her papers a few pages of personal reminiscences, written twenty-one years ago, which probably refer to the period of her life of which I am now speaking. I am sure her friends will listen to her own words with more pleasure than to any thing that I can say. She writes: —

"Through the mists and clouds of later life, remembrance brings a warm glow to our hearts, as we think of the friends we loved, and the books we read. Yes, the books! Who has not some old, torn, dingy favorite of a book, that he remembers with more affection than any volume he has seen for many a year? I remember one that to me, in those years, was a source of never-failing delight. I fondly cherish the memory of that old book, both for itself and its pleasant associations. I chanced to find it in a family where I was allowed to visit, into whose possession it had come in payment of a debt for which nothing else could be obtained. It was a bound volume of a periodical that had been started in Philadelphia by some lover of literature who mistook the tastes of the age; and his magazine soon failed for want of patronage. It *had* been bound; but when I was so happy as to make its acquaintance, its leaves had escaped from their confinement, causing me no little trouble as I turned over the unwieldy mass. It contained no original matter, but choice selections from English and American literature. Here I first read 'L'Allegro' and 'Il Penseroso;' and, though I was delighted with the

> 'Goddess fair and free,
> In heaven ycleped Euphrosyne,
> And by men heart-easing Mirth,'

yet by the time I had read through to —

> 'These pleasures melancholy give,
> And I with thee will choose to live,'

I usually felt like giving in my adhesion to the 'goddess sage and holy.' There, too, I read 'Mazeppa,'—that wild ride related

> 'After dread Pultowa's day,
> When fortune left the royal Swede;'

and I could never understand how, when 'twas done, the king could have been 'an hour asleep.' There were McKenzie's 'Man of Feeling;' Goldsmith's simple, natural, and inimitable 'Vicar of Wakefield;' also those stories of exquisite beauty and pathos, 'The Lights and Shadows of Scottish Life.' And there I first found the letters of our own Dr. Franklin, and his life, written by himself, for his son, which I could never sufficiently admire: it seemed so truthful and honest; as he related the indiscretions of his early years, and remembered his errors, one by one. But I read nothing in that book with more thrilling interest than the old English ballad of 'Chevy Chase.' As I read how that famous hunt fell out, how noble knights and barons bold went down in death, how brave Lord Percy fell, and Scotland's pride, Earl Douglas, too, my enthusiasm was never chilled by a thought that I was reading events 'totally fictitious,' as Spaulding tells us they are. But, of all the treasures I there found, I oftenest read the letters of Lady Mary Wortley Montague, which have always been regarded as models of epistolary composition. It is objected that she sometimes seems unamiable and unfeeling; yet, even then, she is so witty and charming, one is almost tempted to forgive her. Still, I think, there is reason for this charge against her earliest letters. The absurdities and follies of the gay and courtly circle in which she moved appeared so ridiculous, in the light of her strong understanding, that, in letters to her friends, she often hit off those she met with the severest sarcasm. Addison, Pope, and other distinguished writers of that age, were proud of her friendship; but Pope quailed before her peerless wit and sarcasm, and from a most ardent friend turned to an implacable enemy."

After describing, at some length, the character and career of Lady Montague, the manuscript concludes: —

"She [Lady Montague] was proficient in Greek and Latin, and seems to have read almost every thing that had ever been written in any language. In a letter to her daughter, in relation to the education of her granddaughter, she says, 'Learning, if she has a real taste for it, will not only make her contented, but happy. No entertainment is so cheap as reading, nor any pleasure so lasting.' Thus much for the old book. I saw its friendly, honest face, soiled and time-worn, only a few months ago; but it is not so perishable as earth's frail children. I gazed upon it with mingled emotions of pain and pleasure; for I remembered that the dear ones, who in those happy hours had read from that book with me, were all gone. The glad voices of seven children once rang through that home; but now every one is hushed in death, and the poor, stricken parents are left alone. I remembered when the father — a man of uncommon tenderness of feeling — said to me, a few days before his last child was laid in the grave, his voice trembling, and his eyes full of tears, 'Oh! I had hoped the Lord would spare me one child; but his will be done.'

"So that old book is very dear to me."

This charming sketch of the old book is a striking picture of her own mind and heart during the early days of her sorrow.

But, by slow degrees, her sorrow gave place to

ambition for larger culture. In the autumn of 1848 she attended a select school at Mantua Centre, taught by Norman Dunshee, and, among her other studies, began Latin. In the winter of 1849-50 she taught the school in the Darwin-Atwater district; and, in the winter of 1850-51, taught at Hiram Rapids, her last district school. She is still remembered with enthusiastic affection by the people of that neighborhood.

Her success as a teacher was well known to Charles D. Wilber, at whose suggestion President Hayden secured her services to the young Eclectic; and in the spring of 1851 she came here as a teacher in the English department. Up to that time no lady had taught in the Eclectic, except in the primary department, which was established at the opening of the institution, in November, 1850, and maintained for several years. Before the end of her first term, the trustees found that they had drawn a rich prize, in securing her services in the institution.

The Eclectic was compelled to create its own scholarship and culture. Very few of its early students had gone beyond the ordinary studies of the district school; and a large majority of them needed thorough discipline in the common English branches. I doubt if any teacher at Hiram was equal to Miss Booth in the power to inspire such students with the spirit of earnest, hard work, for the love of it.

In August next it will be twenty-five years since I first saw her. I came to the Eclectic as a student, in the fall term of 1851; and, a few days after the beginning of the term, I saw a class of three, reciting in mathematics,— geometry, I think. They sat on one of the red benches, in the centre aisle of the lower chapel. I had never seen a geometry; and, regarding both teacher and class with a feeling of reverential awe for the intellectual height to which they had climbed, I studied their faces so closely that I seem to see them now as distinctly as I saw them then. And it has been my good fortune since that time to claim them all as intimate friends. The teacher was Thomas Munnell; and the members of his class were William B. Hazen, George A. Baker, and Almeda A. Booth.

Let us pause here to consider the situation and attainments of Miss Booth in 1851, at the beginning of what we may call her second life. She was twenty-eight years of age. In many respects her character was fully matured. She had enjoyed somewhat better advantages than most women of that period, who, born of the pioneers and unblessed by wealth, were reared in the narrow circle of country life. Though she had made the most of her opportunities, yet she had hardly entered the circle of that larger scholarship and broader culture which women enjoy in older communities.

As a means of estimating more accurately her abilities and merits, let us contrast her attainments at that time with those of a woman of wider fame who was greatly admired by Miss Booth, and who was very like her in intellectual force.

Margaret Fuller was born at Cambridge, Mass., and from early life breathed the atmosphere of the highest culture of New England. Her father, a graduate of Harvard, and accomplished French scholar, thoroughly read in general history and literature, a prominent lawyer, and for many years a distinguished member of Congress, early devoted himself personally to the work of his daughter's education. At six years of age she was able to read Latin; and soon her young imagination was fired by the strong and beautiful legends of classic history and mythology. Wandering at will in her father's well-filled library, and gathering such food as her young spirit could assimilate, she read, when eight years of age, "Romeo and Juliet," the quaint and wonderful humor of Cervantes, and the bright pictures of Parisian life portrayed in the pages of Molière. In her nineteenth year she had finished a thorough course in one of the best training-schools of Massachusetts. At twenty-two she had mastered the German language, and read its principal authors. At twenty-three she was teaching the languages, and attracting to herself the minds and hearts of all who came within her reach. Ralph Waldo Emerson says of her at that period, " She was an active and inspiring companion and correspondent; and all the heart, thought, and nobleness of New England seemed at that moment related to her, and she to it." At twenty-five she was translating the correspondence of Goethe, was devouring the works of Madame de Staël in French, and of Epictetus in Latin; and was ranging at will through the realms of English literature and philosophy. At twenty-eight she became the editor of a literary journal, and was assisted by Ralph Waldo Emerson, George Ripley, and many other prominent writers. Her wide acquaintance, and still wider correspondence, placed at her command the culture and literary wealth of both hemispheres. From that time forward she rose rapidly from height to height, until a tragic death closed her career in 1850. Her native powers of mind were undoubtedly great; and she would not have remained unknown in any sphere of life, however humble. But it must be acknowledged that very much of her success was due to her rare opportunities for early culture.

Contrast with this brilliant picture the situation of Miss Booth at twenty-eight years of age. We have followed the history of her toilful life up to that period. We saw her moving in a narrow and humble sphere, creating her own means of culture, unaided by the companionship of superior minds to inspire and guide her development. After the light of her young life had been quenched in a great sorrow, we saw her turning sadly away from the wreck of her hopes, and beginning the hard task of creating the new conditions out of which she might gain a broader, deeper culture, and become more useful to her generation.

We found her not farther advanced in technical scholarship at twenty-eight years of age, than Margaret Fuller was at seventeen; and even then her further advancement depended upon what she could accomplish for herself, while teaching six or seven great classes a day, and discharging the other numberless duties which fell to her lot as chief lady teacher in a mixed school of two hundred and fifty scholars.

Highly as I appreciate the character of Margaret Fuller, greatly as I admire her remarkable abilities, I do not hesitate to say, that in no four years of her life did her achievements, brilliant as they were, equal the work accomplished by Miss Booth during the four years that followed her coming to Hiram.

I was never a member of a class that recited to her, and I cannot speak of her work as a teacher as seen from the stand-point of a pupil; but I know from personal observation, and from the unanimous testimony of thousands who were so fortunate as to be her pupils, that her power over classes as a whole, and over every member, was very great and beneficent. In the earlier years of her teaching here, she frequently took advanced classes in grammar and arithmetic, numbering from ninety to one hundred each. Without any parade of authority, without appearing to govern at all, she always held them in most admirable order; and, what was still more remarkable, each pupil felt that his relations to her were those of very direct personal responsibility and sympathy; and that he owed her a personal apology for any dereliction or failure on his part, and a debt of affectionate gratitude for the largest measure of his success. Her classes in botany and astronomy were always filled with enthusiasm for their work, and with affectionate admiration for Miss Booth.

She did not deliver formal lectures on these subjects; but she carried to almost every recitation a memorandum of brief notes, from which, during the course of the lesson, she threw out fertile and striking suggestions which illuminated the subject, and made every pupil feel that to be absent from a recitation of her class was to suffer personal loss. I have found among her papers many of these memoranda, full of strong and beautiful suggestions.

Besides doing her full share of the heavy work of the class-room, Miss Booth had special charge of the ladies, and, from 1852 onward, devoted much time to them as their confidential counsellor and friend. There are hundreds of noble women who have worn the royal crown of maternity these many years, — and some of them are present to-day, — whose hearts are still full of precious memories of those familiar lectures, or rather conversations, in the lower chapel, in which Miss Booth gave them the benefit of her rich experience and wise counsel in the conduct of life. The notes of some of these conversations I have found among her manuscripts. One was written out in full, in which she unfolded her conception of how solemn a thing it is to live, and to perform those duties which fall to the lot of woman.

She aided in organizing and maintaining the first ladies' literary society in the Eclectic, and for several years took an active part in its proceedings. Her essays prepared for its meetings are models of sound judgment and of finished, graceful style.

I first became acquainted with her qualities as a writer during the spring term of 1852, when Corydon E. Fuller and I were appointed to aid her in writing a colloquy for the public exercises at the close of the school year. Having chosen a theme founded on historical events in the time of Pope Leo X., she sketched the outline of the piece, assigned portions to her two associates, set them to reading up the history of the period to which the piece related, directed and corrected their work, and adapted it to her own, cast the parts, criticised and trained those who were to perform them, took the most difficult and least desirable part herself, and put the piece on the stage with such skill as to surprise and delight the great audience that assembled under the bower built among the apple-trees north of the Seminary. I esteemed myself especially fortunate and highly honored in being chosen to aid her in that work. My admiration of her knowledge and ability was unbounded. And even now, after the glowing picture painted upon my memory in the strong colors of youthful enthusiasm has been shaded down by the colder and more sombre tints which a quarter of a century has added, I still regard her work on that occasion as possessing great merit. I have read again some of the pages of the faded manuscript, a few of which survive; and I find that her part of it still justifies much of my early enthusiasm.

To her marked success in this piece is due the fact, that, during many subsequent years, an original drama — or, in the school dialect, a "colloquy" — was the most attractive feature of commencement-days. There are many present to-day who remember these colloquies, — that of 1853, founded on the Book of Esther; "Burr and Blennerhassett," in 1854, when O. P. Miller and Philip Burns played the heavy parts of Adams and Jefferson, and Rhodes, Pettibone, and Williams, the less pious but more exciting *rôles* of Arnold, Burr, and Blennerhassett; "Lafayette," in 1856; "Ivanhoe," in 1857, in which the stirring scenes of the Crusades were revived; "The Conspiracy of Orsini," in 1858 (suggested by the reading of Ruffini's "Doctor Antonio"), in which Elias A. Ford trod the stage as Louis Napoleon, with Electa Beecher as empress, and Amzi Atwater as prime minister, while White, Chamberlin, and Ferry were treacherously seeking his imperial life. Then there was "The Highland Chiefs," in 1859, in which Henry James and Henry White were Lochiel and McAlpine, in deadly feud with Chamberlin and Dudley, Lords of Glencoe and Keppock, mustering their clans for battle to determine which of these fierce knights should win the hands of Sophia Williams and Myra Robbins, the Ellen and the Margaret of the hour. There was "Pickwickian Politics," in 1860, with Brown and Bennett as stars; and "Zenobia," in 1861, in which Mary E. White was the proud Queen of Palmyra, with half a score of young men as bold Romans leading her away in triumph. In all these pieces, the parts which were surest to touch the heart, and win approval, were those written by Miss Booth. They showed how varied were her intellectual resources, and with what power and grace she could employ them.

Occupied as she was in the daily discharge of such exacting duties, one would think she had small leisure for any other work. But we shall see what more she was able to accomplish. She saw, that, so long as she taught only the English studies, the bright and ambitious pupils to whom she was so strongly attached would pass out of her reach by entering upon studies in which she could not guide them. The desire to avoid this gave a new impulse to her ambition for higher scholarship; and in the autumn of 1851 she began those studies necessary to fit her for teaching in the higher grades. When a class was formed in any thing she had not mastered, she arranged to have it recite before or after school-hours, and took her place as one of its members. Thus she kept in advance of her own pupils, and abreast with the foremost students of the institution.

I am not certain when she began Greek; but I remember that she and I were members of the class that began Xenophon's "Anabasis," in the fall term of 1852. Near the close of that term, I also began to teach in the Eclectic, and thereafter, like her, could only keep up my studies outside of my own class-hours. In mathematics and the physical sciences, I was far behind her; but we were nearly at the same place in Greek and Latin, each having studied them about three terms. She had made her home at President Hayden's, almost from the first; and I became a member of his family at the beginning of the winter term of 1852-53. Thereafter, for nearly two years, she and I studied together, and recited in the same classes (frequently without other associates), till we had nearly completed the classical course.

From a diary which I then kept, and in which my own studies are recorded, I am able to state, quite accurately, what she accomplished in the classics, from term to term, in the two following years. During the winter and spring terms of 1853, she read Xenophon's "Memorabilia" entire, reciting to Professor Dunshee. In the summer vacation of 1853, twelve of the more advanced students engaged Professor Dunshee as a tutor for one month. John Harnit, H. W. Everest, Philip Burns, C. C. Foote, Miss Booth, and I were of the number. A literary society was formed, in which all took part. During those four weeks, besides taking an active part in the literary exercises of the society, Miss Booth read thoroughly, and for the first time, the "Pastorals" of Virgil, — that is, the "Georgics" and "Bucolics" entire, — and the first six books of Homer's "Iliad," accompanied by a thorough drill in the Latin or Greek grammar at each recitation. I am sure that none of those who recited with her would say she was behind the foremost in the thoroughness of her work or the elegance of her translations.

During the fall term of 1853, she read one hundred pages of Herodotus, and about the same amount of Livy. During that term also, Professors Dunshee and Hull, and Miss Booth and I, met at her room two evenings of each week, to make a joint translation of the book of Romans. Professor Dunshee contributed his studies of the German commentators De Wette and Tholuck; and each of the translators made some special study for each meeting. How nearly we completed the translation I do not remember; but I do remember that the contributions and criticisms of Miss Booth were remarkable for suggestiveness and sound judgment. Our work was more thorough than rapid; for I find this entry in my diary for Dec.

15, 1853: "Translation Society sat three nours at Miss Booth's room, and agreed upon the translation of nine verses."

During the winter term of 1853–54, she continued to read Livy, and also read the whole of Demosthenes " On the Crown." The members of the class in Demosthenes were Miss Booth, A. Hull, C. C. Foote, and myself.

During the spring term of 1854, she read the " Germania " and "Agricola " of Tacitus, and a portion of Hesiod.

In the autumn of 1854, having secured from the Board of Trustees a leave of absence for one year, she entered the Senior class of Oberlin College. Though she had not yet completed several of the important Junior studies, yet during her one year in college she not only brought up all arrears, but thoroughly accomplished all the work of the Senior year, and in August, 1855, was graduated as Bachelor of Arts in the full classical course, ranking among the very first in her class. Three years later she received the honorary degree of Master of Arts.

A student no farther advanced than Miss Booth was in 1851, usually needs three years of preparatory study to enter the Freshman year, and four years more to complete the course. But in the four years that followed her coming to Hiram, she taught ten full terms, prepared herself for college, and completed with remarkable thoroughness the full course of college study. If any man or woman has done more in the same length of time, I do not know it. It should be mentioned, to the honor of Oberlin College, that, but for the wise and liberal policy which opened the full course of study to women, Miss Booth could hardly have taken the bachelor's degree anywhere in this country.

She returned to Hiram at the beginning of the fall term of 1855, and for ten years, without intermission, devoted herself to the work of teaching. Each year added to her thoroughness in the classroom, and increased her influence over students. Besides taking a few of the more advanced classes in the ordinary studies, she taught the higher mathematics, and Latin and Greek, maintaining her habit of making special preparation for each recitation. She handled these classes also with remarkable thoroughness and success. I cannot speak from personal knowledge of the later teachers of Latin and Greek in this institution; but, during the time she was here, no one of her associates was her superior in those studies.

As the earlier teachers were called away to other fields of duty, their places were supplied by selection from those who had been "Eclectic" students; and thus Miss Booth found herself associated with teachers whose culture she had guided, and who were attached to her by the strongest ties of friendship. I know how apt we are to exaggerate the merits of those we love; but, making due allowance for this tendency, as I look back upon the little circle of teachers who labored here, under the leadership of our honored and venerable friend Mr. Hayden, during the first six years of the Eclectic, and upon the younger group, associated with me from 1856 until the breaking-out of the war, I think I wrong no one of them by saying, that for generous friendship, and united, earnest work, I have never seen, and never expect to see, their like again. Enough new members were added to the corps of teachers from year to year to keep alive the freshness of young enthusiasm; and yet enough experience and maturity of judgment was left to hold the school in a steady course of prosperity.

The influence of Miss Booth, especially during the later period to which I have referred, was not surpassed by any member of that circle. A majority of her associates had been her students,—the children of her intellect and heart. She had watched their growth with something akin to maternal pride; and she welcomed them to that circle with no touch of envy, but with most generous and helpful friendship. I am sure that Rhodes, Everest, Atwater, Hinsdale, Miss Wilson, and the rest can never forget that golden age of our lives; and all will agree with me, that one light at least shone always steady and clear, — the light that beamed upon us from the mind and heart of Almeda A. Booth.

The few spare hours which the school-work left us were devoted to such pursuits as each preferred; but much study was done in common. I can name twenty or thirty books which will forever be doubly precious to me, because they were read and discussed in company with her. I can still read, between the lines, the memories of her first impression of the page, and her judgment of its merits. She was always ready to aid any friend with her best efforts. When I was in the hurry of preparing for a debate with Mr.

Denton in 1858, she read not less than eight or ten volumes, and made admirable notes for me, on those points which related to the topics of discussion. In the autumn of 1859, she read a large portion of Blackstone's "Commentaries," and enjoyed, with keenest relish, the strength of the author's thought, and the beauty of his style. From the rich stores of her knowledge, she gave with unselfish generosity. The foremost students had no mannish pride that made them hesitate to ask her assistance and counsel. In preparing their orations and debates, they eagerly sought her suggestions and criticisms. Everywhere the literary life of Hiram bore abundant marks of her guiding hand.

It is quite probable that John Stuart Mill has exaggerated the extent to which his own mind and works were influenced by Harriet Mill. I should reject his opinion on that subject as a delusion, did I not know, from my own experience as well as that of hundreds of Hiram students, how great a power Miss Booth exercised over the culture and opinions of her friends.

From what I have said of her influence over young men, it must not be inferred that she was wanting in sympathy or influence with her own sex. It is true, that giddy and superficial women, who care more for the adornment of their bodies than for the enlightenment of their minds, were not strongly attracted to Miss Booth; but by all the better class of thoughtful and earnest women she was loved with ardent and enthusiastic devotion.

The war for the Union, which broke up so many happy circles, and changed the plans of so many lives, wrought great changes in Hiram, and swept into the fiery current a hundred of our best students. Their fortunes were watched with patriotic pride and affection by those who remained to sustain the institution, and promote its success. During those trying years, Miss Booth stood at her post of duty, always loyally faithful to her associates, and more indispensable to the institution than ever. In one of her letters to me, written August, 1861, she said, —

"In all my early forecastings of your future, and that of the noble men who went with you, I never counted upon the possibility of war; and I hardly know how to adjust my mind to its dreadful realities. Ah, me! to think what may come! We shall follow you all with our hearts, and do our best to keep the light of the Eclectic burning. The task is a great one; but at a time of such anxiety hard work is a blessing, and just now our hands are very full of it."

Through the darkness of the war, and into the light of victory and peace, she worked on, reaping each year a larger and richer harvest of results.

About the end of 1865, a new and sacred duty called her to leave the field in which for nearly fifteen years she had achieved such remarkable success. Her parents had become old and feeble, and her father had so far failed in body and mind as to need those tender personal services which none but she could render. Without a murmur, she closed the long period of her brilliant career at Hiram; and, leaving a circle of which she was the chief ornament, she removed with her parents to Cuyahoga Falls, established a quiet and unpretending home, and began a new life of uncomplaining self-sacrifice. During the first year of her residence there, she was manager and sole servant of her household, and with the tenderest filial piety devoted herself wholly to the care of her parents. In the autumn of 1866, her father's health had so far recovered, that, in addition to her home cares, she accepted the place of Assistant Principal in the Union Schools at Cuyahoga Falls, then under the superintendence of V. P. Kline, one of her Hiram students, and a cherished friend. There she continued to teach four years, when she was chosen as Superintendent of all the schools of the village, and for three years discharged the duties of that position with her wonted success.

Her life at Cuyahoga Falls exhibited all her peculiar powers, and attracted the same enthusiastic love which she had enjoyed among the students at Hiram. But her long and arduous work had begun to make inroads upon her health; and, withdrawing from the superintendency of the schools, she gave private lessons to select classes in French and German and other advanced studies during the two succeeding years. At the close of 1874, her health was prostrated by a dangerous and painful disease which required the most skilful professional treatment. Few, even of her most intimate friends, knew through what a terrible ordeal of bodily suffering she passed the last year of her life. In the autumn of 1875, she determined to remove to Cleveland, where she could receive the more constant attention of eminent physicians.

Just before leaving Ohio, in October last, I called on her in Cleveland, where she was spending a week near her physicians, and making arrangements for a change of residence. She showed no signs of depression of spirits. Patient and cheerful, she looked forward to the hope of regaining her health, and finding a home near the friends of her earlier life. I expressed the desire that she might yet do me the very great favor to train my boys for college. The tears filled her eyes as she said, "I should dearly love to do that; it would seem like living our own lives over again;" and then, pausing as if in doubt whether it were not self-praise, she added, "I believe I can teach the classics better than I could when I was in Hiram." She spoke of her friends in that warm and earnest way so peculiarly her own; and I bade her good-by with the promise, and in the confident hope, that I would meet her in the Centennial summer, and enjoy again the blessings of that friendship which for nearly a quarter of a century was one of the noblest and richest gifts that Heaven has vouchsafed to me. But it was ordered otherwise by a wisdom higher than ours. She removed to Cleveland on the 10th of November last, with health apparently improving. She set in pleasant order her new home, in the midst of a little colony of her dear old friends. Jennie Eggleston was living with her; Harry Rhodes and his wife, Henry James, and Virgil Kline, all familiar Hiram names, were her neighbors; and she and they looked forward to a pleasant winter, to be made brighter by frequent renewals of old memories; and the re-unions had begun.

On the 8th of December she and Miss Eggleston spent the evening at Kline's, where they read and visited several hours. Almeda read aloud Emerson's essay on "Compensation," and appeared to be all herself again. She seemed so bright and so well that her friends thought a long life of health and happiness was before her. But that re-union was her last. Let me repeat the last half-page she ever read: —

"The compensations of calamity are made apparent to the understanding also after long intervals of time. A fever, a mutilation, a cruel disappointment, a loss of wealth, a loss of friends, seems at the moment unpaid loss and unpayable. But the sure years reveal the deep remedial force that underlies all facts. The death of a dear friend, wife, brother, lover, which seemed nothing but privation, somewhat later assumes the aspect of a guide or genius; for it commonly operates revolutions in our way of life, terminates an epoch of infancy or of youth which was waiting to be closed, breaks up a wonted occupation, or a household, or a style of living, and allows the formation of new ones more friendly to the growth of character. It permits or constrains the formation of new acquaintances, and the reception of new influences, that prove of the first importance to the next years; and the man or woman who would have remained a sunny garden-flower, with no room for its roots, and too much sunshine for its head, by the falling of the walls and the neglect of the gardener, is made the banian of the forest, yielding shade and fruit to wide neighborhoods of men."

I cannot doubt that she felt the truth of these words; for they portray with singular fidelity the course of her own life. Late that night she was taken ill; and after a week of great suffering, borne with uncomplaining fortitude, she died on the morning of Dec. 15, 1875.

One of her friends, who stood by her at the closing scene, wrote me: —

"She passed quietly away. Her face was so peaceful in death, no trace of pain upon it. There she lay before us, as though, weary with labor, she had fallen asleep. All that loving hands could do for her we did. We wreathed her coffin with flowers, and bore her remains to Cuyahoga Falls, where a mournful and tearful audience awaited us at the church. In the hearts of her last pupils, as in the hearts of her earlier ones, there was deepest grief. All felt, as we stood by her grave, that no nobler, grander, purer spirit ever dwelt on the earth, or went up to heaven."

Such is the story of her life, all too poorly told. I have attempted to trace her long and toilful progress through its several stages. We have seen, that, in fact, she lived three lives in one, — first, the life of early struggle promising to culminate in the happy contentment of a home, with the companionship and love of a husband; second, the larger life, born of a great sorrow, but leading her along a rugged path to the calm heights of a broad and beautiful culture, — a life devoted to great and successful achievements, as one of the very foremost teachers of her time; and, third, a life of heroic and unselfish devotion to a sacred filial duty, with added years of noble and beautiful work as a teacher.

It remains to inquire what she has left to us as a legacy and a lesson. Her life was so largely and so inseparably a part of our own, that it is not easy for any of us, least of all for me, to take a sufficiently distant stand-point from which to measure its proportions.

We shall never forget her sturdy, well-formed figure; her head that would have appeared colossal but for its symmetry of proportions; the strongly marked features of her plain, rugged face, not moulded according to the artist's lines of beauty, but so lighted up with intelligence and kindliness as to appear positively beautiful to those who knew her well.

The basis of her character, the controlling force which developed and formed it, was strength,— extraordinary intellectual power. Blessed with a vigorous constitution and robust bodily health, her capacity for close, continuous, and effective mental work was remarkable. No stronger illustration is possible than the fact, already exhibited, that she accomplished, in four years, the ordinary work of ten.

It is hardly possible for one person to know the quality and strength of another's mind more thoroughly than I knew hers. From long association in her studies, and comparing her with all the students I have known, here and elsewhere, I do not hesitate to say, that I have never known one who grasped with greater power, and handled with more ease and thoroughness, all the studies of the college course. I doubt if in all these respects I have ever known one who was her equal. She caught an author's meaning with remarkable quickness and clearness; and, mastering the difficulties of construction, she detected, with almost unerring certainty, the most delicate shades of thought.

She abhorred all shams in scholarship, and would be content with nothing short of the whole meaning. When crowded with work, it was not unusual for her to sit by her lamp, unconscious of the hours, till far past midnight.

Her powers were well balanced. When I first knew her, it was supposed that her mind was specially adapted to mathematical study. A little later, it was thought she had found her fittest work in the field of the natural sciences; later still, one would have said that she had found her highest possibilities in the languages; and Professor Monroe tells us with what ease she fathomed the depths of so severe an argument as Butler's "Analogy."

Her mind was many-sided, strong, compact, symmetrical. It was this symmetry and balance of qualities that gave her such admirable judgment, and enabled her to concentrate all her powers upon any work she attempted.

To this general statement concerning her faculties there was, however, one marked exception. While she enjoyed, and in some degree appreciated, the harmonies of music, she was almost wholly deficient in the faculty of musical expression. After her return from college, she determined to ascertain by actual test to what extent, if at all, this defect could be overcome. With a patience and courage I have never seen equalled in such a case, she persisted for six months in the attempt to master the technical mysteries of instrumental music, and even attempted one vocal piece. But she found that the struggle was nearly fruitless: the music in her soul would not come forth at her bidding. A few of her friends' will remember, that, for many years, to mention " The Suwanee River" was the signal for not a little good-natured merriment at her expense, and a reminder of her heroic attempt at vocal and instrumental music.

The tone of her mind was habitually logical and serious, not specially inclined to what is technically known as wit; but she had the heartiest appreciation of genuine humor, such as glows on the pages of Cervantes and Dickens. Clifton Bennett and Levi Brown will never forget how keenly she enjoyed the quaint drollery with which they once presented, at a public lyceum, a scene from "Don Quixote;" and I am sure there are three persons here to-day who will never forget how nearly she was once suffocated with laughter over a mock-presentation speech by Harry Rhodes.

Though possessed of very great intellectual powers, or, as the arrogance of our sex accustoms us to say, "having a mind of masculine strength," it was not at all masculine in the opprobrious sense in which that term is frequently applied to women. She was a most womanly woman, with a spirit of gentle and childlike sweetness, with no self-consciousness of superiority, and not the least trace of arrogance.

I take pleasure in re-enforcing my own views of the combined strength and gentleness of her character, by quoting the following letter from the Hon. James Monroe, who was one of her esteemed professors at Oberlin:—

"HOUSE OF REPRESENTATIVES, WASHINGTON, D.C.
"May 28, 1876.

"MY DEAR GENERAL,— I learn that you are preparing an address upon the life and character of Miss Almeda A. Booth; and I cannot resist the impulse to write you a note upon this interesting subject, thus contributing my rill of memories to your broader and deeper current.

"It is among the gratifying recollections of my life that Miss Booth was a pupil of mine for a considerable period of time, in connection with a college class at Oberlin. Soon after I began to observe the habit of her mind, I discovered that she was a remarkable woman. What at first struck my attention was the union in her character, in a degree very uncommon, of masculine intellectual strength and perfect womanly gentleness.

"Her intellectual powers were such as would at once have attracted attention in any undergraduate in any college. She had not only great force, but force which worked with evident ease, without friction and without conscious effort. I shall never forget her recitations in Butler's 'Analogy.' Often when one member in the class after another had failed rightly to interpret some difficult paragraph, Miss Booth, when called upon, would at once, without hesitation, without self-consciousness, and with no idea whatever of being superior to others, set the passage in the truest and clearest light, both as to its intrinsic meaning and its relation to the context. She used to recite the 'Analogy' as if she had written it. I remember the pleased expression of relief which passed over the faces of her classmates when she extricated them from some difficulty. They all esteemed and praised her, and her superiority made no one envious.

"Her gentleness of character was as remarkable as her strength of intellect. She seemed to think well of all her acquaintances, and never, to my knowledge, thought she had a grievance. She was noticeably kind and helpful to those who needed attention, and loved her fellow-creatures with the same love which led Christ to die for them. On the whole, she was as good an example of combined 'sweetness and light' as I have met with.

"After she left Oberlin you knew much more of her than I did. I often regretted that I could not continue my acquaintance with her. But I frequently heard of her great usefulness, and of the high esteem in which she was held wherever she resided. She was a large, strong, loving soul;

and any community which was favored with her presence must have been the better for it.

"Yours very truly,

"JAMES MONROE."

Though possessing these great powers, she was not unmindful of those elegant accomplishments, the love of which seems native to the mind of woman.

In her earlier years she was sometimes criticised as caring too little for the graces of dress and manner; and there was some justice in the criticism. The possession of great powers, no doubt, carries with it a contempt for mere external show. In her early life Miss Booth dressed neatly, though with the utmost plainness, and applied herself to the work of gaining the more enduring ornaments of mind and heart. In her first years at Hiram she had devoted all her powers to teaching and mastering the difficulties of the higher studies, and had given but little time to what are called the more elegant accomplishments. But she was not deficient in appreciation of all that really adorns and beautifies a thorough culture. After her return from Oberlin she paid more attention to the "mint, anise, and cummin" of life. During the last fifteen years of her life, few ladies dressed with more severe or elegant taste. As a means of personal culture, she read the history of art, devoted much time to drawing and painting, and acquired considerable skill with the pencil and brush.

She did not enjoy miscellaneous society. Great crowds were her abhorrence. But in a small circle of congenial friends she was a delighted and a delightful companion.

Her religious character affords an additional illustration of her remarkable combination of strength and gentleness. At an early age she became a member of the Methodist Episcopal Church, and continued in faithful and consistent relations with that organization until she united with the Disciples, soon after she came to Hiram.

Her firmness was severely tested by the religious changes which occurred in her own home. Her father's enthusiastic temperament led him to study any new phases of religious opinion, with a somewhat impressible credulity. The Mormon movement of 1830–32 swept him, for a time, into its turbulent current; and, ten or fifteen years later, he was interested in the socialistic theories of the Shakers, with whom, as I understand, he united for a short time. Later still, he paid much attention to the Spiritualistic philosophy. But while Miss Booth thoroughly respected the sincerity of her father's opinions, and from them doubtless became wisely tolerant and liberal in her opinions, she maintained firmly, but without bigotry, her faith in God and in the life to come. She cared little for mere differences of ecclesiastical form, and abhorred every species of ostentatious and noisy piety: but her life was full of the calmness and beauty of religion; her heart was filled with the charity that "suffereth long, and is kind," and, still greater, that "thinketh no evil." At the memorial meeting held here soon after her death, the very just and striking statement was made by one who had known her from childhood, that he "had never heard her speak evil of any human being."

I venture to assert, that in native powers of mind, in thoroughness and breadth of scholarship, in womanly sweetness of spirit, and in the quantity and quality of effective, unselfish work done, she has not been excelled by any American woman. What she accomplished with her great powers, thoroughly trained and subordinated to the principles of a Christian life, has been briefly stated.

She did not find it necessary to make war upon society in order to capture a field for the exercise of her great qualities. Though urging upon women the necessity of the largest and most thorough culture, and demanding for them the amplest means for acquiring it, she did not waste her years in bewailing the subjection of her sex, but employed them in making herself a great and beneficent power. She did far more to honor and exalt woman's place in society than the thousands of her contemporaries who struggle more earnestly for the barren sceptre of power than for fitness to wield it.

She might have adorned the highest walks of literature, and doubtless might thus have won a noisy fame. But it may be doubted whether in any other pursuit she could have conferred greater or more lasting benefits upon her fellow-creatures, than by the life she so faithfully and successfully devoted to the training and culture of youth. With no greed of power or of gain, she found her chief reward in blessing others.

I do not know of any man or woman, who, at fifty-one years of age, had done more or better work. I have not been able to ascertain precisely how long she taught before she came to Hiram;

but it was certainly not less than fifteen terms. She taught forty-two terms here, twenty-one terms in the Union School at Cuyahoga Falls, and, finally, two years in private classes; in all, nearly twenty-eight years of faithful and most successful teaching, to which she devoted the wealth of her great faculties and admirable scholarship.

How rich and how full was the measure of gratitude poured out to her, from many thousands of loving hearts! And to-day, from every station in life, and from every quarter of our country, are heard the voices of those who rise up to call her blessed, and to pay their tearful tribute of gratitude to her memory.

On my own behalf, I take this occasion to say, that for her generous and powerful aid, so often and so efficiently rendered, for her quick and never-failing sympathy, and for her intelligent, unselfish, and unswerving friendship, I owe her a debt of gratitude and affection, for the payment of which the longest term of life would have been too short.

To this institution she has left the honorable record of a long and faithful service, and the rich legacy of a pure and noble life. I have shown that she lived three lives. One of these, the second, in all its richness and fulness, she gave to Hiram. More than half of all her teaching was done here, where she taught much longer than any other person has taught; and no one has done work of better quality.

She has here reared a monument which the envious years cannot wholly destroy. As long as the love of learning shall here survive; as long as the light of this college shall be kept burning; as long as there are hearts to hold and cherish the memory of its past; as long as high qualities of mind and heart are honored and loved among men and women,—so long will the name of Almeda A. Booth be here remembered, and honored, and loved.

All who knew her at any period of her career will carry her memory as a perpetual and precious possession. With the changing of a single word, we may say of our friend what the Poet Laureate of England said of "Isabel:"—

> "The intuitive decision of a bright
> And thorough-edged intellect to part
> Error from crime; a prudence to withhold;
> The laws of friendship charactered in gold
> Upon the blanchèd tablets of her heart;
> A love still burning upward, giving light

To read those laws; . . .
A courage to endure and to obey:
A hate of gossip parlance and of sway;
. . . . the world hath not another
(Though all her fairest forms are types of thee,
And thou of God in thy great charity)
Of such a finished chastened purity."

APPENDIX.

APPENDIX.

THE ARMY POST SCHOOLS.

SINCE the account of these schools given in the "Introduction to Speeches"[1] was written, and even put in type, I have received a mass of valuable information concerning them, some parts of which will be of interest here.

The law of 1866 remained a dead letter until 1875. Chaplain George G. Mullins, of the Twenty-fifth Infantry, discovered the existence of the law, and began to make demands upon his colonel and the War Department that its terms and provisions be carried out.[2] Mullins's work and reports, and a report made by Gen. N. H. Davis of his observations in a tour of inspection in the Department of Texas, led to the organization of the Board that framed the rules and regulations of General Order No. 24, May 18, 1878. These rules form

[1] Pp. 169-173.
[2] Sect. 1,124 of the Revised Statutes made it the duty of chaplains of regiments of colored troops and of post chaplains to instruct the enlisted men in the common English branches of education.

the basis of the post-schools. Rules 1, 2, 3, and 4 provide for the accumulation and management of a post fund. This fund comes from two sources: first, the post-trader at a post is required to pay for his privilege, "not exceeding ten cents a month for every officer and enlisted soldier serving at the post;" second, the troops, when practicable, are required to bake their own bread, and the difference between bread and flour, which is thirty-three and one-third per cent in favor of flour, goes to the post fund. Rule 7 names the objects to which the fund thus accumulated shall be devoted. In their order they are: 1. Expenses of bake-house: 2. Garden seeds and utensils; 3. Post schools; 4. Post library and reading-room; 5. Gymnasium; 6. Chapel; 7. Fruit and shade trees; 8. Fruit-bearing vines and bushes; 9. Printing-press. Order No. 24 contains minute regulations, covering the whole ground of education in the army.

Chaplain Mullins was duly appointed assistant to General McCook, the inspector, and he now holds the office of Supervisor of Education in the Army. He is enthusiastically devoted to the work, and has already done much, through the means appointed by the law, to foster the intelligence and morality of the soldiers. In an able article entitled "Education in the Army," contributed to the "United Service" magazine for April, 1880, the chaplain presents the argument for the schools with great force.

The majority of the twenty-five thousand enlisted men in the army are native-born citizens, and not foreigners. They are not hardened wretches, but hopeful and adventurous young men, generally under thirty years of age, the mass of whom are illiterate, — the larger part not being able properly to sign the muster-rolls. Many of the non-commissioned officers cannot repeat the multiplication-table, know nothing of the history of the country, cannot study the "Tactics," and are wholly unable to write, or to read written orders. He points out the inevitable tendencies of such ignorance under the well-known conditions of army-life, — drunkenness, idleness, shirking duty, want of self-respect, and other vices and immoralities. The tendency of the schools to correct these evils, in great degree, is stated, and well supported by facts. Then he speaks of the multitude of dependent children in the army, or in some way belonging to it, — children of officers, enlisted men, and employees, besides the children of settlers around the posts. He supposes these to be three or four thousand in number. "The majority of these precious *impedimenta* are west of the Mississippi, at the posts upon the wild frontier, far removed from schools, churches, and the thousand refining influences of civil life. To provide teachers, books, and papers for them, to save them from heathenish darkness, to train them up for lives of virtue and usefulness, ought surely to be counted a matter of sufficient gravity to challenge the attention of the wise legislators who are doing so very much in the interest of national education." He then urges the strong claim of the common soldier and his child for an education, and remarks upon the fact, that until the post-schools were organized nothing whatever was done for either.

From the annual report of the Supervisor of Education in the Army, dated St. Louis, Mo., Nov. 1, 1881, it appears that the approximate number of enlisted men in daily attendance upon the reading-rooms for the year is 4,800. The average attendance upon the schools has been, — enlisted men, 912; children of enlisted men, 850; children of officers, 224; children of civilians, 316: total average number, 2,302. Thus far there have been built at the various military posts fifty-two chapels, schools, and reading-rooms, at a total cost of $60,757. Large contributions of reading matter — Bibles, Testaments, song-books, periodicals, tracts, Sunday-school books, and miscellaneous works — have been received through the year from various sources, as the publication societies and private individuals.

This fuller account of the post-schools is given for three reasons: —

1. The public are almost wholly ignorant of the existence of these schools, and of the efforts being made

through them to increase the intelligence and morality of the army.

2. The schools themselves are important. Of course they, and all the related appliances, are still in their infancy; but experience proves conclusively that a foundation was laid in the law of 1866 for incalculable good.

Both these considerations alone would not justify the space here given to the subject, or even a mention. But —

3. In a sense, these are Garfield's schools. Speaking of the law of 1866, he said near the close of his life, "That is one of *my* things." He originated the measure, though it was supported by General R. C. Schenck, and promptly approved by House and Senate. His interest in the post-schools continued to the end. He indorsed Chaplain Mullins as "the man for the work;" and, after he became President, told him that he wished him to remove his headquarters to Washington. He assured the supervisor that he should have the Executive's earnest co-operation in his good work.

www.ingramcontent.com/pod-product-compliance
Lightning Source LLC
Chambersburg PA
CBHW022144300426
44115CB00006B/336